Development-induced Displacement and Human Rights in Africa

Within the context of the 2009 Kampala Convention, this book examines how a balance can be struck between the imperative of development projects and the rights of persons likely to be displaced in Africa.

Following independence, many African states embarked on large-scale development projects such as dams, urban renewal and extraction of natural resources and have had to grapple with how to protect displaced communities while implementing development projects. These projects were considered a panacea for Africa's development and the economic interests of the majority were often considered over and above the interests of the minority of people who were displaced by these projects. This book examines how a balance can be struck between the imperative of development and the rights of displaced persons within the context of the African Union Convention on the Protection and Assistance of Internally Displaced Persons in Africa (the Kampala Convention). Romola Adeola analyses the obligations that are placed on African states by the Kampala Convention in the context of development-induced displacement.

This book will be of interest to scholars of human rights law, forced migration, African Studies and development.

Romola Adeola is the Coordinator of the Global Engagement Network on Internal Displacement in Africa (GENIDA). She is a Postdoctoral Fellow at the Centre for Human Rights, Faculty of Law, University of Pretoria, South Africa and is a Senior Research Associate on Internally Displaced Persons (IDPs) at the Refugee Law Initiative, School of Advanced Studies, University of London, UK.

Routledge Contemporary Africa

Urban Planning in Rapidly Growing Cities
Developing Addis Ababa
Mintesnot G. Woldeamanuel

Regional Development Poles and the Transformation of African Economies
Benaiah Yongo-Bure

Nature, Environment and Activism in Nigerian Literature
Sule E. Egya

Corporate Social Responsibility and Law in Africa
Theories, Issues and Practices
Nojeem A. Amodu

Greening Industrialization in Sub-Saharan Africa
Ralph Luken and Edward Clarence-Smith

Health and Care in Old Age in Africa
Edited by Pranitha Maharaj

Rethinking African Agriculture
How Non-Agrarian Factors Shape Peasant Livelihoods
Edited by Goran Hyden, Kazuhiko Sugimura and Tadasu Tsuruta

Toward an Animist Reading of Postcolonial Trauma Literature
Reading Beyond the Single Subject
Jay Rajiva

Development-induced Displacement and Human Rights in Africa
The Kampala Convention
Romola Adeola

For more information about this series, please visit: www.routledge.com/Routledge-Contemporary-Africa/book-series/RCAFR

Development-induced Displacement and Human Rights in Africa

The Kampala Convention

Romola Adeola

Routledge
Taylor & Francis Group
LONDON AND NEW YORK

First published 2021
by Routledge
2 Park Square, Milton Park, Abingdon, Oxon OX14 4RN

and by Routledge
52 Vanderbilt Avenue, New York, NY 10017

Routledge is an imprint of the Taylor & Francis Group, an informa business

British Library Cataloguing-in-Publication Data
A catalogue record for this book is available from the British Library

Library of Congress Cataloging-in-Publication Data
A catalog record for this book has been requested

ISBN: 978-1-138-10415-0 (hbk)
ISBN: 978-0-367-54625-0 (pbk)
ISBN: 978-1-315-10231-3 (ebk)

Typeset in Baskerville
by Apex CoVantage, LLC

Contents

Foreword

With the reality that millions of individuals are internally displaced on the continent of Africa, the need to give specific attention to this issue and address the various root causes of internal displacement has become an imperative. This is against the backdrop of the fact that IDPs remain within the borders of the state and not having crossed international borders, their protection primarily lies within the state in which they are displaced. Where a state is unable or unwilling to provide adequate protection, IDPs are often exposed to a plethora of challenges and may remain in protracted situations for decades where there are no durable solutions.

Given the prevalence of this issue on the continent, African leaders in 2009 adopted the first continental framework on internal displacement – the African Union Convention for the Protection and Assistance of Internally Displaced Persons in Africa (Kampala Convention). Through its 23-article provisions, the Kampala Convention articulates significant guidance for the furtherance of protection and assistance to IDPs, effectively completing the African Charter on Human and Peoples' Rights as a clear expression of obligations with regards to a specific group of people – the internally displaced. Notably, the Kampala Convention articulates the right not to be arbitrarily displaced and recognizes various root causes of internal displacement in Africa – including armed conflict, disasters, harmful practices, climate change and development projects.

This book by Romola Adeola specifically focuses on development projects as a root cause of internal displacement, also known as, development-induced displacement. Development projects as a root cause of internal displacement, is indeed widely prevalent, however, scarcely discussed. And that this book focuses on the provision of article 10 of the Kampala Convention and provides guidance is both interesting and significant. It is significant because it introduces us to the issue of development projects and gives us prescription on how this pertinent root cause of internal displacement can be addressed. It opens up a space for discussing one of the least discussed root causes of internal displacement that reflects competing imperatives.

The book therefore examines one of the root causes of internal displacement, the least visible, but which reflects competing imperatives. The imperative of development and the rights of persons likely to be displaced. In this narrative is an evident dilemma. The fact that a state wants to advance its economic potentials – which is needful for the realization of peoples' rights to development but also the fact that there are certain populations within the state that may be affected by the furtherance of this imperative who are development-induced displaced persons. These competing imperatives reflect a need to strike a balance. And it is within this context that the provision of article 10 of the Kampala Convention is significant. Indeed, this book presents a classic discussion of this subject and provides a basis for further discussion of the subject of development-induced displacement in Africa and beyond.

It is worth noting that the research initiated by Ms. Romola Adeola has come at a time when Africa is faced with the proliferation of forced displacement, a source of tension for African populations in relation to human rights.

I am glad that this book specifically focuses on this subject area. More importantly, it provides a draft general comment which the African Commission on Human and Peoples' Rights can adopt as the primary institutions for the protection and promotion of human rights in Africa. I laud this book and Romola's masterful work and endorse it in the furtherance of knowledge on internal displacement and specifically, development-induced displacement in Africa.

Mme Sahli Fadel Maya
Commissioner, African Commission on Human and Peoples' Rights
Special Rapporteur on Refugees, Asylum Seekers,
Internally Displaced Persons and Migrants in Africa

Acknowledgements

In March 2013, I attended a Conference on Development-Induced Displacement at the Refugee Studies Centre at the University of Oxford. There was significant discussion on the subject from a plethora of angles, mostly in the fields where initial discussions had occurred: the fields of anthropology, sociology and development studies. This was just barely months after the Kampala Convention had come into force, but there was very limited discussion on how to use this important regional framework to advance protection and assistance of development-induced displaced persons. In conversation with Prof Ted Downing and Prof Michael Cernea, the pertinence of this approach, became ever more evident.

Over the last couple of years, the evident challenge with internal displacement due to development projects has prompted the question: how can a balance be struck between the imperative of development and the rights of persons likely to be displaced? It is against this backdrop that considering this root cause has really been a worthwhile experience. Also, with the knowledge that this is a challenge globally. Not just in Africa. As this book is based on parts of my doctoral thesis, I hope it will inspire some thoughts on the specific article 10. Evidently, to say that I can fully acknowledge everyone who has shaped my perspective along the way would be an exaggeration. But for everyone who has contributed in one way or the other, either in sharing a joke on the elevator or helping me learn to do things better. I am grateful. I am also particularly grateful to my family and friends.

Specifically, I would like to acknowledge the very kind support and excellent mentorship from my doctoral supervisor and mentor, Prof Frans Viljoen. It would be a disservice to say that you were just a doctoral supervisor. For you are also a Professor who takes pleasure in helping others grow in aptitude and character. An extremely rare virtue. I also sincerely appreciate the excellent mentorship received from Prof Francois Crépeau at McGill University. I also appreciate my co-Steinberg Fellow, Marina Sharpe for the lovely conversations and support. I sincerely appreciate the pertinent support I received from Prof Chaloka Beyani, who having drafted the Kampala Convention pleasantly shared insights with me and even allowed me lecture on the Kampala Convention often in his presence, with a reassuring smile and commendation. I am very grateful. I sincerely appreciate the kindness and sincere collegial trust I have enjoyed from Prof David Cantor. Your selfless character is highly commendable. I am very grateful to Prof Walter Kälin and Prof Francis Deng for their very kind support in shaping my perspective on internal displacement through their writings and communications. I would also like to thank Prof Ademola Oluborode Jegede for being a really caring and wonderful adviser. Thank you for your support, also for the conversations on the Kampala Convention. I also sincerely appreciate Prof Elina Pirjatanniemi for the selfless character, support and excellent guidance given to me during my stay at Åbo Akademi University. I am grateful to Mr Cosmas Chanda, Dr Olabisi Dare, Dr Allehone Mulugeta Abebe, Ms Rita Amukhobu and Mr Renny Mike Wafula for the excellent support through the years.

I sincerely appreciate the kind support from Ms Leanne Hinves, the head of the editorial team at Routledge. I am also grateful to members of the editorial team, particularly, Ms Leela Vathenen and Mr Balaji Karuppanan.

Finally, I sincerely appreciate Mme Sahli Fadel Maya for the foreword to this book. I am immensely grateful for the kind words and commendations.

Sincerely,

Romola Adeola

1 The international law on development-induced displacement

1.1 Introduction

From the point of scholarship, a pertinent gap in the field of development-induced displacement is the scanty international law discussion on the subject. It is telling that legal scholarship has largely overlooked this field in which the law has a significant place.

Much of the discussions in this field have proceeded from sociology, anthropology, political economics and development ethics.[1] The absence of significant legal scholarship on the subject is due, in part, to the fact that the relationship between states and their nationals is not a territorial subject for public international law. However, with the emergence of the responsibility to protect and the growing consensus that state sovereignty cannot serve as a shield,[2] the 'territorial business' of public international law has been subject to scholarly queries over the last decade. In the field of development-induced displacement, not many queries have been advanced. The field of internal displacement, from which a discussion on the international law on development-induced displacement emanates, has also not been amply established in international law.

Unlike international refugee law, the international law of internal displacement is regulated by soft law at the level of the United Nations (UN).[3] A soft-law approach was easily favoured, as it was a middle ground between achieving protection for internally displaced populations while not tampering with state sovereignty. The rhetoric at the time of its creation was the prospect that it 'would focus international attention, raise the level of awareness, and stimulate practical measures of alleviating the [internal displacement] crisis.'[4] There was also the compelling rhetoric that a binding instrument will be developed in the long-term[5] and, as such, the soft law was only an 'initial statement of principles'[6] for the 'transitional phase'[7] in which a framework was needed to guide humanitarian action.

The notion of soft law and its relevance within the legal order has garnered much attention among international legal scholars.[8] While there is no universal definition of soft law, there is a general consensus that these laws are not legally binding and, as such, they are not treaties on which state responsibility can be invoked. A wide range of semantics have been adopted in conceptualising these laws. Grnchalla-Wesierski describes soft laws as norms invoking expectations.[9] Abbot and Snidal view soft law as a continuum that 'begins once legal arrangements are weakened along one or more of the dimensions of obligation, precision and delegation.'[10] To Guzman and Meyer, soft laws are 'hortatory.'[11] A golden thread across these conceptions is the fact that their non-binding character creates a significant challenge of legitimacy. Since international law is clear on its sources, when one refers to article 38 of the International Court of Justice (ICJ) Statute, it would appear that the legitimisation of soft law can only be resolved by either admitting that the clarity of international law on its sources needs to be revisited or by determining the relevance of soft law within the definite international legal order. However, whether either of this is pertinent is a question of debate in itself in view of existing contestations on the 'hard' and 'soft' nature of the entire international legal order. While international legal scholars deliberate on this question, it is relevant to highlight two benefits of soft law. First, soft laws can be an avenue to codify comprehensive protection on issues for which there may be little consensus.[12] In this sense, soft laws may aid compromise on sensitive global issues.[13] A clear manifestation of this benefit resonates within the discussion of internal displacement with the level of acceptance of the Guiding Principles among states at different levels of governance.[14] Second, it is pertinent to emphasise that soft laws can serve as normative springboards for the creation of future norms as with the case of the Guiding Principles and subsequent processes in various regions.

While a binding instrument is awaited at the global level, there has been significant progress within the African regional system with the adoption of the African Union Convention for the Protection and Assistance of Internally Displaced Persons (Kampala Convention).[15] Article 10 of the Kampala Convention mandate states to prevent development-induced displacement should be prevented. Within the context of this framework, a discussion on the subject is advanced in this book. Prior to this, however, it is relevant to consider the contributions of general human rights norms and standards of international finance institutions in examining the current state of practice of the international law on development-induced displacement.

1.2 Human rights norms

International human rights law is replete with norms applicable to development-induced displacement. Much of the efforts towards the protection of development-induced displaced persons (DIDPs) have leveraged on these norms in addressing impoverishments that occur due to development-induced displacement.

One such norm of significance is the right to property. Dating back to the 18th century,[16] the right developed out of an understanding that there was a need to protect ownership of assets from exploitative activities.[17] In 1948, it was affirmed in the Universal Declaration on Human Rights (Universal Declaration) that '[e]veryone has the right to own property alone as well as in association with others.'[18] And also, that '[n]o one shall be arbitrarily deprived of his property.'[19] However, there was no further reassertion of this right in the 1966 Covenants[20] due to differences in views on issues such as how the right should be formulated and reflected; whether the right should be subjected to national or international law; the nature of compensation in event of expropriation;[21] and concerns on state sovereignty due, in part, to the 'limits in international law on a state's right in the area of expropriation or nationalization' where foreigners owned land.[22]

At regional levels, the human rights frameworks of the African, inter-American and European systems recognise this right, subject to public interest and law.[23] While states are afforded a margin of discretion in determining public interest, regional institutions have often interpreted law as including international human rights law,[24] a proportionality test involving the legitimacy, necessity and commensurability of the measure is often utilised.[25] In relation to indigenous peoples, the test is 'met with a much higher threshold.'[26] In the *Saramaka* case, the Inter-American Court of Human Rights (IACtHR) emphasised that the restriction on property rights of indigenous peoples will also need to be subject to 'whether the restriction amounts to a denial of their traditions and customs in a way that endangers the very survival of the group and its members.'[27] In the *Endorois* case, the African Commission recognised that the 'continued dispossession and alienation' of the Endorois peoples from their ancestral land threatened the cultural survival of the group, and as such, leans the proportionality test on their side.[28] Although this right has been used significantly in advancing protection of individuals and groups, its emphasis on ownership and the varying interpretation of proportionality across various jurisdictions makes it inadequate to capture the protection needs of DIDPs.

Another relevant norm is the right to development.[29] The right to development was first expressed by Keba M'Baye during an Inaugural Lecture at the International Institute of Human Rights in Austria.[30] Distinguishing between development as 'a legal technique suitable for sustaining the economic and social development of the backward countries'[31] and the notion of development as a human right,[32] M'Baye argued that development should be conceived as a right through which every individual can live better.[33] His argument, premised on moral and political conscientiousness,[34] gained normative ground in international human rights law with the adoption of the United Nations Declaration on the Right to Development.[35] However, it is in the African Charter that the right to development has found its most significant expression.[36]

Article 22 of the African Charter provides that all peoples shall have the right to their social, economic and cultural development.[37] The concept of peoples is crucial to the understanding of this right in this context.

Although the African Charter does not define what 'peoples' mean, there is a strong sense of 'collectivity' that resonates from discussions on rights.[38] In this light, 'peoples' have been used to refer to indigenous communities, national populations and other groups with a bond collectively enjoyed or suffered.[39] The emphasis on collectivity within the context of the right to development is the need to ensure adequate protection for all persons jointly within a group. Within the context of development-induced displacement, a significant implication of this fact is that development plans, programmes and projects must be conceived as a holistic agenda that takes into account the various needs of the collective that will be affected either positively or negatively.

A third relevant norm is the right to adequate housing. In national jurisdictions, this norm has been utilised in advancing protection for persons displaced from informal settlements.[40] Within the context of development-induced displacement, it is relevant to mention the *Nkwantakrom* case in Ghana.[41] The case involved the displacement of 45 people in the Nkwantakrom community in the western region of Ghana to make way for the Ghanaian Australian Goldfields Mining Project. The petitioners, who were neither compensated nor resettled, contended that the displacement violated, among others, the right to housing. Similarly, in the *Mitu-bell* case, the petitioners argued that the displacement of more than 15,000 people from the area of Wilson International Airport without adequate notice and rehabilitation was a violation of the right to adequate housing under article 11 of the International Covenant on Economic, Social and Cultural Rights (ICESCR).[42]

While the first mention of this right is in the Universal Declaration,[43] article 11 of the ICESCR gives the most expression to it. Although the provision of article 11 of the ICESCR links the right to housing to the right to an adequate standard of living as a constituent element, a body of jurisprudence has been developed on the right to housing as a separate norm in view of the global scale of homelessness and the challenge of forced evictions. In this respect, the Committee on Economic, Social and Cultural Rights (CESCR) and the UN Special Rapporteur on Adequate Housing have made significant contributions.[44] Through the state reporting process, the CESCR has often drawn the attention of states to its jurisprudence on forced evictions and adequate housing while expressing concern over cases of displacements.[45] For instance, following the consideration of the state report of Morocco, the CESCR expressed concern over displacements that affected the Amazighs.[46] While calling on Morocco to secure the protection of victims of displacements, the CESCR emphasised its general comments on the right to housing as reference points.[47]

Through an interpretation of the right to privacy, both the CESCR and Human Rights Committee (HRC) have sought to protect DIDPs. In General Comment No 7, the CESCR emphasised that the provision of article 17(1) of the International Covenant on Civil and Political Rights (ICCPR) which recognises the right to be protected against 'arbitrary or unlawful interference' further 'complements the right not to be forcefully evicted without adequate protection.'[48] The HRC has articulated support for this point. In its concluding observation on Kenya, the HRC emphasised that the displacement of thousands of individuals from informal settlement in Nairobi without prior consultation or notice was in violation of article 17 of the ICCPR.[49] Before the European Court of Human Rights, the right to privacy was canvassed to protect persons that were at risk of development-induced displacement in *Yordanova and Others v Bulgaria*.[50] In this case involving an attempted displacement of Roma people from their residence in the Bulgarian capital of Sofia for 'urban development,' the petitioners argued that the removal order purporting to displace them from their homes was contrary to the right to privacy under article 8 of the European Convention on Human Rights (ECHR). The European Court upheld this argument emphasizing that should the removal order be enforced, there would be a violation of the right to privacy, as the removal order was issued under a law which did not afford an opportunity to consider the proportionate nature of interference.[51]

While general human rights norms have contributed to the protection of DIDPs,[52] they have mostly been inadequate, due, in part, to the different interpretations of limitation standards as with the right to property, concerns with implementation and justiciability as with the right to adequate housing and challenges with the normative scope of application as with the right to development.

In the absence of a legally binding framework that specifically addresses development-induced displacement, DIDPs have faced a daunting task not only of utilising these general human rights norms but also the operational policies of international financial institutions such as the World Bank.[53] However, in explicitly setting out state obligations in respect to development-induced displacement and recognising the right not to be arbitrarily displaced within this context, the Kampala Convention affords a basis for fostering adequate protection of DIDPs. Within the context of this framework, this book examines how a balance can be struck between the imperative of development and the right of DIDPs.

1.3 Policy standards

Prior to developments in the field of internal displacement, the narrative on the protection of DIDPs was driven primarily through policies of international financial institutions. A notable policy standard that has served as a significant normative springboard for the protection of DIDPs is the World Bank Operational Policy on Involuntary Resettlement (Operational Policy).[54]

Prior to loan approvals from the World Bank, the Operational Policy requires borrowing states to prepare a resettlement plan that indicates consultation, compensation and development assistance to DIDPs.[55] While the policy does not mention human rights, it emphasises the need for borrowing states to ensure that no harm is done to DIDPs.

However, one the main criticisms of the policy standard relates to implementation by states and the absence of an effective supervisory mechanism at the World Bank. Although the World Bank has an Inspection Panel which is the 'first body of its kind to give voice to private citizens in an international development context,'[56] its lack of independence curtails its full effectiveness.[57] Aside from the fact that its decisions are non-binding,[58] it has no power to issue directives or sanctions for non-compliance.[59] Its investigations are also subject to the approval of the Board of Directors of the World Bank.[60] In view of the need for an improved system of accountability, the World Bank Board of Directors 'commissioned an External Review of the IPN [Inspection Panel] Toolkit'[61] and approved the enhancements to the Bank's accountability system in 2020.[62]

1.4 Conclusion

While there has been some progress in international law with respect to development-induced displacement, much of these improvements have been through human rights norms that have mostly been inadequate and through policy standards of international financial institutions.

With the development of the Kampala Convention, a significant advancement at the African regional level is that there is a binding framework on internal displacement from which the protection of DIDPs may be advanced. Within the context of this framework, this book examines how a balance can be struck between the imperative of development and the right of DIDPs.

Notes

1 M Cernea 'Understanding and preventing impoverishment from displacement: reflections on the state of knowledge' in C McDowell (ed) *Understanding impoverishment: the consequences of development-induced displacement* (1996) 13; MM Cernea 'The risks and reconstruction model for resettling displaced populations' (1997) 25(10) *World Development* 1569; MM Cernea (ed) *The economics of involuntary resettlement: questions and challenges* (1999); MM Cernea 'Risks, safeguards and reconstruction: a model for population displacement and resettlement' (2000) 35(41) *Economic & Political Weekly* 3659; MM Cernea & C McDowell 'Reconstructing resettlers' and refugees' livelihood' in MM Cernea & C McDowell (eds) *Risks and reconstruction: experiences of resettlers and refugees* (2000) 1–8; R Dwivedi 'Models and methods in development-induced displacement' (2002) 33(4) *Development and Change* 709; MM Cernea & K Schmidt-Soltau 'The end of forcible displacements? Conservation must not impoverish people' (2003) 12 *Policy Matters* 42; PK Gellert & BD Lynch 'Mega-projects as displacements' (2004) 55(175) *International Social Science Journal* 15; T Scudder *The future of large dams: dealing with social, environmental, institutional and political costs* (2005);

A Oliver-Smith 'Applied anthropology and development-induced displacement and resettlement' in S Kedia & J van Willigen (eds) *Applied anthropology: domains of application* (2005) 189; C De Wet 'Risk, complexity and local initiatives in forced resettlement outcomes' in C De Wet (ed) *Development-induced displacements: problems, policies and people* (2006) 180–202; A El Jack 'Gendered implications: development-induced displacement in Sudan' in P Vandergeest et al (eds) *Development's displacements: ecologies, economics, and cultures at risk* (2007) 61; T Downing & C Garcia-Downing 'Routine and dissonant cultures: a theory about the psycho-socio-cultural disruptions of involuntary displacement and the ways to mitigate them without inflicting even more damage' in A Oliver-Smith (ed) *Development and Dispossession: The anthropology of displacement and resettlement* (2009) 225–254; S Price 'Prologue: victims or partners? The social perspective in development-induced displacement and resettlement' (2009) 10(4) *The Asia Pacific Journal of Anthropology* 266; A Oliver-Smith *Defying displacement: grassroots resistance and critique of development* (2010); P Penz, J Drydyk & PS Bose *Displacement by development: ethics, rights and responsibilities* (2011); B Terminski 'The concept of human security as a tool for analysing the consequences of development-induced displacement and resettlement' (2012); P Narayan 'Patterns in arbitrariness: resettlement experiences of the unrecognized urban poor in Chennai' in I Satiroglu & N Choi (eds) *Development-induced displacement and resettlement: new perspectives on persisting problems* (2015) 170.

2 FM Deng 'From "sovereignty as responsibility" to the "responsibility to protect"' (2010) 2 *Global Responsibility to Protect* 353; D Kuwali *The responsibility to protect: implementation of article 4(h) intervention* (2011); AJ Bellamy *The responsibility to protect: a defense* (2015); S Breau *The responsibility to protect and international law: an emerging paradigm shift* (2016).

3 UN Commission on Human Rights, Addendum 'Guiding Principles on Internal Displacement' *Report of the Representative of the Secretary-General, Mr. Francis M. Deng, submitted pursuant to Commission on Human Rights resolution 1997/39*, UN Doc. E/CN.4/1998/53/Add.2 (11 February 1998) (Guiding Principles).

4 UN Commission on Human Rights 'Annex: Comprehensive study prepared by Mr Francis Deng, Representative of the Secretary-General on the human rights issues related to internally displaced persons, submitted pursuant to Commission on Human Rights resolution 1992/73' *Note by the Secretary-General*, UN Doc. E/CN.4/1993/35 (21 January 1993) 283.

5 As previously stated, 78.

6 As previously stated, 283.

7 As previously stated, 283.

8 KW Abbott & D Snidal 'Hard and soft law in international governance' (2000) 54(3) *International Organization* 421–456; T Grnchalla-Wesierski 'A framework for understanding "soft law"' (1984) *McGill Law Journal* 29, 44; CM Chinkin 'The challenge of soft law: development and change in international law' (1989) 38 *International and Comparative Law Quarterly* 850–866; AT Guzman & TL Meyer 'International soft law' (2010) 2 *Journal of Legal Analysis* 171; GC Shaffer & MA Pollack 'Hard vs. soft law: alternatives, complements, and antagonists in international governance' (2010) 94 *Minnesota Law Review* 706; P Orchid 'Protection of internally displaced persons: soft law as a norm-generating mechanism' (2010) 36 *Review of International Studies* 281, 286–287; IA Olsson 'Four competing approaches to international soft law' (2013) 58 *Scandinavian Study in Law* 177, 194.

9 Grnchalla-Wesierski (n 8).

10 Abbott & Snidal (n 8) 422.

11 Guzman & Meyer (n 8) 172.

12 ST Kleine-Ahlbrandt *The protection gap in the international protection of internally displaced persons: the case of Rwanda* (2004) 113.

13 Paris Agreement (2015).
14 In 2005, the UN General Assembly adopted a resolution in which UN Member States expressed recognition for the UNGPs as 'an important international framework for the protection of internally displaced persons and resolve to take effective measures to increase the protection of internally displaced persons.' UN General Assembly 'World Summit Outcome' UN Doc A/RES/60/1 (24 October 2005), para 132; Protocol on the Protection and Assistance of Internally Displaced Persons (2006) (the Great Lakes Protocol).
15 African Union Convention for the Protection and Assistance of Internally Displaced Persons in Africa, adopted at the Special Summit of the African Union Heads of States and Government in Kampala, Uganda (19–23 October 2009) (the Kampala Convention).
16 C Golay & I Cismas 'Legal opinion: the right to property from a human rights perspective' Legal Opinion, Centre for Human Rights and Democratic Development (2010) 2.
17 Prior to the incorporation of this right in the French Declaration, Locke argued that 'every man has a "property" in his own "person." . . . The "labour" of his body and the "work" of his hands . . . are properly his.' J Locke *Two treaties of government* (1689); JE Krier 'Evolutionary theory and the origin of property rights' Law & Economics Working Papers, University of Michigan (2009) 14.
18 Universal Declaration of Human Rights, adopted by the UN General Assembly Resolution 217 A (III) of 10 December 1948, art 17(1).
19 As previously stated, art 17(2).
20 International Covenant on Civil and Political Rights, adopted by the UN General Assembly Resolution 2200A (XXI), UN Doc A/6316 (16 December 1966) (ICCPR); International Covenant on Economic, Social and Cultural Rights, adopted by the UN General Assembly Resolution 2200A (XXI), UN Doc A/6316 (16 December 1966) (ICESCR).
21 TRG van Banning *The human right to property* (2001) 43–46; RE Howard-Hassmann 'Reconsidering the right to own property' Human Rights and Welfare Working Paper No 68 (2012); Joseph Korbel School of International Studies (2012).
22 WA Schabas 'The omission of the right to property in the international covenants' (1991) *Hague Yearbook of International Law* 135, 150.
23 African Charter on Human and Peoples' Rights, adopted by the Organisation of African Unity, OAU Doc CAB/LEG/67/3 rev 5 (27 June 1981) (African Charter), art 14; First Protocol to the European Convention on Human Rights (1952) 213 UNTS 262 (ECHR Protocol), art 1; The American Convention on Human Rights (1969) 1144 UNTS 123, art 21.
24 These regional institutions are: the African Commission on Human and Peoples' Rights (African Commission), European Court of Human Rights (ECHR) and the Inter-American Court of Human Rights (IACtHR). In *Malone v the United Kingdom* (2 August 1984), *Amann v Switzerland* ECHR (16 February 2000) and *Rotaru v Romania* (4 May 2000), the European Court of Human Rights stressed the fact that 'the phrase "in accordance with the law" does not merely refer back to domestic law but also relates to the quality of the law, requiring it to be compatible with the rule of law, which is expressly mentioned in the preamble to the [European] Convention.' In *Centre for Minority Rights Development (Kenya) & Minority Rights Group International on behalf of Endorois Welfare Council v Kenya* (2009) (*Endorois* case), the African Commission notes that the requirement of appropriate laws in article 14 of the African Charter must be understood not only as national laws but also international law. See Communication 276/2003, *Centre for Minority Rights Development (Kenya) & Minority Rights Group International (on behalf of Endorois Welfare Council) v Kenya* (2009), paras 218–219.

25 See generally The Siracusa Principles on the Limitation and Derogation Provisions in the International Covenant on Civil and Political Rights, endorsed by the UN Commission on Human Rights, UN Doc E/CN.4/1985/4 (28 September 1984); *Handyside v United Kingdom* (1976) ECHR 5; *Incal v Turkey* (1998) ECHR 48; *Media Rights Agenda and Others v Nigeria* (2000) AHRLR 200 (ACHPR 1998); *Constitutional Rights Project & Others v Nigeria* (2000) AHRLR 227 (ACHPR 1999); *Coster v The United Kingdom* (2001) 33 EHRR 479; *Kimel v Argentina* IACtHR (2 May 2008); M Newton & L May *Proportionality in international law* (2014).

26 *Endorois* case (n 24), para 212. See also ILO Convention 169: Indigenous and Tribal Peoples Convention, adopted by the General Conference of the International Labour Organisation (27 June 1989), arts 4(1) & 16. See also *Case of the Saramaka People v Suriname* IACtHR (28 November 2007) (*Saramaka* case).

27 *Saramaka* case (n 26), para 128.

28 *Endorois* case (n 24), para 235.

29 In the *Endorois* case, the petitioners argued that the displacement of the Endorois indigenous community from their ancestral land in the Rift Valley Province of Kenya violated, among others, the rights development under article 22 of the African Charter on Human and Peoples' Rights.

30 K M'Baye 'Le droit au développement comme droit de l'homme' (1972) 5 *Revue des droits de l'homme* 505; J Donnelly 'In search of the unicorn: the jurisprudence and politics of the right to development' (1985) 15 *California Western International Law Journal* 473, 474; O Oduwole 'Africa's contribution to the advancement of the right to development in international law' in CC Jalloh & O Elias (eds) *Shielding humanity: essays in international law in honour of Judge Abdul G Koroma* (2015) 565.

31 A Dieng 'Background to and growth of the right to development: the role of law and lawyers in development' in P Nobel (ed) *Refugees and development in Africa* (1987) 55.

32 ID Dunn *The right to development and international economic law: legal and moral dimensions* (2012) 41.

33 As previously stated.

34 As previously stated.

35 Declaration on the Right to Development, adopted by the UN General Assembly, Resolution 41/128, UN Doc A/RES/41/128 (4 December 1986).

36 African Charter on Human and Peoples' Rights, adopted by the Organisation of African Unity, OAU Doc CAB/LEG/67/3 rev 5 (27 June 1981), art 22.

37 As previously stated.

38 In, the *African Commission on Human and Peoples' Rights v Republic of Kenya* (*Ogiek* case) African Court on Human and Peoples' Rights emphasised that 'the drafters of the Charter deliberately omitted to define the notion [of peoples] in order to "permit a certain flexibility in the application and subsequent interpretation by future users of the legal instrument, the task of fleshing out the Charter being left to the human rights protection bodies."' While no treaty within the African regional human rights system defines 'peoples,' this concept has been linked to the African philosophy of communitarianism. Not only does the society exist through the individual, the society is integral to the formation of an individual, and the duties within the society are mutually owned in the realisation of the shared ideologies and common vision. According to Kiwanuka, the concept of 'peoples' is an 'embodiment of the African conception of a person in society.' The inclusion of peoples in the African Charter envisions the connection between the life of an individual and the society. As such, the well-being of an individual is integral to the life of the community since it is through this individual that the community exists. P Nobel 'The concept of "peoples"

in the African (Banjul) Charter on Human and Peoples' Rights' in Nobel (n 31) 9, 10; RN Kiwanuka 'The meaning of "people" in the African charter on human and peoples' rights' (1988) 82(1) *American Journal of International Law* 82; F Ouguergouz *The African Charter of Human and People's Rights: a comprehensive agenda for human dignity and sustainable democracy in Africa* (2003) 211; P Ikuenobe *Philosophical perspectives on communalism and morality in African traditions* (2006) 54; S Dersso 'Peoples' rights under the African charter on human and peoples' rights: much ado about nothing' SAIFAC Research Papers Series No 6, 5; *Endorois* case (n 24); SAD Kamga 'The right to development in the African human rights system: the *Endorois* case' (2011) 23 *De Jure* 381, 387; F Viljoen *International human right law in Africa* (2012) 219–228; Application No. 006/2012, *African Commission on Human and Peoples' Rights v Republic of Kenya* (2017), para 196.

39 The African Commission on Human and Peoples' Rights defines peoples as 'a group of individuals having a common identity on account of objective markers of shared language, racial or ethnic makeup, historical experience, religious, cultural or ideological affinity, connection to a particular territory and the subjective manifestations of self-identification and awareness as a distinct group possessing of shared identity.' Peoples are therefore not to be equated solely with 'Nation' or 'State,' but include sub-national groups including communities of a particular region exhibiting the aforementioned characteristics, or people whose resources are exploited under foreign occupation. See African Commission on Human and Peoples' Rights *State Reporting Guidelines and Principles on Articles 21 and 24 of the African Charter Relating to Extractive Industries, Human Rights and the Environment* (2018), para 6.

40 E.g., *Government of the Republic of South Africa v Grootboom* 2000 (11) BCLR 1169; *Modder East Squatters and Another v Modderklip Boerdery (Pty) Ltd, President of the Republic of South African and Others v Modderklip Boerdery (Pty) Ltd* (2004) ZASCA 47; *Nana Kofi Karikari & 44 Others v Ghanaian Australian Goldfields (GAG) Ltd* (2007) Suit No LS.34/97 (*Nkwantakrom* case); *Tswelopele Non-Profit Organisation and Others v City of Tshwane Metropolitan Municipality* (2007) ZASCA 70; *Occupiers of 51 Olivia Road, Berea Township, and 197 Main Street, Johannesburg v City of Johannesburg & Others* (2008) ZACC 1; *Mitu-bell Welfare Society v Attorney General & 2 others* (2013) eKLR (*Mitu-bell* case).

41 *Nkwantakrom* case (n 40).

42 ICESCR (n 20).

43 Universal Declaration (n 18), art 25(1); Centre on Housing Rights and Evictions *The human right to adequate housing: chronology of United Nations activity* (2000).

44 In 1991, the United Nations Committee on Economic, Social and Cultural Rights (CESCR) developed a set of General Comments on this right, asserting the incompatibility of forced evictions with the provisions of the ICESCR. In 1997, the CESCR developed a specific set of comments on forced evictions in relation to the right to housing in which it recognised the practice of evictions 'in the name of development.' Stressing that homelessness should not result from evictions, the CESCR further emphasised that a progressive realisation of the right to housing will 'rarely' be applicable to eviction cases. However, the finite scope of such rarity is not elucidated in the general comments. In 2007, the United Nations Special Rapporteur on the right to adequate housing developed a set of guidelines on development-based evictions within the context of the right to housing. General Comment No 4 on art 11(1): the right to adequate housing, adopted by the UN Committee on Economic, Social and Cultural Rights, UN Doc E/1992/23 (13 December 1991); General Comment No 7 on art 11(1): forced evictions, adopted by the UN Committee on Economic, Social

and Cultural Rights, UN Doc E/1998/22 (20 May 1997); UN Human Rights Council, 'Basic principles and guidelines on development-based evictions and displacement,' *Report of the Special Rapporteur on adequate housing as a component of the right to an adequate standard of living, Mr Miloon Kothari* UN Doc A/HRC/4/18 annex I (5 February 2007) (Kothari Principles).

45 Committee on Economic, Social and Cultural Rights, *Concluding observations on the second periodic report of Honduras,* UN Doc E/C.12/HND/CO/2 (11 July 2016); Committee on Economic, Social and Cultural Rights, *Concluding observations on the fourth and fifth periodic report of Angola,* UN Doc E/C.12/AGO/CO/2 (15 July 2016); Committee on Economic, Social and Cultural Rights, *Concluding observations on the second periodic report of Lebanon,* UN Doc E/C.12/LBN/CO/2 (24 October 2016).

46 UN Committee on Economic, Social and Cultural Rights, *Concluding observations on the fourth periodic report of Morocco,* UN Doc E/C.12/MAR/CO/4 (22 October 2015), para 43.

47 As previously stated, para 44.

48 General Comment No 7 (n 44), para 8.

49 Concluding observations of the UN Human Rights Committee: Kenya, adopted by the UN Human Rights Committee, UN Doc CCPR/CO/83/KEN (29 April 2005), para 22.

50 *Yordanova & Others v Bulgaria* ECHR (24 September 2012) (*Yordanova* case).

51 The ECHR made the point that '[s]ince the loss of one's home is a most extreme form of interference with the right under Article 8 to respect for one's home, any person at risk of an interference of this magnitude should in principle be able to have the proportionality and reasonableness of the measure determined by an independent tribunal in the light of the relevant principles under Article 8, notwithstanding that, under domestic law, he has no right of occupation.' See *Yordanova* case (n 50).

52 Other relevant norms applicable to the protection for DIDPs include the rights to free movement, equality and non-discrimination, life, dignity and social security. See *Sudan Human Rights Organisation & Another v Sudan* (2009) AHRLR 153 (ACHPR 2009) (*Sudan* case), para 189; African Charter (n 36), arts 2, 4 & 5; ICESCR (n 20), art 9; B Pettersson 'Development-induced displacement: internal affair or international human rights issue?' (2002) 12 *Forced Migration Review* 16.

53 Barutciski observes that until a legally binding document exists, 'concerned parties have to pursue their difficult work by making full use of the various human rights norms and existing mechanisms that can provide protections.' See M Barutciski 'International law and development-induced displacement and resettlement' in C De Wet (ed) *Development-induced displacements: problems, policies and people* (2006) 94.

54 Operational Policy 4.12 – Involuntary Resettlement 2001 (revised in 2013), art 6.

55 As previously stated.

56 World Bank *Accountability at the World Bank: the Inspection Panel 10 year on* (2003); See also D Clark & D Hunter 'The World Bank Inspection Panel – amplifying citizen voices for sustainable development' in G Alfredsson & R Ring (eds) *The Inspection Panel of the World Bank: a different complaints procedure* (2001) 167, 170.

57 D Szablowski *Transnational law and local struggles: mining, communities and the World Bank* (2007) 91.

58 J Wouters & C Ryngaert 'Good governance: lessons from international organizations' in DM Curtin & RA Wessel (eds) *Good governance and the European Union: reflections on concepts, institutions and substance* (2005) 83.

59 BS Chimni 'International financial institutions and international law: a third world perspective' in DD Bradlow & DB Hunter (eds) *International financial institutions and international law* (2010) 31, 49.
60 K Lucas 'The Inspection Panel of the World Bank: an effective extrajudicial complaint mechanism?' (2015) 6 *World Bank Review* 531, 533.
61 'Conclusion of the Inspection Panel Toolkit Review' *The World Bank (Factsheet)* (9 March 2020); 'World Bank enhances its accountability' *The World Bank (Press Release)* (9 March 2020).
62 As previously stated.

2 Development projects as a displacement phenomenon in Africa

2.1 Introduction

Significant attention in the literature on internal displacement has principally been around conflict as a principal root cause of internal displacement in Africa. However, the reality of internal displacement in Africa portrays the fact that internal displacement is a consequence of other key factors, one of which is the specific area this book engages, which is the issue of development-induced displacement (DID).

However, before considering development projects as drivers of internal displacement, it is relevant to examine the various root causes of internal displacement in Africa. This discussion is guided by the definition of internally displaced persons (IDPs) under article 1(k) of the African Union Convention for the Protection and Assistance of Internally Displaced Persons in Africa (Kampala Convention),[1] which specifically recognises four drivers of internal displacement, namely, armed conflict, situations of generalised violence, violations of human rights, and natural or human-made disasters.[2]

2.2 Drivers of internal displacement in Africa

2.2.1 Armed conflicts

The primary driver of internal displacement in Africa is armed conflict. However, it is useful to distinguish armed conflict in international law from the general notion of conflict, which also broadly includes generalised violence. Although the notion of armed conflict is not specifically defined in the laws of armed conflict, normative guidance and jurisprudence in international humanitarian law (IHL) recognises armed conflicts as 'a resort to armed force between states or protracted armed violence between governmental authorities and organised armed groups or between such groups within a state.'[3] This description gives an insight into the threshold for categorisation of armed conflicts.

Whenever states resort to armed forces, such scenarios emerge as an armed conflict. Across Africa, incidences of these conflicts in newly independent states emerged between Ethiopia and Somalia in the 1970s over the Ogaden region.[4] Earlier, in the 1960s, there was also an inter-state war between Somalia and Kenya from 1963–1964 in its northern region known as the *Shiftas* War.[5] Following Kenya's independence, ethnic Somalis in the north-eastern region of the state attempted to secede and join Somalia. This attempt was 'supported directly and indirectly by the Somali government.'[6] In the process, a significant population was displaced. One of the prominent manifestations of this form of armed conflict was between Ethiopia and Eritrea prior to its settlement in 2018.[7] However, much of the narrative on armed conflict as a root cause of internal displacement in Africa is driven by hostilities between states and organised armed groups within the context of non-international armed conflicts. In Mozambique, for instance, this was the situation between the government-led Mozambique Liberation Front (FRELIMO) and popular opposition, Mozambican National Resistance (RENAMO).[8] In Somalia and Nigeria, this is also the situation between government forces on the one hand, Al-Shabaab and Boko Haram, respectively, on the other hand.[9] In 2018, at least 16.8 million people were internally displaced by conflict,[10] the majority of which were armed conflicts.

2.2.2 *Situations of generalised violence*

Besides armed conflict, situations of generalised violence significantly drive internal displacement in Africa. Generalised violence emerges mostly in the context of indiscriminate acts against populations within a state and may be orchestrated by public or private actors. Although most often discussed in the context of Latin America, with respect to criminal gangs, situations of generalised violence are also widely prevalent in Africa. For instance, bandit attacks in the northern region of Nigeria have displaced thousands of people with figures rising as high as '4,030 persons from communities in four local government areas of . . . [Niger] state [in Nigeria].'[11] However, incidences of generalised violence are replete in many African countries, mostly through electoral violence. In Kenya, for instance, the 2007/2008 post-election violence displaced at least 255,000 people, with children comprising at least 100,000.[12]

2.2.3 *Natural or human-made disasters*

Natural or human-made disasters are also pertinent drivers of internal displacement in Africa. The connection between disasters and internal displacement has emerged within the context of nomadic movements, particularly in the horn of Africa region. From 2015 to 2017, more than 300,000 pastoralists were displaced by drought in Ethiopia's Somali region.

In this context, displacement is often a blend of disasters, violence and restricted access to grazing areas. In Somalia, where an estimated 60% of the population are pastoralists,[13] the magnitude of disaster-related displacement is evident. While most natural disasters are human-induced, the most prominent dimension of this nexus resonates in the context of climate change. Dimensions of this in Africa include: climate-development projects, climate-exacerbated conflict and climate-exacerbated natural disasters. In many parts of Africa, climate-exacerbated natural disasters have emerged in the climate-displacement discussion as an area where the impact of climate change is increasingly affecting human mobility through extreme weather conditions causing prolonged droughts and torrential rains.[14] There is also an emergence of climate-related conflicts, for instance, in parts of West Africa between agrarian and herder populations over limited resources affected by climate change. It is projected that at least 86 million people will move internally in Africa due to climate change by 2050. While this figure relates both to voluntary and forced migration, the data accentuates the imperative for urgent attention to the climate-displacement nexus, specifically within the context of internal displacement.[15]

2.2.4 Human rights violations

Human rights violations as drivers of internal displacement afford a lens through which to consider a range of circumstances that may give rise to internal displacement in Africa. Overall, understanding this root cause of internal displacement derives from a consideration of human rights norms at various levels: national, regional and global. However, it is useful to spotlight a significant dimension of this form of internal displacement through the lens of harmful practices, a prevalent violation of human rights in many African societies. While prominent, harmful practice-induced displacement is the least discussed in the context of internal displacement. In Africa, one evident manifestation of this is the ritual killing of albinos in some parts of the continent including Tanzania and Malawi.[16] In 2009, at least 10,000 albinos were forced to flee their homes in Tanzania as a consequence of ritual killings based on the belief that the body parts of albinos bring wealth and good luck.[17] In Malawi, this similar practice has caused persons with albinisms to move from rural areas 'to urban areas which are considered to be relatively safe.'[18] Due to their relatively small proportion, the UN Special Rapporteur on the human rights of persons with albinism notes that these persons are at a real risk of extinction.[19] Aside from ritual killing of albinos, another harmful practice is the phenomenon of breast ironing observed in parts of Cameroon.[20] This practice derives, in part, from the belief that promiscuity in young girls may be curbed through flattening of the breasts.[21] There have been other instances of girls fleeing their homes due to female genital mutilation and child marriage.[22] It is significant that the Kampala Convention specifically prohibits harmful practices as a cause of internal displacement.

2.3 Development projects and internal displacement

The Kampala Convention does not specifically mention development projects in the defintion of IDPs; however, it specifically addresses this root cause in article 10 of the Kampala Convention. It is useful, however, to reflect on the nexus between development projects and internal displacement.

Post-independence, many African countries embarked on development projects in fostering economic growth. Early pioneers of African development were unequivocal in describing these projects as imperatives for national economic futures.[23] While these ideological persuasions were mostly borne out of a strong belief that Africa's potential was reliant on these projects, they were not entirely premised on convictions without facts. There were good, valid reasons to adopt this rhetoric. Importantly, African states were particularly influenced by the evident success in Europe post-World War II.

At the end of the World War, following the establishment of the Bretton Wood Institutions, a Europe Recovery Programme (the Marshall Plan) was launched by the United States to provide assistance to Western European countries that had been economically affected by the war. The Marshall Plan, which was geared towards stimulating economic development in Western Europe, was to 'provide a cure rather than a mere palliative.'[24] While emphasising the need for the United States to 'do whatever it is able to do to assist in the return of normal economic health in the world,' Marshall underscored the fact that the initiative 'must come from Europe' and that the 'program should be a joint one.'[25] A favourable response from Western European states led to the initiation of the Marshall Plan. Between 1948 and 1951, the Marshall Plan provided significant finance in the furtherance of large-scale industries for countries in the region. The success of the Europe Recovery Programme in boosting economic recovery in Western European states provided an evidence base and a significant motivation for pursuing development projects that could modernise and shift societies to industrialised economies.

When African states started attaining independence, the allure of this approach was rooted in the evident progression towards economic growth and liberation from the colonial past. That Africa was richly endowed with natural resources gave an impetus to this ideology. Vast expanses of land and rich deposits of mineral resources in comparison with other parts of the world meant that Africa stood a good chance if these projects were established to achieve modernisation. In order to stimulate economic growth, these development projects have become an evident feature of national economic policies. Since the 1950s, development projects including dams, natural resource extraction, urban renewal, large-scale agricultural investments, and, in more recent years, climate carbon projects have become economic imperatives at a high human cost, particularly to those fated to make way for these projects.

2.3.1 Dams

The value of power generation to the industrialisation of Africa has justified the imperatives for large dams across several African countries. In Nkrumah's speech on the Volta River Project to the National Assembly in the 1960s, Nkrumah emphasised that[26]

> [t]he abundant supply of electrical power will bring light to thousands of homes in the country-side where darkness now prevails. It will make available power practically at the doorsteps of businessmen and entrepreneurs in urban areas, and offer them a powerful stimulus for the modernization of existing industries and the development of new ones. The increased use of electricity will help to reduce the foreign exchange expenditure on imported fuel oil. The production of aluminium ingots will add to the range of Ghana's exports and stimulate a greater development of our rich bauxite resources.

The metaphor of bringing 'light to thousands of homes in the country-side where darkness now prevails' created a compelling narrative. But Nkrumah was not alone in these positions. Earlier in the 1950s, Nasser compared the Aswan High Dam to the Great Pyramids of Egypt, stating that[27]

> For thousands of years the Great Pyramids of Egypt were fore-most among the engineering marvels of the world. They ensured life after death to the Pharaohs. Tomorrow, the gigantic High Dam, more significant and seventeen times greater than the Pyramids, will provide a higher standard of living for all Egyptians.

The allures of the project, encased in its potential benefits, made the human cost less of an imperative. The Volta River Project displaced 'over 80,000 people from more than 700 villages.'[28] But resettlement was done 'into just 52 villages with the promise of housing and the foundations for productive agriculture.'[29] Johnson, Howell and Evered observe that '[i]n the process, land resources and local economic vitality was lost, to say nothing of the populations' traditional identities and cultural practices.'[30] According to Tamakloe, 'planners overemphasised the national interest of the Volta River Project, as against the local interest of the resettlers.'[31] Houses provided in resettlement were not constructed with due consideration for the size of the household.[32] The economic livelihoods of some of those displaced were heavily impacted and some communities had to find alternative means of sustenance following the loss of their former means of livelihood. While these consequences were positively reframed,[33] the enduring effect of the displacement and poorly planned resettlement are still being felt by the displaced communities.[34]

In the case of the Aswan High Dam, at least 100,000 Nubians were displaced and not properly resettled.[35] Aside from challenges relating to basic amenities such as water and health services, the 'New Nubia' resettlement site was not built with a consideration of the socio-cultural lifestyle of the Nubians. Agha observes that the 'Nubians refused to call these settlements New Nubia and instead called it Tahgeer, meaning place of displacement.'[36] Since the 1960s, this rhetoric has continued to characterise the realities of displaced communities in various states, for instance with the Cahora Bassa Dam in Mozambique in the 1970s, the Manantali dam in Mali in the 1980s, and the Katse and Muela dams in Lesotho in the 1990s. The Merowe dam in Sudan, which led to the displacement of over 50,000 people, exposed the displaced population to a range of socio-economic deprivations. Askouri observes that '[p]roposed resettlement sites are barren, windswept places with no groundwater supply.'[37] Moreover, the impacts of these dams on downstream communities are consequences that are sometimes left out of analytical studies. For instance, in the case of the Merowe dam, this was a pertinent concern.[38]

2.3.2 Natural resource extraction

Natural resource extraction is also a prevalent cause of DID in Africa. Within this context, displacement principally emerges from activities geared towards the recovery of oil and natural gas. While examples of this cause of internal displacement have received attention in oil-rich countries such as Nigeria,[39] there have also been instances of this in Guinea with gold mining and in Zimbabwe with diamond mining. In the Kintinian village of Guinea, for instance, more than 1,000 individuals were displaced for the expansion of mining activities by South Africa's Anglo-Gold Ashanti in Area One. Kaufman indicates that the government of Guinea[40]

> sent military and police force in over alarming numbers to intimidate the community into leaving the land. The community was resisting but they were forced to concede the land because corporate representatives accompanied by heavily armed soldiers went door to door forcing them to agree to an inventory of their assets and eventually sign over the land.

This rhetoric has also characterised the nature of displacement in Zimbabwe, particularly with regards to the displacement of members of the Chiadzwa community to make way for the Marange diamond mines. Community members were not properly consulted on resettlement choices.[41] Inadequate compensation and issues of improper resettlement have emerged in other contexts, for instance, with regards to the displacement of families from the Dambankhoto village in Senegal's Sabodala region for gold mining activities. While consultations with the community were held and a resettlement agreement was negotiated between local authorities, corporate representatives and the chief of Dambankhoto, the provisions of the agreement were not fully complied with. A report by Amnesty International indicates that[42]

> [w]hen the families arrived at the new site [in April 2011] they found that the facilities were not what they had been promised. The housing provided was inadequate – including buildings without doors in some cases. Of particular concern to the Dambankhoto community was the loss of access to land on which they depended for subsistence agriculture and grazing cattle, and the loss of access to their local water sources, including a nearby stream, which they used for water for domestic purposes and crop irrigation. The relocation included a vegetable garden for the women, who had maintained gardens at the original site. However, there was no access to agricultural land at the new site.

Initially, only houses were offered as compensation to the displaced persons. Upon refusal, financial compensation was proposed. However, only a few families received the monetary compensation.[43] Some of the housing units were not completed prior to displacement, contrary to the assurances that had been given to the affected communities. At the resettlement site, there was limited access to agricultural land, even though it is known that these families depend on agricultural sustenance. Although a socio-economic and environmental impact assessment was prepared prior to the grant of an Environmental Compliance Certification by the Senegalese government,[44] the consent of the families was only sought and obtained after the government had approved the corporation's occupation of the land. As a result, '[t]he families concerned . . . had only limited ability to negotiate the terms of . . . displacement.'[45]

2.3.3 Urban renewal

Infrastructure projects generally seek to enhance and sustain the necessary conditions for daily exercise of economic and social life within societies. These projects include highways, tunnels, telecommunications, pipelines, sewage, bridges, rails, airports, seaports and roads. While they are imperative to the business life of a nation, they are often carried out at a significant cost to local populations in many parts of Africa. Issues of inadequate compensation and consultation with affected populations often emerge in the implementation of these projects. In Egypt, for instance, an estimated 2,000 people were displaced to make way for the extension of the Suez Canal without adequate compensation.[46] In situations where compensation is paid for the implementation of these projects, there have been issues with delay. For instance, those displaced to make way for the Julius Nyerere International Airport experienced significant delays in receiving their compensation package. Mteki, Murayama and Nishikizawa observe that 'the Tanzania Airports Authority (TAA), the main implementing agent, failed to pay compensation in a timely way and, as a result, there was a 12-years delay.'[47] Concerns over such situations of delay and inadequate compensation have raised apprehension over megaprojects such as the Lamu Port South Sudan Ethiopia Transport (LAPSSET) project. The LAPSSET project is a multi-billion dollar project aimed at creating essential infrastructure including railways, resort cities, pipelines, sea port and airports.[48] While being imperative to stimulate development in Ethiopia, Kenya and South Sudan, the human cost has been a major concern, particularly for indigenous populations in Kenya.

In recent years, displacements for urban development have been widespread across Africa.[49] In Zimbabwe, over 700,000 individuals were displaced in Operation *Marambatsvina* carried out by Zimbabwean authorities in 2005.[50] An objective of the Operation *Marambatsvina*, which translates to 'drive out rubbish'[51] or 'clean out the filth,'[52] was to clean up slums.[53] Thousands of individuals were displaced and several properties were destroyed.[54] Although the government had previously stated that the operation would begin on 30 June 2005, police officials destroyed several properties, homes and businesses on 24 May 2005.[55] Similar urban renewal strategies have led to widespread displacements in Kenya in places such as Kibera and Mitumba village.[56]

In Nigeria, several urban renewal projects have led to displacements in cities such as Abuja, Lagos and River State.[57] In 2009, the Rivers State Government (RSG) unveiled its Greater Port Harcourt City Development (GPHCD) plan – an urban development project initiated to attract investment and tourism into Rivers State. For the implementation of the project, the RSG established a GPHCD Authority with the vision to[58]

> transform the Greater Port Harcourt Area into a world class city, internationally recognized for excellence, and the preferred destination for investors and tourists. The objective is to build a well planned city, through the implementation and enforcement of policies that will ensure the provision of first-rate infrastructure and delivery of quality services to enhance the standard of living and well being of the people.

The GPHCD was to be implemented in phases and, as part of the process, communities living in waterfront areas of the state such as Njemanze, Abonnema, Bundu, Elechi Beach, Okrika and Marine base[59] were to be displaced. As justification for the displacement, the RSG Information and Communication Commissioner claimed that residents of the waterfront communities lived 'demeaning lives' and the government desired to take them out of such conditions.[60] Although the 2003 River State Physical Planning and Development Law provided alternatives to displacements and contains provisions on consultation, its procedural requirements were not adequately complied with.[61] On 28 August 2009, about 17,000 individuals were forcibly displaced in Njemanze. According to a statement by Amnesty International[62]

> [p]eople living in the Njemanze waterfront were given only a week's notice and there was no genuine consultation with residents to identify alternatives to the eviction. People were not provided with legal remedies and very few provided with compensation or alternative housing. Thousands of people, including children, women, and the elderly were left homeless and vulnerable to other human rights violations.

In 2012, the RSG demolished the Abonnema Wharf waterfront slum displacing between 10,000 and 20,000 people.[63] Prior to displacement, the RSG had agreed to compensate all land owners and resolve disputes arising from the compensation process.[64] The RSG further promised that displacements would only occur after a month's notice had been given.[65] However, the displacement of residents in the communities occurred before compensation was fully paid to all the land owners.[66] The RSG did not provide alternative housing, nor did it consider the socio-economic impact that displacement would have on the affected communities.

In addition, sufficient notice was not given, nor was temporary shelter provided to ensure that those displaced were not rendered homeless.[67] On the day of eviction, heavily armed men were employed to supervise the demolition of houses. With little time to recover property and make arrangements for alternative accommodation, some residents lost their belongings and slept on the streets and in cars.[68] The displacement was carried out not only in disregard of the agreement between the state and members of the community, but it was also conducted in disregard of a high court injunction restraining the government from carrying out demolitions.[69] Some members of the community were also violently evicted. According to the Social and Economic Rights Action Centre (SERAC), '[r]esidents that attempted to salvage personal properties were brutally beaten by members of the demolition squad.'[70] Further, compensation was imposed in a 'take it or leave it' style.[71]

2.3.4 Large-scale agricultural investments

Large-scale agricultural investments have also occasioned significant population displacement in several parts of Africa. Often described in the rhetoric of 'land grabs,' these investments create dire consequences for Africa, where 70% of the population are 'dependent on agriculture for livelihoods.'[72] Reports indicate that an estimated 15–20 million hectares of land 'in developing countries have been subject to transactions or negotiations involving foreign investors'[73] in the period between 2006 and mid-2009, with a significant majority in Africa.[74] In Madagascar, the proposed acquisition of 1.3 million hectares of land for maize production by a South Korean corporation galvanised attention to this issue.[75] In many cases across Africa, the narrative of large-scale agricultural investments have been driven by the economic imperative, not only to supply food to foreign markets but also to stimulate national economic growth.

In Uganda, for instance, the government entered into an investment agreement with the Neumann Kaffee Gruppe for the establishment of a large-scale coffee plantation in 2001. Earlier in 2000, the Ugandan government developed a Poverty Eradication Action Plan (PEAP). Primarily, the PEAP sought to transform Uganda 'into a modern economy in which people in all sectors can participate in economic growth.'[76] Part of the objective of the PEAP was to stimulate economic growth through modernised agriculture and for the furtherance of this, a Plan for Modernization of Agriculture (PMA) was developed. The mission of the PMA was to tackle poverty through a shift from 'subsistence agriculture to commercial agriculture.'[77] Modernising agriculture was considered an imperative in 'increasing incomes of the poor by raising farm productivity, increasing the share of agricultural production that is marketed, and creating on-farm and off-farm employment.'[78] Given that the large-scale coffee plantation fit within the national priority, it provided an evident advantage. But establishing the plantation meant that a significant proportion of land was required. Land was acquired from a registered title holder; however, Uganda's law creates a dual system of land tenure under which interest in land could be held by a title holder and *bona fide* occupants. In this case, there were bona fide occupants on the land who were not adequately compensated as lawfully required. Occupants of the land were told to leave by 31 August 2001. However, before the expiration of the notice, they were displaced. Kasoma Aminadabu, one of those displaced, recalls that[79]

> [t]hey ruined my banana and coffee plantation. They took away all my livestock. They ruined all my houses. I lost everything. One of my children was killed when we had to flee. Then soldiers came with an excavator and tore down our house when we had to flee.

Tumwine Evaristo further describes the incidence, noting how they[80]

> saw a military truck coming, it was full of soldiers. Behind that was a second car with civilians. They weren't wearing any uniforms. They were armed with clubs and sticks. They went to the houses and yelled 'everybody out!' Whoever tried to save things from the inside of their house was beaten with billy clubs and had to flee. The children were afraid and ran in all directions. Some tried to save their goats and household goods but they didn't know how. They even had to leave their chickens

behind. Then they burned down my beehives and my house. Many people were sitting in the car. They split up into groups and barged into every house, every house. Those who weren't able to save themselves quickly enough had to watch as they cut the banana trees and threw them into their car. Those who weren't able to save themselves quickly enough had to watch them cut the fruit down from off the trees and throw them into their car. Some hit the community members as they did so.

2.3.5 Climate projects

In the previous section, one of the identified dimensions of climate change and internal displacement was climate projects. These projects may be geared towards climate adaptation or mitigation. Under the United Nations Framework Convention on Climate Change (UNFCCC), the imperative of this project is underscored by the need to address the concentration of greenhouse gases in the atmosphere. This has led to the initiation of projects such as the Batéké Plateau project in the Democratic Republic of Congo (DRC) initiated to enhance carbon sinks while also providing wood in parts of the DRC. A significant challenge with this project, however, is the fact that land belonging to the indigenous Batwa peoples were plundered.[81] Consultation with the indigenous peoples also resonates as a concern. Adrien observed that Batwas were not seen to be included in 'the preparation of the Ibi Carbon Sink project on the ground, no more than we see them benefitting from the realization of the project activities on the Batéké Plateau.'[82] These groups were also not distinctively provided for and, as such, were made to endure 'discrimination and servitude.'[83] Other similar projects in countries such as Kenya and Uganda have unveiled the challenge of climate-related development-induced displacement – an emerging phenomenon in Africa that requires more studies and significant attention in view of the impact of climate change and the imperative of addressing it.

2.4 Conclusion

This chapter has considered the main dimensions of DID in Africa drawing on situations in various countries and the challenge that emerges from the furtherance of these projects. Not only do these cases reveal the magnitude of the problem in Africa, they also reveal an inadequate balance between the imperative of development and the rights of persons likely to be displaced. To states, the issue of DID poses a complex question on how to resolve a majority/minority tension. When faced with this challenge, states often resort to pitching the interest of a majority over the needs of the minority and, as such, fail to protect development-induced displaced persons. However, this decision is often met with counter-hegemonic resistance from displaced communities who challenge the notion that development comes at a human sacrifice. Hence, the daunting question has always been: how can a balance be struck between the imperative of development and the rights of displaced persons? In answering this question, the fourth chapter analyses the provision of article 10 of the Kampala Convention. Before engaging this provision, it is relevant to consider the legal framework on internal displacement and, in particular, the Kampala Convention as a regional response to the issue of internal displacement in Africa.

Notes

1 African Union Convention for the Protection and Assistance of Internally Displaced Persons in Africa, adopted at the Special Summit of the African Union Heads of States and Government in Kampala, Uganda (19–23 October 2009) (the Kampala Convention). Cross-referencing is to endnotes in this chapter.

2 Article 1(k) of the Kampala Convention defines IDPs as 'persons or groups of persons who have been forced or obliged to flee or to leave their homes or places of habitual residence, in particular as a result of or in order to avoid the effects of armed conflict, situations of generalized violence, violations of human rights or natural or human-made disasters, and who have not crossed an internationally recognized State border.' Kampala Convention (n 1), art 1(k).

3 P Rowe 'The application of international humanitarian law to attacks on education in armed conflict' in United Nations Educational, Scientific and Cultural Organization (ed) *Protecting education from attack: a state-of-the-art review* (2010) 179, 180; International Committee of the Red Cross 'How is the term "armed conflict" defined in international humanitarian law?' (Opinion paper, March 2008).

4 A Adepoju 'The politics of international migration in post-colonial Africa' in R Cohen (ed) *The Cambridge survey of world migration* (1995) 170.

5 K Weitzberg 'Rethinking the *Shifta War* fifty years after independence: myth, memory, and marginalization' in MM Kithinji, MM Koster and JP Rotich (eds) *Kenya after 50: reconfiguring historical, political, and policy milestones* (2016) 65, 77.

6 O Otunnu 'Factors affecting the treatment of Kenyan-Somalis and Somali refugees in Kenya: a historical overview' (1992) 12(5) *Refuge* 21, 23.

7 A Underwood 'The sudden end of the Ethiopia-Eritrea war, explained' *Vox* 31 July 2018; R Bereketeab *The Ethiopia-Eritrea rapprochement: peace and stability in the horn of Africa* (2019).

8 S Funada-Classen *The origins of war in Mozambique: a history of unity and division* (2012); SA Emerson *The battle for Mozambique: the Frelimo-Renamo struggle, 1977–1992* (2014).

9 SJ Hansen *Al-Shabaab in Somalia: the history and ideology of an Islamist group, 2005–2012* (2013); D Joseph & H Maruf *Inside Al-Shabaab: the secret history of Al-Qaeda's most powerful ally* (2018); B Thurston *Boko Haram: the history of an African jihadist movement* (2018); EE Anugwom *The Boko Haram insurgence in Nigeria: perspectives from within* (2019).

10 Internal Displacement Monitoring Centre *Africa report on internal displacement* (2019) 37.

11 'Bandits displace 4,030 persons in Niger – NSEMA' *The Guardian* 3 February 2020.

12 'Kenya post-election violence displaces over 100,000 children – UNICEF' *UN News* 17 January 2008.

13 F Jibrell 'Pastoralism in Somalia: a lifestyle under threat' https://afrikansarvi.fi/issue1/15-artikkeli/41-pastoralism-in-somalia-a-lifestyle-under-threat (accessed 16 February 2020).

14 R McKie 'Global heating to inflict more droughts on Africa as well as floods' *The Guardian* 16 June 2019; 'East Africa reels from deadly floods in extreme weather' *News24* 2 November 2019; K Silverstein 'For Southern Africa, climate change is real as prolonged droughts are creating food shortages' *Forbes* 7 November 2019; R Washington 'How Africa will be affected by climate change' *BBC (News)* 15 December 2019.

15 World Bank *Groundswell: preparing for internal climate migration* (2018).

16 Under the Same Sun *Reported attacks of persons with albinism* (2016).

17 'Report: scores of albinos in hiding after attacks' *CNN* 29 November 2009; T Odula 'East African albinos flee murder, dismemberment' *The Toronto Star* 29 November 2009; UN General Assembly 'Enjoyment of human rights by persons with albinism,' prepared by Ms Ikponwosa Ero, UN Special Rapporteur on the enjoyment of human rights by persons with albinism,' *Note by the Secretary-General,* UN Doc A/71/255 (29 July 2016), para 58.

18 Amnesty International *"We are not animals to be hunted or sold" Violence and discrimination against people with albinism in Malawi* (2016) 35.

19 'In Malawi, people with albinism face "total extinction" – UN rights expert' *UN News Centre* 29 April 2016; Statement by the United Nations Independent Expert on the enjoyment of human rights by persons with albinism, Ms Ikponwosa Ero, upon conclusion of her official visit to Malawi – 18 to 29 April, 2016 www.ohchr.org/EN/NewsEvents/Pages/DisplayNews.aspx?NewsID=19903&LangID=E (accessed 21 May 2020).

20 See R Tapscott 'Understanding breast "ironing": a study of the methods, motivations, and outcomes of breast flattening practices in Cameroon' Feinstein International Center, Tufts University (2012) 2 http://fic.tufts.edu/assets/Understanding-breast-flattening.pdf (accessed 21 May 2020).

21 BR Ngunshi *Breast ironing . . . a harmful practice that has been silenced for too long* (2011).

22 R Jelimo 'Nandi girl walks 50km to flee forced marriage' *The Standard Media* 22 June 2015; 'The Kenyan girls who fled their families to escape FGM' *BBC News (Africa)* 14 July 2016; Amnesty International *Coerced and denied: forced marriages and barriers to contraception in Burkina Faso* (2016) 4.

23 A significant discussion of this issue was originally published in R Adeola 'The legal protection of development-induced displaced persons in Africa' (2017) 10(1) *African Journal of Legal Studies* 91.

24 C Tarnoff 'The Marshall Plan: design, accomplishments, and significance' Congressional Research Service (CRS) Report (18 January 2018); Remarks by the Secretary of State (George C Marshall Jr) at Harvard University (5 June 1947) (Marshall Plan Speech) 6.

25 Marshall Plan Speech, (n 24) 7.

26 Speech by Dr Kwame Nkrumah of Ghana on the Volta River Project (25 March 1963); J Woddis 'Ghana's changing economy' (1964) www.sahistory.org.za/sites/default/files/archive-files4/Acn1764.0001.9976.000.017.Apr1964.4.pdf (accessed 16 February 2020).

27 J Joestan 'Nasser's daring dream: the Aswan High Dam' (1960) 16(2) *The World Today* 55, 59.

28 LB Johnson, JP Howell & KT Evered ' "Where nothing was before": (re)producing population and place in Ghana's Volta River Project' (2015) 32(2) *Journal of Cultural Geography* 195, 204.

29 Johnson, Howell & Evered (n 28) 204.

30 As previously stated.

31 MA Tamakloe 'Long-term impacts of resettlement: the Akosombo dam experience' in CC Cook (ed) *Involuntary resettlement in Africa: selected papers from a conference on environment and settlement issues in Africa* (1994) 99, 101–102.
32 P Gyau-Boakye 'Environmental impacts of the Akosombo dam and effects of climate change on the lake levels' (2001) 3(1) *Environment, Development and Sustainability* 25.
33 Johnson, Howell & Evered (n 28) 205.
34 D Darko *et al* 'The context and politics of decision making on large dams in Ghana: an overview' Future Dams Working Paper 002 (2019) 27–28; 'Ministry prioritizes communities displaced by Volta Lake Project' *Citi 97.3 FM* 2 February 2018.
35 HM Fahim *Dams, people and development: the Aswan High Dam Case* (1981) 59.
36 M Agha 'Nubia still exists: on the utility of the nostalgic space' (2019) 8(1) *Humanities* 24. Fahim also observed that in the Aswan High Dam resettlement, official statistics confirmed an increase in mortality rate among the Nubians during the two years after relocation. See HM Fahim 'Community-health aspects of Nubian resettlement in Egypt' (1979) 55–56 *Kroeber Anthropological Society Papers* 81.
37 AK Askouri 'The Merowe dam: controversy and displacement in Sudan' (2004) 21 *Forced Migration Review* 56.
38 R Abbas 'Sudan: no clear studies on impact of Merowe Dam' *Inter Press Service* 2 January 2012.
39 See O Oluduro *Oil exploitation and human rights violations in Nigeria's oil producing communities* (2014) 271.
40 'Guinea: South Africa's Anglo-Gold Ashanti accused of wrongful eviction of villagers' *West Africa Democracy Radio* 2 February 2017.
41 C Madebwe *et al* 'Involuntary displacement and resettlement to make way for diamond mining: the case of Chiadzwa villagers in Marange, Zimbabwe' (2011) 1(10) *Journal of Research in Peace, Gender and Development* 292, 297.
42 Amnesty International *Mining and human rights protection in Senegal: closing the gaps in protection* (2014) 16–17.
43 As previously stated.
44 The socio-economic and environmental impact assessments were prepared by Tropica Environmental Consultants in 2006 for TGC. In 2008, the *Ministère de l'Environnement et de la Protection de la Nature* granted the Environmental Compliance Certification. AMC Mining Consultants (Canada) Ltd 'Technical report Sabodala gold project, Senegal, West Africa: prepared for Teranga Gold Corporation' (2012) 177.
45 Amnesty International (n 42) 37.
46 '"New Suez Canal" construction displaces over 2,000 people in Egypt' *Middle East Eye* 13 February 2015.
47 N Mteki, T Murayama & S Nishikizawa 'Social impacts induced by a development project in Tanzania: a case of airport expansion' (2017) 35(4) *Impact Assessment and Project Appraisal* 272.
48 'What is the LAPSSET Corridor Program' www.lapsset.go.ke/#1461328856794-2dee9bba-e774 (accessed 19 February 2020).
49 See AL Oseni 'Mega city projects leave slum dwellers with uncertain future' *Premium Times* 31 May 2013; Amnesty International 'Public statement: state of housing rights and forced evictions in Africa: African Commission on Human and Peoples' Rights during its 50th ordinary session, to be held in Banjul, The Gambia 24 October–7 November 2011' www.refworld.org/pdfid/4eba7e912.pdf (accessed 21 May 2020).
50 Report of the Fact Finding Mission to Zimbabwe to assess the scope and impact of Operation Marambatsvina by the UN Special Envoy on Human Settlements Issues in Zimbabwe: Mrs. Anna Kajumulo Tibaijuka (2005) 7 (Tibaijuka Report).

51 'Million squatters face eviction' *News24* 24 May 2005.
52 'Zimbabwe "forced child evictions": Amnesty' *Times Live* 5 October 2011.
53 J Nicolai 'Operation Marambatsvina: a crime against humanity under the Rome statute?' 21(5) *American University International Law Review* 813, 819–819.
54 Tibaijuka Report (n 50) 7; Human Rights Watch *Zimbabwe: evicted and forsaken: internally displaced persons in the aftermath of Operation Marambatsvina* (2005) 10.
55 As previously stated.
56 M Masava 'Mitumba slum dwellers evicted, land fenced off' *The Star* 9 January 2012.
57 'Police displace thousands in Nigeria's Otodo-Gbame slum' *Al Jazeera* 18 March 2017; IJ Ike & A Esiebo ' "They came while we were asleep": Lagos residents tell of brutal evictions' *The Guardian (UK)* 31 May 2017; O Olawoyin 'Displaced Otodo-Gbame residents protest in Lagos' *Premium Times (Nigeria)* 15 November 2017; BN Obiadi, AO Onochie & PU Uduak 'Where is home for the Abuja, Nigeria urban poor' (2019) 8(1) *Mgbakoigba, Journal of African Studies* 50; 'Many rendered homeless as Navy evicts residents from Tarkwa Bay' *Punch* 21 January 2020; O Jonathan 'Tears as soldiers evict Tarkwa Bay residents from home' *Premium Times (Nigeria)* 21 January 2020; 'Tarkwa Bay residents storm Alausa, protest forceful eviction' *Channels Television* 28 January 2020; 'Nigeria court orders halt to Lagos waterfront evictions' *News24* 30 January 2020; 'Court orders halt to Tarkwa Bay waterfront evictions' *The Guardian (Nigeria)* 31 January 2020; T Ahemba 'Nigeria evicted 800,000 Abuja residents: report' *Reuters* 15 May 2008; Amnesty International *"Just move them" forced evictions in Port Harcourt, Nigeria* (2010); 'Lagos state government displaced the people of Makoko community' *CNN iReport* 19 July 2012; A Adegbite 'The tragic end of Makoko' *The Guardian (Nigeria)* 22 July 2012; E Sessou 'The untold story of Badia as 40,000 displaced persons groan in pain' *Vanguard* 2 March 2013; E Sessou 'Ijora-Badia proposed 1008 housing project: govt can't be trusted on the project' *Vanguard* 9 March 2013; EBA Agbaje 'Modernisation, urban renewal and the social cost of development' (2013) 4(10) *Mediterranean Journal of Social Sciences* 318, 321.
58 Greater Port Harcourt City Development Authority 'The Authority' http://www.gph-city.com/about/authority.php (accessed 21 May 2020).
59 'Fresh battled on Port Harcourt's waterfronts' *Daily Trust* 6 November 2010.
60 T Morford 'Demolition of Abonnema and other water front communities (2)' *Vanguard* 27 August 2012.
61 Amnesty International *Nigeria: forced eviction of Abonnema wharf waterfront: 'Pack and Go!'* (2012) 22–23.
62 'Nigeria: Two years after Njemanze community was demolished – Nigerians need a housing policy that respects human rights' *Amnesty International (Joint Public Statement)* 26 August 2011.
63 'Urgent action (bad news): Nigeria. Thousands forcibly evicted in Port Harcourt' *Amnesty International* 20 August 2012.
64 Amnesty International 2012 (n 61) 19.
65 As previously stated.
66 As previously stated (n 21).
67 A Akujobi 'RSG defends Abonnema wharf demolition' *The Tide* 29 June 2012; 'Amnesty International condemn forced evictions in Abonnema Wharf' *Vanguard* 6 July 2012.
68 Amnesty International 2012 (n 61) 5.
69 *Jim George & Others v The Executive Governor of Rivers States & Others* (2011) (PHC/2286/2009); V Obia 'SERAC condemns demolition of Abonnema' *This Day Live* 01 July 2012; F Morka 'Abonnema wharf community demolished by the Rivers State Government in flagrant disregard of judicial process' *Social and Economic Rights Action Center (SERAC)* 29 June 2012; Amnesty International 2012 (n 61) 5.

70 SERAC (n 69) 1.
71 T Morford 'Demolition of Abonnema wharf community and other waterfronts communities: Rivers State Government must end demolition and pay adequate compensation' *Socialist Democracy* 6 July 2012.
72 M Biteye '70% of Africans make a living through agriculture, and technology could transform their world' *World Economic Forum (News)* 6 May 2016.
73 Large-scale land acquisitions and leases: a set of core principles and measures to address the human rights challenge, Mr Olivier De Schutter, Special Rapporteur on the Right to Food (11 June 2009); T Kachika 'Land grabbing in Africa: a review of the impacts and the possible policy responses' (2010) 20 www.oxfamblogs.org/eastafrica/wp-content/uploads/2010/11/Land-Grabbing-in-Africa.-Final.pdf (accessed 2 March 2020); 'Foreign land investments in developing countries – contribution or threat to sustainable development?' (Swedish FAO Committee Publication Series No 7, 2010) 7; J Cherian 'Grabbing Africa' *Frontline* (20 April 2010).
74 A Spieldoch & S Murphy 'Agricultural land acquisitions: implications for food security and poverty alleviation' in M Kugelman & SL Levenstein *Land grab? The race for the world's farmland* (2009) 39, 42; C Stebbins 'African land grab threatens food security: study' *Reuters* 27 July 2011.
75 'Land leased to secure crops for South Korea' *Financial Times* 18 November 2008; B Head 'Deal brings many jobs, but at what price?' *The Guardian (UK)* 22 November 2008; 'Madagascar scraps Daewoo farm deal' *Financial Times* 18 March 2009; V Vinciguerra 'How the Daewoo attempted land acquisition contributed to Madagascar's political crisis in 2009' Paper presented at the International Conference on Global Land Grabbing (6–8 April 2011); 'The global farmland grab in 2016: how big, how bad?' *GRAIN* 14 June 2016; R Vellvé & M Rakotondrainibe 'The Daewoo-Madagascar land grab: ten years on' *Reuters* 16 November 2018.
76 Ministry of Finance, Planning and Economic Development (Kampala) 'Uganda's poverty eradication action plan: summary and main objectives' Poverty Reduction Strategy Paper (2000) 3; Republic of Uganda 'Plan for Modernisation of agriculture: eradicating poverty in Uganda' https://semuwemba.files.wordpress.com/2010/03/uga-plan-for-modernisation-of-agriculture.pdf (accessed 19 February 2020).
77 Republic of Uganda (n 76) vi.
78 Republic of Uganda (n 76) vi.
79 FIAN International 'Coffee to go – with a taste of eviction' A Film from: Michael Enger (2012).
80 As previously stated.
81 A significant discussion of this issue was originally published in R Adeola & F Viljoen 'Climate change, development projects and internal displacement in Africa' (2018) 62(3) *Journal of African Law* 335–350; SM Adrien 'The DRC case study: The impact of the "Carbon Sinks of Ibi-Batéké Project" on the indigenous pygmies of the Democratic Republic of Congo' in M Abhainn, KM Bernard & S Grey (eds) *Indigenous peoples and climate change: vulnerabilities, adaptation and responses to mechanisms of the Kyoto Protocol: a collection of case studies* (2007) 65.
82 Adrien (n 81) 61.
83 Adrien (n 81) 62–63.

3 The development of the Kampala Convention as a regional response

3.1 Introduction

This chapter discusses the regional normative law on internal displacement – the African Union Convention for the Protection and Assistance of Internally Displaced Persons in Africa (Kampala Convention).[1] Over the last decade, the Kampala Convention has become a significant framework for the furtherance of protection and assistance to IDPs. The Kampala Convention has shaped action at various levels of governance on internal displacement and has become the primary text for understanding the extent of protection and assistance to Internally Displaced Persons (IDPs) in Africa. With nearly two-thirds ratification, its significance on the regional map as a normative framework on IDP issues is evident. This chapter focuses on the instrument, particularly on its development as a regional response to internal displacement. However, before considering the Kampala Convention, it is useful to examine the global framework on internal displacement – the United Nations (UN) Guiding Principles of Internal Displacement, which predates the Kampala Convention and from which the latter draws normative strength.

3.2 The Guiding Principles

During a UN meeting on refugees and stateless persons in 1949, the representative of Greece drew attention to the importance of assisting persons who were not outside the territory of their state. Greece asserted that while this did not raise the issue of 'legal protection,' the 'material distress' of these persons 'was causing grave anxiety to the Greek Government.'[2]

However, not until the 1980s did the imperative for international protection of IDPs emerge on the global agenda.[3] At the 1988 International Conference on the Plight of Refugees, Returnees and Displaced Persons in Southern Africa (SARRED), held in Oslo, Norway,[4] the absence of a specific international mechanism for internally displaced persons (IDPs) was highlighted.[5]

One of the recommended action points in the Oslo Declaration and Plan of Action on the Plight of Refugees, Returnees and Displaced Persons (adopted at SARRED) was that the United Nations (UN) Secretary-General should 'undertake studies and consultations in order to ensure . . . timely implementation and overall co-ordination of relief programmes for these people.'[6] After SARRED, the UN General Assembly asked the UN Secretary-General to examine the need for the development of a UN structure for relief to IDPs.[7] The UN Economic and Social Council also urged the UN Secretary-General to carry out a 'United Nations system-wide review'[8] and 'recommend ways of maximising co-operation and co-ordination among . . . various organisations of the United Nations system in order to ensure an effective response . . . to the problems of refugees, displaced persons and returnees.'[9]

With ongoing global deliberations on relief-based assistance,[10] there were groups that called for a more substantive approach, such as the Friend World Committee for Consultation (Quakers).[11] In 1992, the UN Commission on Human Rights (CHR) requested the UN Secretary-General to designate an IDP representative.[12] The representative was to seek 'views and information from Governments on the human rights issues relating to internally displaced persons.'[13] The CHR further urged states to 'make known their views on the subject.'[14] Francis Deng, a seasoned diplomat, was appointed by the UN Secretary-General.[15]

When Deng and his team began to execute the mandate, they decided early on to adopt a soft law approach.[16] Indeed, there were those who would have preferred a more binding instrument. However, there were obvious challenges with the creation of a binding instrument at the time. The first challenge relates to state sovereignty and the attendant consequences of seeking to elaborate a norm that would regulate the internal affairs of states. Indeed, Deng observed that states 'saw the formulation of a convention as a long-term objective, but argued for developing guiding principles or a declaration that would pave the way for a legally binding instrument in the future.'[17] Another part of the challenge was the fact that proposing a hard law would mean developing a treaty that would have to be negotiated by states. This could affect the elaboration of a comprehensive approach to IDP protection. Moreover, there was a pressing need to respond to the gap in IDP protection and assistance at the global level.[18] Hence, having 'an initial statement of principles' that could be utilised to enhance global attention to IDP issues was imperative.[19] This initial statement would 'prepare the ground for a more legally binding document.'[20] Through a thorough and inclusive consultative process,[21] a set of Guiding Principles on Internal Displacement (the Guiding Principles)[22] was developed in 1998. In the last two decades, this initial statement has emerged as a global rhetoric for advancing protection and assistance to IDPs.[23] A notable manifestation of its value is in the development of the Kampala Convention.

3.3 The Kampala Convention

Prior to the development of the Kampala Convention, the imperative for a regional framework that responds to the issue of internal displacement was first advanced in the Great Lakes region. In 2006, African countries in the Great Lakes developed a Protocol on the Protection and Assistance to Internally Displaced Persons (the Great Lakes Protocol)[24] as part of the Declaration on Peace, Security, Democracy and Development. Article 2(1) provides that one of the aims of the Great Lakes Protocol is to '[e]stablish a legal framework in the Great Lakes region for ensuring the adoption by [m]ember [s]tates of the Guiding Principles on Internal Displacement.'[25]

Owing to the severity of the issue of internal displacement in Africa,[26] in 2004 the African Union (AU) Executive Council took a decisive step towards a regional approach to the issue of internal displacement.[27] Deciding that a legal document was needed, the AU Executive Council[28] mandated the AU Commission to come up with a solution securing the protection of IDPs.[29] The Division of Humanitarian Affairs, Refugees and Displaced Persons in the Department of Political Affairs of the AU Commission had the responsibility of ensuring the accomplishment of this mandate.[30] For this purpose, Dr Chaloka Beyani, a Zambian international law expert and the former UN Special Rapporteur on the Human Rights of IDPs, was requested to prepare a draft document. A concept note was developed and discussed by experts in 2005.[31] At this meeting, an 'annotated framework' was prepared,[32] and was then presented and adopted at the second AU Ministerial Conference on Refugees, Returnees and Internally Displaced Persons (the second Ministerial Conference) in Ouagadougou, Burkina Faso.[33] Beyani notes that at this conference, 'the ministers resolutely affirmed "zero" tolerance for refugees and internally displaced persons in Africa and called upon member states to achieve this objective.'[34]

In 2006, the AU Executive Council endorsed the outcome of the second Ministerial Conference meeting[35] and requested the AU Commission to start preparations for an AU Assembly summit.[36] The AU Executive Council also asked the AU Commission to 'expedite . . . efforts in collaboration with the PRC Sub-Committee on Refugees, Returnees and Internally Displaced Persons and with the participation of relevant partners at the appropriate instance.'[37] Following pertinent deliberations on the Kampala Convention,[38] a draft Convention was adopted at the Third Ministerial Conference on Refugees, Returnees and Internally Displaced Persons in 2008. Following a series of postponements, a Special Summit of Heads of State and Government (AU Assembly) was eventually held in Kampala, Uganda,[39] at which the Kampala Convention was adopted on 23 October 2009.

The Kampala Convention is a set of 23 articles divided into four pertinent themes: prevention of internal displacement, protection during internal displacement, humanitarian assistance and durable solutions.[40] As with the Guiding Principles, the Kampala Convention is emphatic on the primary responsibility of the state in the protection and assistance of IDPs. However, it notably reinforces international assistance and state cooperation in the protection of IDPs. As with the Guiding Principles, the Kampala Convention incorporates the right not to be arbitrarily displaced, which is pertinent to addressing internal displacement.[41] While the Kampala Convention draws normative strength from the Guiding Principles, there are certain novelties of the Kampala Convention such as its recognition of harmful practices as a root cause of internal displacement, and also the issue of climate change.[42] The Kampala Convention further extends to non-state actors, recognising the evident reality of these actors on the scene of internal displacement in Africa.[43] While making reference to existing regional mechanisms such as the African Peer Review Mechanism (APRM) and the African Commission on Human and Peoples' Rights (ACHPR), the Kampala Convention establishes a Conference of State Parties for monitoring the implementation of its provisions.[44] Overall, the Kampala Convention creates a regional standard for the protection and assistance of IDPs, which is binding on state parties.[45]

Since its formation, the Kampala Convention has had significant impacts in the furtherance of protection and assistance for IDPs in Africa. From a normative perspective, the impact of the Kampala Convention resonates at national and regional levels. Since the development of the Kampala Convention, at least seven AU member states have developed normative frameworks on the Kampala Convention. Notable among these are Niger and Somalia, with law and policy on IDPs, respectively. In 2018, Niger adopted the first national legislation leveraging on the Kampala Convention. As with the Kampala Convention, Niger's IDP Law recognises protection from arbitrary displacement and incorporates the idea of the Kampala Convention in relation to DID, with an emphasis on the fact that in the implementation of development projects, the state or other organisations, groups or individuals involved have an obligation to prevent the risk of internal displacement.[46]

Somalia's normative landscape on IDP has flourished from a policy perspective, both within the regional governments of Somalia and at the federal level.[47] The Puntland IDP policy reinforces the objective of creating synergy with the Kampala Convention.[48] Likewise, Somalia's national IDP Policy, adopted in 2019, references the Kampala Convention and its prohibition of arbitrary displacement. The federal policy reflects protection from DID, in fairly similar terms to the Kampala Convention, adopting the phrase 'as far as possible.'[49]

At the regional level, other standards have been developed based on the Kampala Convention including the Model Law on the Kampala Convention and a General Comment by the African Commission on Human and Peoples' Rights (African Commission) relating to the free movement of persons within state borders in Africa. Developed through the African Union Commission on International Law (AUCIL), the Model Law on the Kampala Convention offers guidance for the development of national law on internal displacement. Adopted in 2018 by the AU Assembly, the Model Law provides 'an exposition on the Kampala Convention and reinforces the interpretation of national legislation in line with the Kampala

Convention.'[50] In 2019, the African Commission adopted a General Comment on Free Movement of Persons, which provides specific safeguards for IDPs within the context of free movement, referencing the Kampala Convention.[51] The Kampala Convention is also reflected in the Protocol to the African Charter on Human and Peoples' Rights on the Rights of Persons with Disabilities in Africa.[52]

3.4 Conclusion

While drawing on the Guiding Principles, the Kampala Convention contextualises IDP protection with a significant understanding of the regional context and challenges. Over the last decade, the Kampala Convention has emerged as an important framework for the protection and assistance of IDPs in Africa, recognising various root causes of internal displacement including DID. Article 10 of the Kampala Convention sets out the obligation of the states in the context of DID. While there is no absolute obligation to prevent DID, there is a duty on states to prevent arbitrary displacement. The next chapter examines the extent of the obligation in article 10 with a focus on how a balance can be struck between the imperative of development and the rights of persons likely to be displaced.

Notes

1 African Union Convention for the Protection and Assistance of Internally Displaced Persons in Africa, adopted at the Special Summit of the African Union Heads of States and Government in Kampala, Uganda (19–23 October 2009) (the Kampala Convention). Cross-referencing is to endnotes in this chapter.

2 UN General Assembly *Provisional summary record of the two hundred and fifty-seventh meeting held at Lake Success, New York, on Tuesday, 8 November 1949, at 3 p.m.* (9 November 1949), para 17; For further discussion, see also P Orchard *Protecting the internally displaced: rhetoric and reality* (2019).

3 See R Cohen & F Deng *Masses in flight: the global crisis of internal displacement* (1998) 1; DA Korn *Exodus within borders: an introduction to the crisis of internal displacement* (1999).

4 According to Richter '[t]he conference brought together most of the African countries, many of the Western and Socialist states and a substantial number of IGOs [intergovernmental organisations] and NGOs [non-governmental organisations]. Some 100 delegations were represented at SARRED, which was attended by about 600 people.' R Richter 'International Conference on the Plight of Refugees, Returnees and Displaced Persons in Southern Africa (SARRED), Oslo, 22–24 August 1988' (1989) 2(2) *Journal of Refugee Studies* 284; The Conference was organised pursuant to a resolution 42/106 of the General Assembly made on 7 December 1987. The Resolution requested the 'Secretary-General of the United Nations, in close cooperation with the UN High Commissioner for Refugees, to give all possible assistance to the Secretary-General of the Organization of African Unity in the preparation and organisation of the Conference.' International Conference on the Plight of Refugees, Returnees and Displaced Persons in Southern Africa, adopted by the UN General Assembly Resolution 42/106, UN Doc A/RES/42/106 (7 December 1987).

5 UN General Assembly *International Conference on the Plight of Refugees, Returnees and Displaced Persons in Southern Africa: Report of the UN Secretary-General*, UN Doc A/43/717 (19 October 1988).

6 Oslo Declaration and Plan of Action on the Plight of Refugees, Returnees and Displaced persons in Southern Africa, adopted at the International Conference on the Plight of Refugees, Returnees and Displaced Persons in Southern Africa, held at Oslo, Norway (22–24 August 1988), para 21.

7 International Conference on the Plight of Refugees, Returnees and Displaced Persons in Southern Africa, adopted by UN General Assembly Resolution 43/116, UN Doc A/RES/43/116 (8 December 1988).

8 Refugees, Displaced Persons and Returnees, UN Economic and Social Council Resolution 1990/78, UN Doc E/RES/1990/78 (27 July 1990) (Resolution 1990/78), para 7.

9 Resolution 1990/78 (n 8), para 8.

10 UN Economic and Social Council, Addendum, 'Annex: Report on refugees, displaced persons and returnees, prepared by Mr. Jacques Cuénod, Consultant,' *Note by the Secretary-General*, UN Doc. E/1991/109/Add.1 (27 June 1991); a significant discussion of the Guiding Principles was originally published in R Adeola & F Viljoen 'The right not to be arbitrarily displaced in Africa' (2017) 25(4) *African Journal of International and Comparative Law* 459.

11 R Cohen 'The guiding principles on internal displacement: an innovation in international standard setting' (2004) 10 *Global Governance* 459, 462; R Cohen 'UN human rights bodies should deal with the internally displaced' presented at a meeting for delegates to the UN Commission on Human Rights by the Quaker United Nations Office and the World Council of Churches (7 February 1990) 5; 'Human rights protection for internally displaced persons' an international conference convened by the Refugee Policy Group (24–25 June 1991).

12 Internally Displaced Persons, adopted by the UN Commission on Human Rights Resolution 1992/73, UN Doc. E/CN.4/RES/1992/73 (5 March 1992).

13 As previously stated, para 2.

14 As previously stated, para 4.

15 FM Deng 'The global challenge of internal displacement' (2001) 5(1) *Washington University Journal of Law and Policy* 141.

16 W Kälin 'How hard is soft law? The Guiding Principles on Internal Displacement and the need for a normative framework' Brookings/CUNY Project on Internal Displacement (19 December 2001) 1.

17 UN Commission on Human Rights 'Annex: Comprehensive study prepared by Mr Francis Deng, Representative of the Secretary-General on the human rights issues related to internally displaced persons, submitted pursuant to Commission on Human Rights resolution 1992/73' *Note by the Secretary-General* UN Doc. E/CN.4/1993/35 (21 January 1993), para 78.

18 As previously stated, paras 280–284.

19 As previously stated, para 283.

20 As previously stated.

21 UN Commission on Human Rights, 'Internally displaced persons' *Report of the Representative of the Secretary-General, Francis M. Deng, submitted pursuant to Commission on Human Rights resolutions 1993/95 and 1994/68*, UN Doc. E/CN.4/1995/50 (2 February 1995); UN Commission on Human Rights 'Internally displaced persons: compilation and analysis of legal norms' *Report of the Representative of the Secretary-General, Mr Francis M Deng submitted pursuant to the UN Commission on Human Rights resolution 1995/57*, UN Doc. E/CN.4/1996/52/Add.2 (5 December 1995).

22 UN Commission on Human Rights, Addendum, 'Guiding Principles on Internal Displacement' *Report of the Representative of the Secretary-General,*

Mr. Francis M. Deng, submitted pursuant to Commission on Human Rights resolution 1997/39, UN Doc. E/CN.4/1998/53/Add.2 (11 February 1998) (the Guiding Principles).

23 See generally Cohen (n 56) 459–480; C Phuong *The international protection of internally displaced persons* (2005); TG Weiss & DA Korn *Internal displacement: conceptualization and its consequences* (2006); ED Mooney 'Something old, something new, something borrowed . . . something blue? The protection potential of a marriage of concepts between R2P and IDP protection' in Sara E Davies & Luke Glanville (eds) *Protecting the displaced: deepening the responsibility to protect* (2010) 59; R Adeola 'The right not to be arbitrarily displaced under the United Nations Guiding Principles on Internal Displacement' (2016) 1 *African Human Rights Law Journal* 84, 90; DJ Cantor 'Returns of internally displaced persons during armed conflict: international law and its application in Colombia (2018) 15–17; D Casalin 'The Guiding Principles in international human rights courts' (2018) 59 *Forced Migration Review: Twenty Years of the Guiding Principles on Internal Displacement* 42–43.

24 Protocol on the Protection and Assistance of Internally Displaced Persons (2006) (the Great Lakes Protocol). There are 12 countries in the Great Lakes Region, namely, Angola, Burundi, Central African Republic, Democratic Republic of Congo, Kenya, Republic of Congo, Rwanda, South Sudan, Sudan, Uganda, Tanzania and Zambia. International Refugee Rights Initiative 'Comparison of the Kampala Convention and the IDP Protocol of the Great Lakes Pact' (2014). See W Kälin 'The Great Lakes Protocol on Internally Displaced Persons: responses and challenges' *Brookings* 27 September 2007.

25 The Great Lakes Protocol (n 24), art 2(1).

26 In 2003, over half of the world's 25 million IDPs were recorded as being in Africa. 'African Union addressing the challenge of forced displacement in Africa' Conference Background Paper, Special Summit on Refugees, Returnees and Displaced Persons in Africa held in Addis Ababa, Ethiopia (5–11 November 2008).

27 Civil society organisations within and outside Africa were also involved. See 'Forced displacement, citizenship and statelessness in Africa: report of a civil society consultation on African Union mechanisms and the protection of refugees, internally displaced persons and citizenship rights' (2009).

28 AU Executive Council, fifth ordinary session 25 June–3 July 2004, Addis Ababa, Ethiopia, Decision on the meeting of experts on the review of OAU/AU treaties, Doc EX/CL/95 (V) para 4(i).

29 AU Executive Council, fifth ordinary session 25 June–3 July 2004, Addis Ababa, Ethiopia, Decision on the Situation of Refugees, Returnees and Displaced Persons Doc EX. CL/108 (V), para 8.

30 AU Economic, Social and Cultural Council 'Making the Kampala Convention work for IDPs: Guide for civil society on supporting the ratification and implementation of the Convention for the Protection and Assistance of Internally Displaced Persons in Africa' (2010) 20.

31 'On the occasion of the commemoration of the entry into force of the African Union Convention for the Protection and Assistance of Internally Displaced Persons in Africa (the Kampala Convention)' Statement made by Chaloka Beyani in Addis Ababa, Ethiopia (6 December 2012).

32 'Implementation of the African Union Convention for the Protection and Assistance of Internally Displaced Persons (IDPs) 2009 (The Kampala Convention)' Speech delivered by Chaloka Beyani at the first ministerial meeting of the Economic Community of West African States (ECOWAS) on internally displaced Persons in Abuja, Nigeria (7 July 2011).

33 As previously stated.

34 C Beyani 'Recent developments: the elaboration of a legal framework for the protection of internally displaced persons in Africa' (2006) 50(2) *Journal of African Law* 187, 195.
35 AU Executive Council, ninth ordinary session, 25–29 June 2006, Banjul, the Gambia, Decision on the ministerial conference on refugees, returnees and internally displaced persons, Doc EX.CL/259 (IX), para 4.
36 As previously stated, para 7.
37 AU Executive Council, ninth ordinary session, 25–29 June 2006, Banjul, the Gambia, Decision on the situation of refugees, returnees and displaced persons, Doc EX.CL/254 (IX), para 9.
38 'Explanatory note on the African Union Convention on the Protection and Assistance of Internally Displaced Persons in Africa (Kampala Convention)' 2.
39 AM Abebe 'The African Union convention on internally displaced persons: its codification background, scope and enforcement challenges (2010) 29(3) *Refugee Survey Quarterly* 28, 40.
40 See MT Maru *The Kampala Convention and its contribution to international law: legal analyses and interpretations of the African Union Convention for the Protection and Assistance of Internally Displaced Persons* (2014); AM Abebe 'Legal and institutional dimensions of protecting and assisting internally displaced persons in Africa' (2009) 22(2) *Journal of Refugee Studies* 155; P Kamungi 'Beyond good intentions: implementing the Kampala Convention' (2010) 34 *Forced Migration Review* 53; M Stavropoulou 'The Kampala Convention and protection from arbitrary displacement' (2010) 36 *Forced Migration Review* 62; W Kidane 'Managing forced. Displacement by law in Africa: the role of the new African Union IDPs Convention' (2011) 44(1) *Vanderbilt Journal of Transnational. Law* 1; FZ Guistiniani 'New hopes and challenges for the protection of IDPs in Africa: the Kampala Convention for the Protection and Assistance of Internally Displaced Persons in Africa' (2011) 39(2) *Denver Journal of International Law and Policy* 347; L Groth 'Engendering protection: an analysis of the 2009 Kampala Convention and its provision for internally displaced women' (2011) 23(2) *International Journal of Refugee Law* 1; K Ridderbos 'The Kampala Convention and obligations of armed groups' (2011) 37 *Forced Migration Review* 36; C D'Orsi 'Strengths and weaknesses in the protection of the internally displaced persons in Sub-Saharan Africa' (2012) 28(1) *Connecticut Journal of International Law* 73; L Bailey 'Out of Africa: toward regional solutions for internal displacement' (2014) 39(1) *Brooklyn Journal of International Law* 353; A Abebe *The Emerging Law of Forced Displacement in Africa: Development and Implementation of the Kampala Convention on Internal Displacement* (2016); R Adeola & F Viljoen (n 10); A Dieng 'Protecting internally displaced: the value of the Kampala Convention as a regional example' (2017) 99(904) *International Review of the Red Cross* 263–282; R Adeola 'The Kampala Convention and the right not to be arbitrarily displaced' (2018) 59 *Forced Migration Review* 15.
41 Kampala Convention (n 1), art 4(4); Guiding Principles (n 22), principle 6.
42 Kampala Convention (n 1), arts 4(4)(e) & 5(4).
43 Kampala Convention (n 1), art 2(4) & 3(1)(h) & (i).
44 Kampala Convention (n 1), art 14.
45 Article 2 of the Kampala Convention provides that the objectives are to: '(1) Promote and strengthen regional and national measures to prevent or mitigate, prohibit and eliminate root causes of internal displacement as well as provide for durable solutions; (2) Establish a legal framework for preventing internal displacement, and protecting and assisting internally displaced persons in Africa; (3) Establish a legal framework for solidarity, cooperation, promotion of durable solutions and mutual support between the States Parties in order to

combat displacement and address its consequences; (4) Provide for the obligations and responsibilities of States Parties, with respect to the prevention of internal displacement and protection of, and assistance, to internally displaced persons; (5) Provide for the respective obligations, responsibilities and roles of armed groups, non-state actors and other relevant actors, including civil society organizations, with respect to the prevention of internal displacement and protection of, and assistance to, internally displaced persons.' Kampala Convention (n 1), art 2.

46 Specifically, it provides in the French text that '[d]ans le cadre de la réalisation des projets de développement, l'Etat, toute organisation, tout organisme ou tout individu intervenant dans la prise en charge des personnes déplacées internes a l'obligation de prévenir les risques de déplacement interne.' Niger Law No 2018–74 (10 December 2018), art 8.

47 Puntland Policy Guidelines on Displacement (2014); Bandir Regional Administration and Municipality of Mogadishu *Internally Displaced Person and Refugee Returnees Policy* (2019); Somalia: National Policy on Refugee-Returnees and Internally Displaced Persons (IDPs) (2019).

48 Puntland Policy Guidelines on Displacement (n 47).

49 Somalia: National Policy on Refugee-Returnees and Internally Displaced Persons (n 47) 10.

50 R Adeola 'The impact of the African Union Convention on the Protection and Assistance of Internally Displaced Person in Africa' (2019) 19 *African Human Rights Law Journal* 591, 601; see also R Adeola 'The African Union Model Law on Internally Displaced Persons: a critique' in O Shyllon *The Model Law on Access to Information for Africa and other regional instruments: Soft law and human rights in Africa* (2018) 234.

51 General Comment on art 12(1) of the African Charter on Human and Peoples' Rights (2019).

52 Protocol to the African Charter on Human and Peoples Rights on the Rights of Persons with Disabilities, adopted by the AU Assembly at the 30th Ordinary Session in Addis Ababa, Ethiopia (29 January 2018).

4 Development projects and human rights

Striking a balance between the imperative and the rights of persons likely to be displaced

4.1 Introduction

The crux of this chapter is article 10 of the African Union Convention for the Protection and Assistance of Internally Displaced Persons in Africa (the Kampala Convention).[1] Article 10 of the Kampala Convention reads:

> States Parties, as much as possible, shall prevent displacement caused by projects carried out by public or private actors;
>
> States Parties shall ensure that the stakeholders concerned will explore feasible alternatives, with full information and consultation of persons likely to be displaced by projects;
>
> States parties shall carry out a socio-economic and environmental impact assessment of a proposed development project prior to undertaking such a project.

This provision sets out the obligation of states with respect to development-induced displacement (DID). Within the context of this provision, this chapter examines how a balance can be struck between the imperative of development and the rights of persons likely to be displaced.

4.2 The principle in article 10(1)

Article 10(1) of the Kampala Convention sets out the crux of state obligation on DID. While it provides that 'States Parties, as much as possible, shall prevent displacement caused by projects carried out by public or private actors,'[2] it does not define the scope of this obligation, in particular its usage of the term 'as much as possible.' However, the Kampala Convention, overall, seeks to prevent arbitrary displacement. Article 3(1)(a) of the Kampala Convention is emphatic on this, requiring states to '[r]efrain from, prohibit and prevent arbitrary displacement of populations.'[3] Article 4(4) also protects the right not to be arbitrarily displaced.[4] From its ordinary meaning,[5] the word 'arbitrary' may mean 'groundless,' 'unjustifiable' or 'unreasonable.'[6] Generally, this indicates that the word 'arbitrary' connotes an unbalanced action. In the *Elettronica Sicula S.p.A. (ELSI) (United States of America v Italy)*,[7] the International Court of Justice (ICJ) offered a useful insight on the word 'arbitrary,' stating that more than 'unlawfulness,' which 'may well be relevant to an argument that. . . [an act] was also arbitrary,'[8] the notion of arbitrary implies 'a wilful disregard of due process.'[9] In determining what constitutes arbitrary displacement, there are two principal emphases: legality of the root cause of internal displacement and due process in the context of the specific act of displacement.

The question of the legality of internal displacement resonates from the permissibility of the specific root cause of internal displacement in international law. Article 4(4) of the Kampala Convention offers an insight into permissible and impermissible forms of internal displacement. Although it does not specifically recognise DID, in sub-paragraph (h) it prohibits internal displacement that 'is not justified under international law, including human rights and international humanitarian law.'[10] Generally, development projects are permissible grounds of internal displacement,[11] where they serve 'compelling and overriding public interests.'[12] Earlier drafts of the Kampala Convention incorporated this provision in similar terms to the Guiding Principles, however, this was subsequently removed. Nonetheless, the Kampala Convention does not permit DID where it is 'arbitrary,' or put differently, where it constitutes 'a wilful disregard of due process.' The notion of due process may be categorised in three dimensions: general, cause-specific and group-based guarantees. While general guarantees relate to a wide-range of safeguards on internal displacement in the Kampala Convention, group-based guarantees relate to safeguards that apply to specific categories of persons as provided under international human rights law. Cause-specific guarantees relate to specific safeguards with respect to the root cause of internal displacement, which in this context is DID. Pertinently, there are two cause-specific guarantees in the DID context: participation and prior-impact assessments. With reference to articles 10(2) and 10(3), the next section examines these guarantees.

4.3 Participation and prior impact assessments: prerequisites in striking a balance in development-induced displacement

Article 10(2) of the Kampala Convention encapsulates the prerequisite of participation in requiring states to 'ensure that stakeholders concerned will explore feasible alternatives, with full information and consultation of persons likely to be displaced by projects.'[13] However, nowhere in the Kampala Convention are the terms used in this provision explained. In analysing this obligation, it is relevant to proceed from an understanding of its key elements, namely: 'stakeholders,' 'consultation,' 'information,' 'feasible alternatives' and 'persons likely to be displaced.'

4.3.1 Participation – article 10(2)

4.3.1.1 Stakeholders

Depending on its contextual use, the word 'stakeholder' is polysemic. In business, the word 'stakeholder' is used with reference to persons with an interest in the activities of a corporation.[14] To understand its use in the context of DID, it is relevant to consider the policies of international financial institutions in which the term has been defined in relation to development projects.[15]

The World Bank defines stakeholders as 'those affected by the outcome – negatively or positively – or those who can affect the outcome of a proposed intervention.'[16] Three specific categories are identified, namely, the government, those who will be directly affected by the project and those who are indirectly affected by the project. Within those directly affected are beneficiaries and those who are bound to be negatively affected, such as persons likely to be displaced. The World Bank recognises that '[t]he poor and marginalized are often among this group.'[17] Those indirectly affected include persons who 'because of their technical expertise or public and private interest in Bank-supported policies or programs' are relevant. Civil society, professionals and corporations are included in this category.[18]

The African Development Bank takes a similar position with respect to its definition of stakeholders in stating that stakeholders are 'people/communities who may – directly or indirectly, positively or negatively – affect or be affected by the outcomes of projects or programs.'[19] It proposes certain questions in identifying stakeholders. These questions encompass: project beneficiaries, those who will be negatively affected, vulnerable groups, project promoters, project oppositions, project implementers, financiers and those '[w]hose behaviour has to change for the intervention to succeed.'[20] Broadly, these groups can be categorised into primary and secondary stakeholders. Similar to direct stakeholders recognised in the World Bank Sourcebook, primary stakeholders are those on whom the development project will either have a positive or negative effect. Comparable with indirect stakeholders recognised in the World Bank Sourcebook, secondary stakeholders are those whose actions can influence the implementation of development projects, such as civil society, development actors, state agencies and private sector firms.

In light of the foregoing, 'stakeholders' in article 10(2) of the Kampala Convention need to be understood as encompassing both primary and secondary stakeholders. As such, stakeholders include individuals, communities, corporate bodies and institutions connected with the implementation of a project, including those that are bound to be affected negatively and positively. However, given that article 10(2) of the Kampala Convention specifically requires that consultation should be done between stakeholders and persons likely to be displaced, persons likely to be displaced represent a distinct category.

4.3.1.2 Consultation

In defining consultation, it is essential to consider the generic concept from which it derives, which is the concept of participation.[21] There is wide consensus about the fact that participation is crucial not only for legitimising decision-making processes but also for ensuring that decisions from these processes are durable. In the development discourse, participation has been described in metaphors such as 'shibboleth of development'[22] and 'development orthodoxy.'[23] While a single definition of participation has proved challenging, scholars such as Oakley, Cornwall and Cleaver agree that it requires an engagement of individuals in decision-making.[24] Scholars such as Ake, Diamond, Linz and Lipset agree that participation is integral to the realisation of democracy.[25] In the literature, participation has been described from various angles including 'community participation,' 'public participation,' 'popular participation' and 'citizen participation.'

The rhetoric of community participation dwells in its emphasis on people-driven development. In the development discourse, community participation has been recognised as 'an active process by which beneficiary/client groups influence the direction and execution of a development project with a view to enhancing their well being.'[26] While popular, public and community participation have been identified as one and the same,[27] citizen participation holds a different meaning. Citizen's participation emphasises the involvement of the governed in government, and is closely linked with political participation. According to Arnstein, citizen participation is 'the redistribution of power that enables the have-not citizens, presently excluded from the political and economic processes, to be deliberately included in the future.'[28]

An underlying emphasis of these forms of participation is the need for meaningful involvement of individuals and groups in decision-making processes. However, in development practice, participation has been watered-down in semantic formulations such as 'utilisation,' 'contribution,' 'enlistment' and 'consultation.'[29] Smith notes that consultation is 'the weakest form of participation in decision-making.'[30] According to Cornwall, consultation 'is widely used, north and south, as a means of legitimating already-taken decisions.'[31] Consultation, as a weak form of participation, is conceived as a process through which 'affected populations are asked to offer their opinions, suggestions, and perspectives but are not involved in decision-making or implementation of projects.'[32] Although conceptual distinctions are drawn between consultation and other forms of participation (such as contribution, utilisation and enlistment), a significant question which needs to be answered is: should consultation in the context of article

10(2) of the Kampala Convention be conceived as a means of legitimising already-made decisions or merely gathering opinions?

Such interpretation will be an anomaly, as it goes against the object and purpose of the Kampala Convention. In understanding the object and purpose of the Kampala Convention, it is relevant to consider specific provisions of the Kampala Convention including the Preamble which is 'the natural place in which to look for, an express or explicit general statement of the treaty's objects and purposes.'[33] Paragraph 3 of the Preamble emphasises the commitment of states to 'providing durable solutions' as an underlying reason for the creation of the Kampala Convention. Under article 11(1) of the Kampala Convention, states are obligated to 'seek lasting solutions to the problem of displacement by promoting and creating satisfactory conditions for voluntary return, local integration or relocation on a sustainable basis.'[34] A significant indicator of durable solutions emphasised by the Inter-Agency Standing Committee on Durable Solutions for IDPs is that such solution must result in a situation where IDPs 'no longer have any specific assistance and protection needs that are linked to their displacement and [as such] can enjoy their human rights without discrimination on account of their displacement.'[35] The idea which resonates from this fact is that durable solutions should involve 'a workable balance between the development agenda and protection schemes for communities already displaced or in danger of being displaced.'[36] In achieving a workable balance, there must necessarily be an agreement between the state and persons likely to be displaced. However, such agreement cannot be realised where consultation is regarded as a means of merely gathering opinions or legitimising already-made decisions.

Interpreting 'consultation' as merely a means of gathering opinions or legitimising already-made decisions equally goes against the obligation of states to formulate development plans based on the active, free and meaningful participation of persons involved.[37] Active, free and meaningful participation of individuals in development processes means a purposeful engagement of individuals in development plans, programmes and projects (bound to affect them) in a manner devoid of coercion. Such participation must necessarily be a two-way process and should drive development outcomes. Hence, if states are to ensure free, active and meaningful participation in development processes, 'consultation' cannot merely be a form of legitimising already-made decisions relating to development projects.

Having emphasised that consultation cannot be regarded as a means of merely gathering opinions or legitimising already-made decisions, an important question which needs to be answered is: how should the process of consultation be understood?

In view of the accepted wisdom of proffering African solutions to African problems, it is essential to consider the nature of consultation in African traditions and customs. In Southern Africa, among the Tswana people of

Botswana, there is a *kgotla* system, recognised by the government as a traditional institution for settling matters.[38] At the *kgotla*, members of a community gather to deliberate on issues affecting them and decisions are reached through consensus.[39] Similar practices exist under the *baito* system in Eritrea and in the *gumi gayo* system among the borana of Kenya and Ethiopia.[40] Under these systems, the local assembly gather to deliberate on issues of concern to the community and decisions are taken by consensus.[41] Bereketeab notes that 'the *baito* system of local governance . . . was marked by three salient features (i) direct democracy, (ii) consensus-based decision making, and (iii) the three functions of governance incorporated in one.'[42] Among the Akans of Ghana, the lineages are the political entities.[43] These lineages are represented in the town council by an *abusua panyin* who ensures that members of the lineages are consulted in issues that affect them. The significance of this dwells in the proverb that 'one head does not go into council'[44] and that 'wisdom is like a baobab tree; no one individual can embrace it.'[45] These traditional mechanisms illustrate that consensual decision-making processes are integral to African traditional systems. Lending credence to this assertion, Ake argues that 'traditional African political systems were infused with democratic values. They were invariably patrimonial and consciousness was communal; everything was everybody's business, engendering a strong emphasis on participation.'[46] Factually, consultation in these traditions are deliberative processes geared towards resolving issues and reaching certain goals.

Consultation, in the context of article 10(2) of the Kampala Convention, should be construed as a consensual decision-making process geared towards exploring feasible alternatives and not just a project-legitimising performance where opinions are merely gathered.

4.3.1.3 Information

The need for information is closely linked to the process of consultation. Article 10(2) of the Kampala Convention requires that persons likely to be displaced are fully informed. Under international human rights law, the right to information is often associated with freedom of expression.[47] In article 19 of the ICCPR, the right to freedom of expression includes the right to 'seek, receive and impact information and ideas of all kinds.'[48] McDonagh argues that '[t]he foundation of the argument for including a right to information under the umbrella of freedom of expression is that access to information is a pre-condition of the full exercise of the right to freedom of expression.'[49] Freedom of expression entails the right to voice an opinion or a thought without fear of intimidation or coercion by the state or a third party.

In response to the political repressions of absolutism in Europe in the 17th and 18th century, scholars including Locke, Rousseau and Milton emphasised the concept of liberal democracy through writings on social contract and the importance of the human agency in the creation of the state.[50] Central to this ideology is the fact that state institutions must reflect the will of the people. States are therefore to be accountable to the people 'who . . . [are] the rightful owners of their destiny,'[51] and have only submitted their will collectively in exchange for its protection. As integral as their active participation is to the state's legitimacy, so also is their right to be informed. Schauer argues that '[i]f everyone is to participate equally, then everyone must have the information necessary to make that participation meaningful.'[52]

In light of this link between information and consultation, the pertinent question in the context of this discussion is: what is 'information' as required under article 10(2)? In answering this question, it is relevant to consider what information means. For this purpose, the Model Law on Access to Information for Africa (Model Law), which 'serves as a benchmark for measuring compliance with regional and international human rights standards,'[53] is considered. Article 1 of the Model Law defines information as including[54]

> [a]ny original or copy of documentary material irrespective of its physical characteristics, such as records, correspondence, fact, opinion, advice, memorandum, data, statistic, book, drawing, plan, map, diagram, photograph, audio or visual record, and any other tangible or intangible material, regardless of the form or medium in which it is held, in the possession or under the control of the information holder to whom a request has been made.

In light of article 7 of the Model Law, information relating to the policies and operations of public and private bodies, and those setting out the processes of engagement with the public, are to be provided. In view of article 5 of the Model Law, which emphasises the consideration of international standards favourable to the interpretation of the right to access information, it is also relevant to consider the report of the UN Special Rapporteur on the promotion and protection of the right to freedom of opinion and expression (the UN Special Rapporteur).[55] In the 2013 report, the UN Special Rapporteur notes that the right to access information encompasses (1) the right of the public and of individuals to access information relating to public interest, (2) the right of the media to access information, and (3) the right of individuals to receive information that may infract on their rights.[56]

In light of the foregoing, certain criteria relevant to the interpretation of 'full information' in article 10(2) of the Kampala Convention are inferable. First, all information requested with regards to the development project must be provided to persons likely to be displaced. Second, information with regards to the likely environmental and socio-economic impacts of the development project on the rights of these persons or communities should be provided. Third, information on state policies and corporate guidelines on how the concerns of these persons or communities will be addressed are to be provided. Fourth, since the primary objective of the consultation process in article 10(2) of the Kampala Convention is to explore feasible alternatives, all other information relevant to this process must be provided.

4.3.1.4 Feasible alternatives

From its ordinary meaning,[57] 'feasible' alternatives can also imply 'likely' options.[58] However, the Kampala Convention does not given an inclination on what likely options are to be considered with persons likely to be displaced. To understand what these feasible alternatives or likely options entail in the context of DID, it is relevant to consider existing international standards.[59]

A. NO-ACTION PLAN

An option that should be considered is the 'no-action' plan.[60] This implies that the possibility of not carrying out the development project should be considered. A significant justification for considering this alternative is the need to avoid the consequences of DID.

B. ALTERNATIVE PROJECT LOCATION

Another alternative that may be considered is the possibility of implementing the project in an alternative project location where displacement is likely to be non-existent or minimal. This evidently derives from the need to avoid the negative effects of displacement to a great extent.

C. PROJECT IMPLEMENTATION IN COLLABORATION WITH PERSONS LIKELY TO BE DISPLACED

Another alternative is the option of implementing the project in collaboration with persons likely to be displaced should be considered.[61]

D. ADOPT STRATEGIES TO MINIMISE DISPLACEMENT

Pertinently, strategies for minimising displacements should be duly considered. In paragraph 31 of the Kothari Principles, states are required to give priority to strategies that can minimise displacements.[62] One of the strategies that may be adopted is to create an alternative project design.

However, where an alternative project design is not feasible, another strategy that can be adopted is to adjust the intended project design to minimise the socio-economic and environmental impacts of the project.

For instance, in the case of a large-scale dam, the operational regime of the dam can be altered to mimic natural water flows so as to mitigate its negative impact on the ecosystem, which may in turn affect the livelihood of fishing communities.[63] In Zambia, this mitigation strategy was adopted by the World Wide Fund for Nature and other partners along with Zambian authorities to address issues of water management and restore the environmental flows of the Itezhi-tezhi and Lower Kafue Gorge dams in the Kafue Flats, which is a major tributary of the Zambezi River.[64]

E. LEASE NEGOTIATIONS

But where mitigation strategies are not feasible, another feasible alternative could be for stakeholders to negotiate a lease with persons and communities likely to be displaced for the part of the land sought to be utilised for the development project. In negotiating a lease, ownership of the lands and properties will remain with those likely to be displaced for the duration of the project. Such practice was done in Japan in the 1950s with the creation of the three Jintsu Gawa Dams.[65] Rather than expropriating the lands of the peasant owners, the government leased the land from these persons to build reservoirs.[66]

F. VOLUNTARY COMPENSATION

However, where lease negotiation is not feasible due to the nature and magnitude of the project, voluntary compensation should be given priority. Under article 12 of the Kampala Convention, states are mandated to develop legal mechanisms for providing 'fair and just' compensation to internally displaced persons.[67] Just compensation is compensation provided for loss of properties at the fair market value. In determining what amounts to a fair market value, the pecuniary sum which a seller and a buyer would offer for the property sought to be expropriated should be examined.[68] However, it has been argued that this valuation standard is inadequate for various reasons. Among these reasons are that it does not take into account the sentimental value of the property which the owner may have,[69] nor the replacement cost of the property in circumstances where replacement is higher than the fair market value.[70] Further, it does not take into account the disturbances which displacement may occasion such as psychological stress, attorney fees and livelihood reconstruction.[71] Hence, there have been calls for a more comprehensive approach,[72] such as a disturbance-integrated compensation approach, which involves compensation for losses aside from real estate.[73] These losses include 'removal costs, relocation costs, loss of livelihood, loss of income, psychological damages . . . and possibly other unique circumstances of affected parties which should be captured to ensure adequate compensation.'[74] As the kind of losses that are compensable as disturbances are not exhaustive,[75] a case by case approach should be adopted. Principle 60 of the Kothari Principles further stipulates losses, such as[76]

> physical or mental harm; lost opportunities, including employment, education and social benefits; material damages and loss of earnings, including loss of earning potential; moral damage; and costs required for legal or expert assistance, medicine and medical services, and psychological and social services.

However, compensation alone is not sufficient to restore livelihood capacities. According to Cernea,[77]

> empirical analysis demonstrates, contrary to received wisdom, that the magnitude of the combined material and non-material losses and the impoverishment imposed on those displaced far surpass the redeeming power of compensation 'solutions.'

Cernea argues that compensation 'must be supplemented by investments for development.'[78] Investments for development involve financing the livelihood reconstruction of displaced persons and channelling funds towards improving their capacities. These funds may be derived from a plethora of sources, such as project windfalls and project-generated revenues.[79] For instance, the lump sum amount with which natural resource extraction projects are concluded between states and corporations is a windfall through which displaced persons may be rehabilitated.[80] Through these windfalls, funds may be earmarked for investing in the development of persons likely to be displaced. Besides these windfalls, project-generated revenues may also serve as funds for reconstructing the livelihood of displaced persons. Between 2010 and 2011, Ghana's revenue from mining reportedly doubled from 210 million dollars to 500 million dollars.[81] In Mozambique, revenue from extractive industries in 2011 reached an estimate of 100 million dollars.[82] Whaley notes that '[o]ver the years hundreds of billions of dollars have flowed into Nigeria from oil revenues contributing over 90% of the country's total economy.'[83] Evidently, these revenues are viable sources of funds which states can utilise in furthering the livelihood capacities of affected communities so as to 'avoid displacees' pauperization.'[84]

However, in determining fair and just compensation, consultation with persons likely to be displaced is imperative. Supporting this view, article 9(2)(k) of the Kampala Convention mandates states to 'consult internally displaced persons and allow them to participate in decisions relating to their protection and assistance.'[85] Such consultation in determining compensation has the potential of instilling trust in the form of compensation given.[86] Where compensation is given without prior consultation, it may be perceived as 'a tool merely intended to "buy" local support,'[87] such as the case in the compensation given to land owners in the Abonnema community displaced by the Greater Port-Harcourt City Development in Nigeria.[88] Morford notes that 'compensation was imposed on the landlords without prior negotiation in a "take it or leave it" approach.'[89] Had compensation been negotiated prior to displacement, it would not have been perceived as a mere tool. Further, meaningful consultation prior to compensation has the potential of ensuring that the needs of different categories of persons are met and that choices are exercised on the form of compensation. Principle 21 of the UN Principles on Housing and Property Restitution for Refugees and Displaced Persons (the Pinherio Principles) recognises that compensation 'may be monetary or in kind.'[90] In addition, it is pertinent that the right to resettlement is recognised.[91]

Paragraph 56 of the Kothari Principles requires states to adhere to certain criteria in any case of resettlement. One of these criteria is that, prior to resettlement, a comprehensive resettlement policy conforming to international standards should be developed. In line with paragraph 16 of the Kothari Principles, resettlement should entail the provision of substitute land of a similar or an improved quality and adequate housing. For housing to be deemed adequate, seven criteria must be met, namely; 'accessibility, affordability, habitability, security of tenure, cultural adequacy, suitability of location, and access to essential services such as health and education.'[92] In General Comment No 4 of the Committee on Economic, Social and Cultural Rights (CESCR), these criteria are also emphasised.[93]

In addition, paragraph 56 of the Kothari Principles obligates states to ensure that the specific needs of different categories of persons likely to be displaced are taken into account. As such, the cultural lifestyle of indigenous peoples should be given due consideration in resettlement planning. Likewise, where persons with disabilities are bound to be affected, states must ensure that impairment-specific measures are taken into account in resettlement processes. Laying emphasis, article 18(7) of the Kampala Convention Model Law provides that '[r]elocation measures should safeguard the rights of women, children, and other groups and individuals requiring particular protection.'[94]

Further, paragraph 56 of the Kothari Principles requires that '[t]he right of affected persons, groups and communities to full and prior consent regarding relocation must be guaranteed.'[95] Under international human rights law, the application of free, prior and informed consent (FPIC) to indigenous peoples has been fairly established.[96] With regards to non-indigenous communities, the application of FPIC is unsettled. However, this raises a concern as to whether non-indigenous communities are not also entitled to decide on matters affecting their own development and voice consent on matters touching on their right to development. It further raises concerns about the adherence of a state to democratic values. According to Goodland, part of the justifications for FPIC is 'inclusion, freedom to choose one's fate, meaningful participation in decisions affecting one's community; in short, democracy.'[97] If democracy is an underlying justification, then it would be a contradiction of the democratic value of equal participation if non-indigenous communities are excluded from deciding on issues affecting their livelihood capacities.

From an ethical perspective, it would be a denial of autonomy which, as expounded by Kant, is the 'ground of the dignity of a human.'[98] Further, it would be a contradiction of relevant norms in international law relating to DID to exclude the application of the doctrine of FPIC to non-indigenous communities. As noted earlier, paragraph 56(e) of the Kothari Principles recognises FPIC.[99] Article 7(3)(c) of the Guiding Principles also requires that the 'free and informed consent' of persons likely to be displaced should be sought.[100]

To understand the doctrine of FPIC, it is relevant to consider the Guidelines on Free, Prior and Informed Consent,[101] developed by the UN Programme on Reducing Emissions from Deforestation and Forest Degradation (UN-REDD) which provides guidance on the content of FPIC. There are four main components of the doctrine of FPIC encased in the words 'free,' 'prior,' 'informed' and 'consent.' The word 'free' contemplates the absence of coercion, intimidation and manipulation. The UN-REDD Guidelines outlines certain requirements for 'free consent.'[102] First, affected groups should set the timeline of the deliberation process, its duration and the structure of the decision-making.[103] Second, affected groups should receive information, upon request, in a manner that is 'transparent and objective.'[104] Third, the deliberation process should neither be induced nor manipulated.[105] Fourth, the deliberation process should occur at a venue and for the specified duration as decided by the affected groups, and also in the 'languages and formats' decided by them.[106] Fifth, participation should be without recourse to age, gender or status.[107]

'Prior consent' suggests that a process of deliberation must have occurred before the implementation of a project and consent must have been obtained. In enumerating the criteria for prior consent, the UN-REDD Guidelines stipulate that (1) there should be time for the comprehension and consideration of information on the intended project; (2) information must precede the initiation, process or phase of a project's implementation; and (3) the duration of the rights-holders' consideration of the deliberation process must be respected.[108]

The word 'informed' in relation to consent requires that adequate knowledge should guide the decision-making process. The UN-REDD Guidelines provide that information should 'be complete, covering the spectrum of potential social, financial, political, cultural, environmental impacts, including scientific information with access to original sources in appropriate languages.'[109] What this implies is that the information on which consent is based must be comprehensive and not altered or misrepresented.

The UN-REDD Guidelines define consent as four things, namely (1) a decision given without inducement, which can be a yes or no, with the likelihood of reconsideration upon alteration of the proposed project or other subsequent information; (2) a communal decision made by the affected groups 'in accordance with their customs and traditions'; (3) the exercise of rights; and (4) a continuous process across phases of the project.[110]

There is a question as to the extent to which FPIC is required.[111] With respect to indigenous peoples, the UN Special Rapporteur on Indigenous Peoples has emphasised that where a project will 'not substantially affect indigenous peoples in the exercise of any of their substantive rights in relation to the lands and resources within their territories,' FPIC need not be obtained.[112] However, both the IACtHR and the African Commission have stressed that where a project will have a 'major impact' on indigenous peoples land rights, their FPIC must be obtained.[113] The rationale for this position derives from the fact that the survival of indigenous peoples is intrinsically linked to the lands and territories they occupy, which is not often the case with non-indigenous communities. For non-indigenous communities, Bojosi notes that 'land . . . is apparently primarily economical and lacks cultural and spiritual value.'[114] Wachira further makes this point in emphasising that indigenous peoples' way of life 'are best sustained by the particular lands they inhabit, unlike some other communities who would thrive on any productive lands they elect to occupy.'[115] Agreeing with MacKay that the special attachment of indigenous peoples is not merely to any land but to the particular lands and territories on which they reside, Wachira emphasises that[116]

> [i]t is on the specific territories that indigenous peoples' relationship with the lands they occupy takes a deep special connection that is basic to their existence and is linked to their beliefs, customs, and traditions and culture. They are therefore attached to specific traditional lands and not just any piece of land.

In view of this special attachment, their FPIC must be sought and obtained where projects will have a major impact on their capacities to survive on their lands and territories. With respect to non-indigenous communities, article 7(2)(c) of the Guiding Principles requires that FPIC should be sought.[117]

It is crucial that an external review mechanism exist in order to sanction the actions of public and private actors and to ensure compliance with the Kampala Convention and other relevant international standards including human rights. In addition, access to justice must be protected and the jurisdiction of the courts to determine matters relating to the process, such as the adequacy of compensation, must not be restricted.

4.3.1.5 Persons likely to be displaced

Article 10(2) of the Kampala Convention require states to ensure that concerned stakeholders explore feasible alternatives with persons likely to be displaced. As with other words and phrases in this provision, the Kampala Convention does not set out who these persons are. While it may be argued that these persons may easily be identified with reference to the intended coverage of the project, certain categories of persons may not be adequately protected if they are not specifically identified. In clarifying this phrase, the next section discusses the different categories of persons likely to be displaced, notably, indigenous peoples, property rights holders, squatters, minorities, women, children and persons with disabilities.

A. INDIGENOUS PEOPLES

The concept of indigenous peoples has a long history linked to colonialism.[118] Between the 16th and 19th centuries, it was used to describe the original inhabitants on the land occupied by settlers. These inhabitants were often considered as 'savages' or 'barbarians' in need of 'the gift of civilisation.'[119] The idea of savagery and barbarism in the writings of political thinkers in this era was of a people who could not govern with civility and were in need of external help.[120] Montesquieu described savages as those who could not form lasting social ties due to the fact that they 'wonder about the forests.'[121] Rousseau draws a distinction between a savage and a civilised individual, arguing that the savage 'sighs for nothing but repose and liberty; he desires only to live and to be exempt from labour.' On the other hand, the civilised man 'always in motion, is perpetually sweating and toiling, racking his brains to find out occupations still more laborious.'[122] Rousseau further asserts that the[123]

> savage man, destitute of every species of knowledge, experiences no passion . . . his desires never extend beyond his physical wants . . . he fears no evil but pain and hunger; I say pain and not death; for no animal, merely as such, will ever know what it is to die.

In light of these perceptions, the ideas of 'conquest,' 'discovery' and 'just wars,' which were sometimes brutal, were justified.[124] Lands belonging to original inhabitants of territories were acquired by settlers who considered the original inhabitants as backward and uncivilised. As the powers of these settlers were consolidated and the need arose to ethically legitimise their presence in these territories, the idea of colonial trusteeship was developed.[125] Wilde notes that 'the concept of trust was understood . . . as a way of placing colonial rule on an ethical humanitarian footing.'[126]

In view of this idea, policies were pursued with the goal of raising the status of original inhabitants to that of civilised men across various continents. Anaya describes this 'civilising mission' as 'one of "elevating" the savage from his backward condition, while keeping him subordinated to colonial rule or a segregated status.'[127] In the General Act of Berlin Conference on Africa, the administrative governments were obligated to 'watch over the preservation of the native tribes, and to care for the improvement of the conditions of their moral and material well-being.'[128] In legitimising this concept of trusteeship, the 1919 Covenant of the League of Nations (the Covenant) noted that there were colonies and territories 'inhabited by peoples not yet able to stand by themselves under the strenuous conditions of the modern world.'[129] For these colonies and territories, the Covenant stated that 'there should be applied the principle that the well-being and development of such peoples form a sacred trust of civilisation.'[130] This idea of trusteeship, used to legitimise colonial rule, greatly consolidated the powers of foreign administrations.

However, as international law evolved – influenced in part by the experiences of World War II – the normative justification for foreign domination of indigenous territories began to lose its appeal. The advancement of ideological principles such as self-determination of peoples, dignity and human rights underscored the need for decolonisation. As decolonisation began to occur, the term 'indigenous' used with reference to the colonised began to fade.[131] Over time, it gained a new meaning within the context of independent states. Within this context, it was used in the International Labour Organisation (ILO) Convention 107 to refer to (1) groups with cultural, political and social traditions distinct from those of the dominant society; and (2) groups belonging to the lineage of the original inhabitants of a region at the time of conquest or colonisation.[132] In ILO Convention 169, a further criterion of 'self-identification'[133] was added. But while recognition for the rights of indigenous peoples has gained momentum in international law over the last decade, some African states have resisted this concept.

One justification for this resistance is the ethnic plurality in Africa, which makes it daunting to identify the original inhabitants across different regions of the continent.[134] Further, African states have resisted this concept for fear that the right to self-determination of indigenous peoples may challenge the territorial integrity of the state.[135] However, in *Katangese Peoples' Congress v Zaire*,[136] the African Commission made a distinction between internal and external self-determination, which may serve to assuage this fear. In light of its jurisprudence, it may be inferred that in a political clime of good governance, rule of law and democracy, external self-determination cannot be asserted. As such, this fear is unfounded.

Despite the resistance of some African states, there is a weight of evidence in support of the existence of certain groups in Africa as indigenous peoples.[137] The African Commission has recognised some groups in Africa as indigenous peoples such as the Amazigh in Algeria, the Mbororo in Central African Republic, the Endorois in Kenya and the San in southern African countries such as Botswana, Namibia and South Africa.[138] The African Commission has equally set out the criteria for identifying these groups, stating that indigenous peoples are culturally distinct from the dominant society; they identify themselves as indigenous; their ways of life are dependent on their access to the ancestral lands they occupy; and they have suffered marginalisation, subjugation and are extremely vulnerable to the interest of the dominant societies.[139]

In article 10 of the UN Declaration on the Rights of Indigenous Peoples (UNDRIP), displacement of indigenous peoples from their lands and territories without their FPIC is prohibited. However, a joint reading of articles 10, 19 and 46(2) of the UNDRIP reveals that the obligation to obtain FPIC is not absolute. In view of these provisions, it is relevant to consider the extent of the obligation to obtain the FPIC of indigenous peoples.

As earlier noted, the UN Special Rapporteur on Indigenous Peoples has emphasised that consent need not be obtained where a development project will have minimal impact on the land rights of indigenous peoples.[140] But, where a project will have a substantial impact, there is an obligation to seek and obtain consent.[141]

But where it is argued, for instance, that a project sought to be done on indigenous territories is for a compelling and overriding public interest in terms of article 4(5) of the Kampala Convention, is the obligation to obtain FPIC subject to such interests?[142] Hence, it appears that states are required to protect indigenous communities from displacement only to the extent that the protection does not affect its power of eminent domain. But a relevant question arising from this provision is: should the obligation on states to seek the FPIC of indigenous peoples in situations where their lands are to be expropriated be subject to such instances where the development projects sought to be implemented by states are for a compelling and overriding public interest?

In the *Endorois* case, the African Commission emphasised that in situations where the lands of indigenous peoples are to be encroached, the public interest test 'is met with a much higher threshold' as against encroachment of individual land and property.[143] In the *Ogiek* case, the African Court on Human and Peoples' Rights (African Court) examined the argument of Kenya that the basis for the displacement of Ogieks from their ancestral land was 'the preservation of the natural ecosystem.'[144] The African Court emphasised the need for the government to adduce evidence in this regard that 'the Ogiek's continued presence in the area is the main cause for the depletion of natural environment in the area.'[145] However, available evidence from various reports suggested differently, that 'the main cause of the environmental degradation are encroachments upon the land by other groups and government excisions for settlements and ill-advised logging concession.'[146] Consequently, the African Court noted that 'the continued denial of access to and eviction from the Mau Forest of the Ogiek population cannot be necessary or proportionate to achieve the purported justification of preserving the natural ecosystem of the Mau Forest.'[147] In General Recommendation 23, the UN Committee on the Elimination of Racial Discrimination (CERD Committee) emphasised that where the rights and interests of indigenous peoples are to be affected, such as in circumstances of DID, states are expected to ensure that their FPIC is obtained.[148] In its concluding observation following a consideration of Cameroon's state report, the CERD Committee highlighted the need for the state to consult with the indigenous populations 'in order to obtain their free and informed consent, before approving any project that affects their lands, territories or . . . resources.'[149]

Domestic institutions have taken similar positions. In the *Sesana* case, the High Court of Botswana (HCB) stated that there was an obligation on the state to obtain the consent of the San peoples prior to displacement. The HCB emphasised that '[t]he current wisdom, which should inform all policy and direction in dealing with indigenous peoples is the recognition of their special relationship to their land.'[150] In view of this special relationship, it is important that they are meaningfully consulted and their consent is obtained. In the *Endorois* case, the African Commission emphatically states that where[151]

> projects . . . would have a major impact . . . the [s]tate has a duty not only to consult with the community, but also to obtain their free, prior, and informed consent, according to their customs and traditions.

From the jurisprudence of the African Commission and the IACtHR, a major impact is one which threatens the survival of indigenous peoples.[152] In the *Saramaka* case, the IACtHR observed that although the Saramaka people did not use gold, gold mining activities on the land of the Saramaka peoples will 'necessarily affect other resources that are vital to their way of life.'[153] In the same case, the IACtHR also noted that the Saramaka people had 'traditionally harvested, used, traded and sold timber and non-timber forest products, and continue to do so.'[154] Hence, it was wrong for the state to conclude that as long as there were no 'sacred sites, cemeteries and agricultural plots,'[155] there was no need for consent. The IACtHR jurisprudence suggests that, in addition to impacts that threaten the cultural survival of indigenous peoples, major impacts also extend to economic sustenance. In addition, the UN Special Rapporteur on Indigenous Peoples identifies other 'principal effects' as including[156]

> (a) loss of traditional territories and land, (b) eviction, migration and eventual resettlement, (c) depletion of resources necessary for physical and cultural survival, (d) destruction and pollution of the traditional environment, social and community disorganization, (e) long-term negative health and nutritional impacts as well as, in some cases, (f) harassment and violence.

But since it will be difficult to limit the rights of these peoples without rendering such rights illusory,[157] an indigenous-controlled or co-managed approach should be adopted when their consent cannot be obtained.[158]

Within the context of natural resource extraction, the UN Special Rapporteur on Indigenous Peoples described this approach as an indigenous-controlled resource extraction. This approach seeks to vest control of extraction projects in indigenous peoples' owned enterprises. According to the UN Special Rapporteur on Indigenous Peoples,[159]

> [t]his alternative of indigenous-controlled resource extraction, by its very nature, is more conducive to the exercise of indigenous peoples' rights to self-determination, lands and resources, culturally appropriate development and related rights, in accordance with the United Nations Declaration on the Rights of Indigenous Peoples and other international sources of authority.

Placing indigenous peoples at the centre of these projects can foster sustainability. Research has shown, for instance, that the wisdom and skills of indigenous peoples are integral to natural resource conservation.[160] According to Clay, Alcorn and Butter, '[t]hroughout the world, there is a strong correlation between the last remaining relatively intact forests and the presence of indigenous peoples.'[161] Sobrevila further notes that[162]

> [i]ndigenous [p]eoples are carriers of ancestral knowledge and wisdom about . . . biodiversity. Their effective participation in biodiversity conservation programs as experts in protecting and managing biodiversity and natural resources would result in more comprehensive and cost-effective conservation and management of biodiversity worldwide.

B. PROPERTY RIGHTS HOLDERS

The obligation of states towards property rights holders derives from their legal ownership of property. The right to property is recognised in nearly all national constitutions in the world.[163] While the recognition of the right at the global level dates back to the UDHR,[164] the idea of property rights dates back to the writings of scholars such as Locke.[165] However, it is yet to be concretely recognised at the global level.'[166] In 1990, the UN General Assembly requested the UN Commission on Human Rights (CHR) to 'consider the means whereby and the degree to which respect for the right to own property alone as well as in association with others contribute to the development of individual liberty and initiative.'[167] In a subsequent report by an Independent Expert appointed by the CHR, it was generally concluded that the right to property was yet to emerge as a 'universal human right.'[168] However, within regional frameworks, the right to property has gained traction.[169] Under the African Charter, the right to property is 'guaranteed,'[170] subject to the limitation of 'appropriate laws.'[171] Laws in this context are not just national legislations but international human rights law.[172] Moreover, it is imperative that limitation on the right does not have the consequence of rendering it illusory.[173]

In situations of DID, states have an obligation to consider feasible alternatives with property rights holders for the purpose of seeking their FPIC. Where strategies for mitigating displacement cannot be adopted, states should consider negotiating a lease agreement where the development project will only be for a period of time. However, where a lease cannot be negotiated, voluntary compensation and resettlement should be given priority.

C. SQUATTERS

In the law of real property, squatters are generally not entitled to legal protection. This is in line with the fact that they have no legal title and, as such, have no right that can be protected in law. An exception to this rule is when a squatter remains in possession of a land for a period of time without any action from the legal owner. In such circumstances, the squatter acquires an interest in the land. Under South African law, for instance, this mode of acquisition of interest is recognised as prescription. Section 1 of the Prescription Act of 1969 provides that a 'person shall by prescription become the owner of a thing which he has possessed openly and as if he were the owner thereof for an uninterrupted period of thirty years.'[174]

In common law jurisdictions such as Ghana, Nigeria, Uganda, Tanzania and Kenya, this mode of acquisition of interest in real property is contained in Limitation Acts and is called adverse possession.[175] To succeed in a claim as an adverse possessor, a person must be in possession for a period of 12 years without interruption from the legal owner. This doctrine seeks to protect a person in long possession and ensures that a legal owner does not 'sleep on his rights.'

However, the principle of adverse possession does not apply to state-owned land. In the Kenyan case of *Peter Mwashi & Another v Javan Mwashi & 4 Others*,[176] the High Court of Kenya (HCK) made this point in stating that the doctrine of adverse possession does not apply to government land. In *Mitu-bell Welfare Society v Attorney General* (*Mitu-bell* case),[177] the HCK further stressed this point emphasising that '[t]he law that one cannot maintain a claim to government or public land by way of adverse possession is . . . well articulated in our jurisdiction.'[178] The HCK held that though the residents of Mitumba village could not claim title to public land on the doctrine of adverse possession, their forced eviction by the Kenya Airport Authority was in violation of Kenya's international human rights obligation. The HCK stated that[179]

> the state had an obligation to protect the petitioners' existing homes, rudimentary as they were, while doing what it could, to the extent of its available resources, to ensure their progressive access to adequate

> housing. It cannot properly argue, as it has in this case, that since the petitioners had no right to the land, their houses in Mitumba Village could be demolished arbitrarily without providing them with alternative accommodation.

In a view similar to the position of the HCK, the UN Committee on Economic Social and Cultural Rights (CESCR) notes that '[e]victions should not result in individuals being rendered homeless or vulnerable to the violation of other human rights.'[180] The CESCR also emphasised that where affected persons cannot provide for themselves, a state 'must take all appropriate measures, to the maximum of its available resources, to ensure . . . adequate alternative housing.'[181] However, considering that the right to adequate housing is subject to progressive realisation under article 2(1) of the International Covenant on Economic, Social and Cultural Rights (ICESCR),[182] should the provision of alternative housing in circumstances of forced evictions be progressively realised?

In General Comment No 7, the CESCR stated that 'in view of the nature of the practice of forced evictions, the reference in article 2(1) to progressive achievement based on the availability of resources will rarely be relevant.'[183] The CESCR further refers to the provision of article 17(1) of the ICCPR, which 'complements the right not to be forcefully evicted without adequate protection'[184] and which is not subject to 'considerations relating to . . . available resources.'[185] In light of this, a relevant question is: how should states implement the obligation of providing adequate housing significantly with respect to squatters who – as required by the CESCR's General Comment and the Kothari Principles – 'are not to be rendered homeless'? In answering this question, it is relevant to consider two positions – the minimum core obligation and reasonableness.

General Comment No 3 of the CESCR require states to guarantee – at the very least – the minimum essentials for the realisation of a particular right.[186] In justifying this position, the CESCR emphasised that '[i]f the Covenant were to be read in such a way as not to establish such a minimum core obligation, it would be largely deprived of its *raison d'être*.'[187] In the *Government of the Republic of South Africa v Grootboom*,[188] the South African Constitutional Court (SACC) stated that ascertaining the minimum core for the progressive realisation of the right to adequate housing is not possible without a consideration of the 'needs and opportunities' involved, which is a daunting process requiring information.[189] In reflecting on a feasible standard, the SACC emphasised that the act of the state in relation to the right to adequate housing should be weighed against the standard of reasonableness.[190]

The Optional Protocol to the International Covenant on Economic, Social and Cultural Rights follows this reasoning by requiring the CESCR to consider the 'reasonableness of the steps' taken by a state in the determination of communications instituted on the basis of the ICESCR.[191] In the

Grootboom case, the SACC noted that for a measure to be considered reasonable, it cannot exclude those whose needs are 'the most urgent.'[192] A significant justification for this standard derives from the concept of human dignity.[193] According to the SACC, '[a] society must seek to ensure that the basic necessities of life are provided to all if it is to be a society based on human dignity, freedom and equality.'[194] Hence, denying a group in society the basic necessities of livelihood, such as temporary shelter, goes against the obligation of the state to guarantee the rights to an adequate standard of living, health, life, non-discrimination and development.[195]

Hence, in respecting international human rights obligations and the obligation under article 10 of the Kampala Convention, states should ensure that squatters have access – at the very least – to temporary shelter so as not to be rendered homeless while the state develops a long-term plan for the progressive realisation of the right to adequate housing for all in the society, including squatters.

D. MINORITIES

While no agreed definition for minorities exists sufficient to capture the ethnic, linguistic and cultural diversities,[196] certain criteria are used to recognise minorities, namely: numerical size, non-dominant position in the society and distinctiveness from the rest of the society. According to Capotorti:[197]

> [a]n ethnic, religious or linguistic minority is a group numerically smaller than the rest of the population of the [s]tate to which it belongs and possessing cultural, physical or historical characteristics, a religion or a language different from those of the rest of the population.

Khan and Rahman highlight five characteristics of minorities, namely: '(a) numerical inferiority; (b) non-dominant position; (c) nationality; (d) distinguishing ethnic, religious or linguistic characteristics; and (e) collective will.'[198] On the point of numerical inferiority, Dersso observes that '[t]he norm on minorities were developed on the basis of the minority/majority dichotomy.'[199] The essence of recognising this dichotomy is two-fold; namely, to address the imbalances in power relations within a society and, secondly, to ensure that adequate protection is provided to those groups that are not as prominent in size. However, a significant flaw of this characteristic in determining minorities is that a numerical minority may not necessarily be a 'minority' in light of its political position.[200] Hence, the criterion of 'non-dominant position' should instead be considered an essential characteristic in determining minorities. While some states have often utilised the criterion of nationality, the Human Rights Committee has emphasised that the criterion of nationality is not an essential criterion in determining minorities.[201] Hence, 'migrant workers or even visitors in a

[s]tate party constituting such minorities are entitled not to be denied the exercise of those rights.'[202]

Although indigenous peoples are often minorities, it is pertinent to emphasise that minorities are distinct from indigenous peoples. One obvious distinction between these two groups relate to the normative source of their protection. On a practical level, however, scholars such as Henrard have argued that distinguishing between indigenous peoples and minorities in Africa is not clear-cut 'mainly due to the uncertainties of the use of the former term on a continent that was colonised.'[203] But considering the centrality of indigenous peoples' claim framed around attachment to their ancestral land, a distinction can be drawn between these two groups. Giving credence to this assertion, the Office of the UN High Commissioner for Human Rights has emphasised that '[m]inorities . . . do not necessarily have the long ancestral, traditional and spiritual attachment and connection to their lands and territories that are usually associated with self-identification as indigenous peoples.'[204] A distinction can also be drawn on the basis that while minority rights aim at 'ensuring a space for pluralism in togetherness, the instruments concerning indigenous peoples are intended to allow for a high degree of autonomous development.'[205]

Minority rights are primarily protected by article 27 of the ICCPR and the Declaration on the Rights of Persons Belonging to National or Ethnic, Religious and Linguistic Minorities.[206] Under article 27 of the ICCPR, states are obligated to ensure that minorities have 'the right, in community with the other members of their group, to enjoy their own culture, to profess and practice their own religion, or to use their own language.'[207] Article 2(2) of the Minorities Declaration guarantees their 'right to participate effectively in cultural, religious, social, economic and public life.'[208]

In the context of DID, the essence of minority protection emanates from the fact that while certain groups may not qualify as indigenous communities, their culture, for instance, may be affected in displacement. Hence, it is essential that states – in keeping with the obligation to preserve their culture, religion or language – protect them.

E. WOMEN

In General Comment No 7, the CESCR observed that women are particularly vulnerable to violence when rendered homeless.[209] The UN Special Rapporteur on Adequate Housing also notes that in forced evictions, women are vulnerable to loss of relationship and support systems, physical and psychological trauma, increased morbidity, mortality and breakdown in family relations.[210] Article 2(a) of the Convention on the Elimination of All Forms of Discrimination against Women (CEDAW) obligate states to 'ensure, through law . . . the practical realization of. . . [equality of men and women].'[211] In the Maputo Protocol, the law is recognised as one of the ways through which states are to combat discrimination against women.[212]

In the context of DID, securing the rights of women – such as the right to equality and property in national laws – serve to ensure that women are not marginalised or denied access to compensation. It further serves to ensure that women are engaged in the consultation processes and are ensured the right to decide on their own development.

Besides protecting the rights of women in national legislation, states are to ensure that they train relevant actors on the rights of women.[213] Paragraph 34 of the Kothari Principles mandate states to ensure that 'adequate training in applying international human rights norms. . . [is] provided for relevant professionals . . . involved in the design, management and implementation of development projects' and 'this must include training on women's rights.'[214] The aim of this training is two-fold. First, it is to create awareness on the rights of women. Second, it is to prevent violations of these rights and guide relevant actors in designing compensation plans. In addition to training relevant actors on women's rights, it is essential for states to monitor the consultation process under article 10(2) of the Kampala Convention so as to ensure that women are adequately consulted and that they are fully informed.[215] Paragraph 38 of the Kothari Principles provides that states are to ensure that 'women . . . have the right to relevant information, full consultation and participation throughout the entire process, and to propose alternatives that authorities should duly consider.'[216] Hence, states must ensure that in considering feasible alternatives, women are actively engaged and are not marginalised by socio-cultural practices that affect gender equality.

Furthermore, states are to implement socio-economic rehabilitation policies to ensure that women enjoy the 'rights to housing, food, water, health, education, work, security of the person, security of the home, freedom from cruel, inhuman or degrading treatment, and freedom of movement.'[217]

F. CHILDREN

In situations of DID, children are particularly vulnerable where adequate measures are not in place to ensure protection. According to Lundberg and Wuermli, 'children . . . are among the most vulnerable to crisis because of their lack of agency, and more importantly, because of the sensitive developmental milestones they must achieve during those years.'[218] Nampungu and Kasabiiti describe some of the impacts of DID on children in the context of the Bujagali dam-induced displacement.[219] They note that due to the financial incapacities of families, children were exposed to sexual and physical abuses.[220] There were several instances of sexual exploitation of girls in hopes of financial support. Some had to drop out of school due to poverty; in one instance, a boy had to work in order to pay his school fees due to the fact that his parents – who had lost their source of income following displacement – were incapable of doing so.

Under Article 18(2) of the Convention on the Rights of the Child (CRC), states are obligated to 'render appropriate assistance to parents and legal guardians' for the purpose of realising the rights recognised in the CRC.[221] In line with article 3 of the CRC and article 4(1) of the African Children's Charter, states are required to ensure that in situations where children are concerned, the best interest of the child should be considered. Article 4(1) of the African Children's Charter is emphatic on best interest as '*the* primary consideration' in actions concerning children.[222]

In the context of DID, these provisions impose an obligation on states to ensure that when children are likely to be displaced, their best interest – which also includes the capacities of their caregivers to continuously give care to them – must be the primary concern. In General Comment No 14, the UN Committee on the Rights of the Child (CRC Committee) emphasised that the concept of the best interest of the child is threefold. It is a substantive right, an essential interpretative principle of law and a procedural rule.[223] The implication of this threefold conceptualisation is that the best interest of a child must not only guide the interpretation of the rights of children, but it must also frame policies and legislation of states that are bound to affect children.

States must recognise the specific vulnerability of children and ensure that in the consultation process required under article 10(2) of the Kampala Convention, stakeholders are guided by the best interest of children. States must also ensure that children are involved in this process in line with article 12 of the CRC and article 7 of the African Children's Charter.[224]

States are to ensure the implementation of compensation regimes that – while also taking into account the interests of other vulnerable groups – uphold the best interest of the child.[225] For this, it is recommended that states should integrate a child-rights impact assessment[226] as part of its socio-economic impact assessment under article 10(3) of the Kampala Convention.

G. PERSONS WITH DISABILITIES

Persons with disabilities (PWDs) are at a higher risk of marginalisation in situations of DID.[227] Persons with physical disabilities may lack access to physical structures at resettlement sites where their specific needs are not taken into consideration or where facilities are far away from them. For instance, in the Bujagali Dam resettlement, social amenities like schools and markets were far away from the Naminya resettlement site, placing PWDs at a disadvantage.[228] Where basic structures are built at a distance to PWDs, it may also heighten their vulnerability to risks such as sexual abuse. Lending credence to this assertion, Stein and Lord note that '[l]ocations of latrines can mean the difference between safety and sexual violence for women and girls with disabilities due to their remoteness within the [displaced] camp setting and lack of lighting.'[229] Persons with hearing impairments may also be excluded from consultation where there are no sign language interpreters and assistive devices are not provided. In a post-conflict reconstruction programme in northern Uganda, Ngirabakunzi and Malinga observed that 'consultation [with affected persons] was inadequate because it did not take care of the information needs of the deaf and the visually impaired.'[230] As there were no sign language interpreters and Braille, persons with hearing impairments experienced communicative difficulties in expressing their needs and accessing information.[231]

Where disability intersects with gender or age, vulnerability may be compounded. During the conflict situation in northern Uganda, there were several incidences of sexual and physical violence against women with disabilities.[232] These incidences thrived on the vulnerability of these women as a result of 'isolation, lack of support structures, limitation in physical mobility, communication barriers and also because of myths that women with disabilities are weak, stupid, or asexual.'[233] In one instance, a woman with physical and communication disability was raped by a neighbour while her husband went to another camp in search of food.[234] In another instance, a woman with disability was repeatedly beaten by her husband as a result of her disability.[235] When exposed to displacement, children with disabilities are also at a higher risk of abuse. The 1990 World Summit on Children recognised that children with disabilities are in 'especially difficult circumstances'[236] and, as such, require special protection. The International Labour Organisation observes that 'disabled children are routinely sold or stolen – usually from rural areas – to be used by criminals or gangs of beggars.'[237] Traces of such practices have been recorded,[238] including situations where children with disabilities are rented to beggars by their guardians.[239] Children in displacement context are also prone to neglect. In the Dadaab refugee camp in Kenya, children with disabilities were reportedly tied to trees while stones were thrown at them.[240] Access to education may also be a challenge. In the case of the Bujagali Dam-induced resettlement, Nampungu and Kasabiiti observed that '[m]any children with disabilities showed no interest in school because of the difficulty in accessing schools which explains why one particular girl with a physical disability decided to drop out of school completely.'[241]

Protecting PWDs in displacement situations require states to adopt specific measures,[242] leveraging on the provisions of applicable standards, including the UN Convention on the Rights of Persons with Disabilities (CRPD) and the Protocol to the African Charter on Human and Peoples rights on the Rights of Persons with Disabilities (Disability Rights Protocol).[243] Article 2 of the CRPD and article 3 of the Disability Rights Protocol outline the principles which should inform the protection of PWDs. These principles include: respect for dignity and autonomy, non-discrimination, participation and inclusion, respect for difference, equality of opportunity, accessibility, gender equality and respect for the evolving capacities of children with disabilities. Central to the tenets of the CRPD and the Disability Rights Protocol is the principle of dignity and autonomy.[244] This principle requires states to ensure that PWDs are treated humanely and that their capacities to make choices are upheld. In relation to DID, this will require that resettlement and compensation policies are developed with respect for the right of PWDs to exercise choices and that PWDs are adequately consulted in line with the principle of participation and inclusion. Article 29(b) of the CRPD mandates states to '[p]romote actively an environment in which persons with disabilities can effectively and fully participate in the conduct of public life, without discrimination and on an equal basis.'[245]

Creating an environment suitable for the participation of PWDs in DID necessarily require states to ensure that negative perceptions on disabilities among affected communities in which PWDs live are addressed through advocacy prior to consultation. Further, it requires states to ensure that assistive devices and interpreters are provided during consultation and that consultation processes are closely monitored so that negative societal perceptions do not hinder the capacities of PWDs to express their views and make choices. Closely linked to participation and inclusion is the principle of non-discrimination.

The principle of non-discrimination require states to ensure that PWDs are not excluded from policies and plans initiated for the benefits of society based on their disability. Linked to this principle is respect for difference and equality of opportunity, which contemplates inclusivity and non-marginalisation of PWDs. Article 5 of the CRPD and article 5 of the Disability Rights Protocol echoes this principle in requiring states to prohibit all forms of discrimination based on disability. In realising this obligation, article 5(3) of the Kampala Convention mandate states to make reasonable accommodation. As such, states are to ensure that individualised needs are taken into account so as to promote equality and ensure non-discrimination.

The principle of gender equality and respect for the evolving capacities of children are integral to the realisation of the principle of non-discrimination. As noted earlier, due to social structures of marginalisation, women and children with disabilities are prone to multiple layers of discrimination. In recognition of this fact, articles 6 and 7 of the CRPD and articles 27 and 28 of the Disability Rights Protocol mandate states to protect women and children with disabilities. With regards to children with disabilities, states are to ensure that their 'best interests' are taken into account and that these children are given the opportunity to express their views in line with article 7(3) of the CRPD and article 28(4) of the Disability Rights Protocol. Explicitly, article 6(2) of the CRPD require states to 'take all appropriate measures to ensure the full development, advancement and empowerment of women.'[246] In the context of DID, such measures must necessarily involve integrating gender into resettlement and compensation policies. This is important in light of the fact that women are sometimes excluded from compensation policies. For instance, in the Lesotho Highland Water Project, Braun notes that 'policies were implemented in such a way that men were designated to receive . . . compensation.'[247] Further, the yearly food packages were 'delivered to men, even though food and its preparation are the responsibility of women.'[248]

4.3.2 Prior impact assessments – article 10(3)

In line with article 10(3) of the Kampala Convention, states are required to conduct socio-economic (SEIA) and environmental (EIA) impact assessments prior to the implementation of development projects. The rationale for carrying out these assessments in relation to the obligation in articles 10(1) and 10(2) of the Kampala Convention is to determine the effect of the project and inform consultations in order to avoid harm. But, while article 10(3) of the Kampala Convention specifically mentions these impact assessments, it does not explicitly set out the content of these assessments. This section examines these impact assessments.

4.3.2.1 Socio-economic impact assessment

The socio-economic impacts of a project are the likely consequences that a project may have on the social orderings and the economic sustenance of persons likely to be displaced. From an interdisciplinary perspective, two categories of impact are contemplated, namely, social impact and economic impact.

In the field of social sciences, Armour describes social impacts as alterations in people's lifestyle, culture and community. Building on this definition, Vanclay describes social impact as changes in the lifestyle, cultural and political systems, well-being, property rights, environment and aspirations.[249] In the Guidelines and Principles for Social Impact Assessment, developed by the Interorganisational Committee on Guidelines and Principles for Social Impact Assessment, social impacts are described as[250]

> the consequences to human populations of any public or private actions that alter the ways in which people live, work, play, relate to one another, organize to meet their needs and generally cope as members of society.

Economic impacts focus on assessing the economic dimension of the development project, within the context of the livelihood of persons likely to be displaced. Reflecting on economic impacts with respect to natural disasters, Navrud and Magnussen observe that[251]

> [e]conomic assessments of damage caused by extreme events are conducted both *ex post* in order to assess the need for compensatory and

alleviating measures, and *ex-ante* in cost-benefit analysis of preventive/mitigating measures that will prevent natural hazards or reduce their impact.

From a rights-based perspective, socio-economic rights provide a useful reference for reflecting on these assessments given the existence of specific state obligations with respect to these rights, such as the right to an adequate standard of living,[252] work,[253] health,[254] development,[255] education,[256] culture[257] and social security.[258]

4.3.2.2 Environmental impact assessment

The need for an EIA prior to the implementation of a development project derives from the fact that harming the environment can affect the livelihood capacities of those dependent on it. While campaigns against the consequences of oil exploration on the environment in some parts of the continent have signalled this fact,[259] oil extraction activities in the Niger-Delta region of Nigeria[260] and in the northern region of Cabinda in Angola[261] have proven it. Between 1976 and 1990, about 2,796 spillage incidences were recorded in the Niger-Delta region of Nigeria.[262] Since oil exploration activities began in 1958, the amount of oil spilled in the Niger Delta region has reportedly ranged between nine and 13 million barrels of oil,[263] affecting the ecosystem and destroying food sources.

In Angola, environmental degradation from oil exploration activities has also occurred. However, instances of these are sometimes underreported.[264] One justification for this, as noted by Danda, is that '[t]here is this real culture of secrecy between the government and holding companies to account . . . when these spills happen, the government says nothing and does nothing.'[265] As a consequence, the environmental effects of oil exploration on the livelihood capacities of affected communities are trivialised. But it is such trivialisation that the Kampala Convention seeks to avoid in requiring states to perform EIAs prior to carrying out development projects.

Moreover, in light of the right to the environment specifically recognised in the African Charter, conducting an EIA is important. Article 24 of the African Charter provides that 'all peoples shall have the right to a general satisfactory environment.' In *Socio-Economic Rights and Accountability Project (SERAP) v Nigeria*,[266] the Economic Community of West African States (ECOWAS) Court of Justice noted that this provision must be read in line with article 1 of the African Charter. Under article 1, states are required to take 'legislative or other measures' to realise the rights in the African Charter. Other measures, in the context of this provision, include a wide range of means for the implementation of the obligation in the African Charter. In *Social and Economic Rights Action Centre (SERAC) & another v Nigeria* (*SERAC* case), the African Commission emphasised that '[t]he right to a general satisfactory environment, as guaranteed under article 24 of the African Charter . . . requires the state to take . . . measures to prevent pollution and ecological degradation.'[267] Since the primary objective of carrying out an EIA is to evaluate the environmental consequences of a proposed project, it is an important measure in preventing pollution and ecological degradation and, as such, states are required to perform it in compliance with the obligation in article 24 of the African Charter.

States are also required to carry out EIAs in view of the interrelationship between environmental protection and human rights. This link resonates in Knox's assertion that 'strong compliance with procedural duties produces a healthier environment, which in turn contributes to a higher degree of compliance with substantive rights such as rights to life, health, property.'[268] In national jurisprudence, this recognition has also emerged.[269] In the *Gbemre* case, the Nigerian Federal High Court noted that the failure of Shell and Nigeria to carry out an EIA in the applicant's community was not only a violation of the environmental law of Nigeria, but also a violation of fundamental human rights.[270]

Having established its importance to human rights protection, the pertinent question which needs be answered in the context of article 10(3) is: how should an EIA be conducted? In answering this question, it is relevant to consider relevant international standards.[271]

The EIA Principles stipulate 14 basic notions and ten operational standards of EIAs. In light of the basic notions, EIAs must be '(a) purposive, (b) rigorous (c) practical (d) relevant (e) cost-effective (f) efficient (g) focused (h) adaptive (i) participatory (j) inter-disciplinary (k) credible (l) integrated (m) transparent (n) systematic.'[272]

That EIA must be purposive requires that it should be carried out with a goal of making decisions that will not diminish the livelihood capacities of persons and communities that are within contemplation. The notion of rigour requires that EIAs should be done with the best scientific practices and methods. The notion of practicality demands that EIAs should provide information that can be implemented and utilised in solving the problems identified. The idea of relevance contemplates that EIAs should be geared towards providing adequate, genuine and viable information for planning and decision-making. Cost-effectiveness requires that EIAs should be realised within the specified duration and with the resources and information that are available. Efficiency requires that the EIA should be conducted in a manner that is not burdensome in terms of logistics and duration. The requirement that EIA should be focused requires that it should be geared towards identifying environmental issues specific to a project. Adaptiveness requires that it should be flexible and consider the 'current condition of the environment and likely future changes to it without the development.'[273]

The notion that an EIA should be participatory derives from an understanding that public participation enhances sustainable environmental decisions.[274] According to Fagbohun, where environmental decision-makers give premium to public participation in environmental decision-making processes, 'the public through its very scepticism and willingness to question expert and scientific claims, will ultimately provide important decision-making resources.'[275] Participation in environmental decision-making not only ensures that better environmental decisions are made, but it also compels decision-making authorities to act in conformity with international standards.[276]

The idea that EIAs should be inter-disciplinary requires that experts in various disciplines, such as physical sciences, biological sciences and social sciences, are engaged in the process. While the notion of credibility requires that EIAs should be done impartially and objectively, the idea of integration contemplates that EIAs should address the interconnection of socio-economic and biophysical environmental concerns. Moreover, the idea that EIA should be systematic demands that it should 'result in full consideration of all relevant information on the affected environment, of proposed alternatives and their impacts, and of the measures necessary to monitor and investigate residual effects.'[277]

Aside from these basic notions, there are ten operational standards which can be grouped into three phases: pre-EIA, EIA and post-EIA.[278] In the pre-EIA phase, the first step is environmental screening.[279] This involves a determination as to whether a project requires an EIA. Where an EIA is considered necessary, then the extent to which it is required is to be considered. Following this consideration, the next step, which is 'scoping,' should be geared towards identifying environmental concerns and creating a 'term of reference for the EIA'[280] to serve as a guide through the EIA process. The UN Environment Programme highlights three main informational elements that a term of reference should contain, namely, (1) the likely environmental impacts to be discovered, envisaged, appraised, ameliorated and observed; (2) alternative designs; and (3) a timeline for the EIA and schedule for consultation.[281] Following the preparation of the term of reference for the EIA, the next step is examination of the alternatives. This requires a consideration of procedures for carrying out the EIA in order to determine a procedure that is 'environmentally sound.'[282]

When this has been done, the first step in the EIA phase, which is the 'impact analysis,'[283] should be carried out. Following this, mitigation and impact management measures for avoiding the environmental consequences of projects or minimising the impacts should be considered. Following this consideration, the next step is 'evaluation of significance.' At this stage, the relative significance of impacts that will remain and cannot be mitigated should be considered.

Afterwards, the post-EIA phase should commence first with the preparation of an EIA report. The UN Environment Programme highlights certain relevant details which the EIA report should contain, namely, '(a) an executive summary, (b) results from EIA studies, (c) information on data gaps and major sources of uncertainties, (d) technical appendices; and (e) visual aids and easy to read text.'[284] Following the preparation of the EIA report, the next step is to crosscheck the EIA report with the terms of reference prepared in the pre-EIA stage to determine whether the EIA meets the term of reference. Afterwards, the decision-making process, which is participatory and based on the EIA report, should commence. When this is finalised, a follow-up mechanism should be set up to ensure that (1) the conditions for the environmental approval of the project are met, (2) the impacts of the project are observed, and (3) mitigation strategies are employed and appropriately monitored.

4.4 Conclusion

This chapter discusses the obligation in article 10 of the Kampala Convention. The prevention of arbitrary displacement is integral to an understanding of the principle in article 10(1). This requires that the root cause of internal displacement must be permissible in international law and that due process must be followed. For the purpose of understanding due process in the context of DID, the provisions of article 10(2) and 10(3) of the Kampala Convention are significant.

Article 10(2) of the Kampala Convention emphasises the need for full information and consultation with persons likely to be displaced. In examining the provision of article 10(2) of the Kampala Convention, this chapter elaborates on key terms of the provision. This chapter describes stakeholders as those connected with the implementation of a project, including those bound to be affected negatively and positively. With regards to consultation, this chapter notes that consultation cannot be conceived as a means of legitimising already-made decisions, but it must be rightly understood as a means through which persons likely to be displaced are meaningfully engaged. On the content of information, this chapter emphasises that every vital piece on the development project – including details on the environmental and social impacts – must be provided.

Six feasible alternatives are considered: the possibility of not implementing the project in order to avoid displacement; the possibility of implementing the project in another location where individuals will not be affected; the possibility of implementing the project in collaboration with persons likely to be displaced; strategies for minimising displacements; lease agreements, where projects are for a period of time, so as to ensure that those with ownership rights do not lose their ownership. But in circumstances where these alternatives are not feasible, voluntary compensation should be given priority coupled with investment in development. It is important that an external review mechanism exists to sanction the actions of public and private actors and ensure compliance with the Kampala Convention and other relevant international standards including human rights. Further, access to justice must be protected and the jurisdiction of courts should not be restricted on issues relating to the process, for example, in the determination of the adequacy of compensation.

Prior to the implementation of development projects, the socio-economic and environmental impacts of these projects must be assessed in accordance with article 10(3) of the Kampala Convention.

Notes

1 African Union Convention for the Protection and Assistance of Internally Displaced Persons in Africa, adopted at the Special Summit of the African Union Heads of States and Government in Kampala, Uganda (19–23 October 2009) (Kampala Convention). Cross-referencing is to endnotes in this chapter.
2 The Kampala Convention (n 1), art 10(1).
3 As previously stated, art 3(1)(a).
4 As previously stated, art 4(4).
5 Vienna Convention on the Law of Treaties 1969 1155 UNTS 331 (VCLT), art 31(1).
6 Oxford Dictionaries 'Arbitrary' https://www.lexico.com/synonym/arbitrary (accessed 26 May 2020).
7 *Elettronica Sicula S.p.A. (ELSI) (United States of America v Italy)* (Judgement) (1989) (*ELSI* case) ICJ Rep 15.
8 *ELSI* case (n 7), para 124.
9 *ELSI* case (n 7), para 128.
10 The Kampala Convention (n 1), art 4(4)(c).
11 See UN Commission on Human Rights, Addendum, 'Guiding Principles on Internal Displacement' *Report of the Representative of the Secretary-General, Mr. Francis M. Deng, submitted pursuant to Commission on Human Rights resolution 1997/39,* UN Doc. E/CN.4/1998/53/Add.2 (11 February 1998) (the Guiding Principles).
12 Guiding Principles (n 11), art 6(2)(c).
13 The Kampala Convention (n 1), art 10(2).
14 T Donaldson & LE Preston 'The stakeholder theory of the corporation: concepts, evidence, and implications' (1995) 20(1) *Academy of Management Review* 65, 76.
15 European Investment Bank *The EIB statement of environmental and social principles and standards* (2009) 35.
16 World Bank *The World Bank participation sourcebook* (1996) 125 (World Bank Sourcebook).
17 As previously stated.
18 Civil society organisations are particularly relevant in this narrative in view of their ability to ensure the legitimacy of processes and protect persons likely to be displaced from being marginalised.
19 African Development Bank (AfDB) *Handbook on stakeholder consultation and participation in ADB operations* (2001) 2.
20 As previously stated, 25–26.
21 SR Arnstein 'A ladder of citizen's participation' (1969) 35(4) *Journal of the American Institute of Planners* 216, 219; BC Smith 'Participation without power: subterfuge or development?' (1998) 33(3) *Community Development Journal* 197; BC Smith *Good governance and development* (2007) 152; JE Stiglitz 'Participation and development: perspectives. From the comprehensive paradigm' (2002) 6(2) *Review of Development Economics* 163.
22 S Hickey & G Mohan 'Relocating participation within a radical politics of development' (2005) 36(2) *Development and Change* 237.
23 A Cornwall 'Historical perspectives on participation in development' (2006) 44(1) *Commonwealth & Comparative Politics* 62.
24 P Oakley 'The concept of participation in development' (1991) 20 *Landscape and Urban Planning* 115; F Cleaver 'Paradoxes of participation: questioning participatory approaches to development' (1999) 11 *Journal of International Development* 597, 605; A Cornwall 'Unpacking "participation": models, meanings and practices' (2008) 43(3) *Community Development Journal* 269.
25 L Diamond *et al* (eds) *Democracy in developing countries, Volume 2* (1988) extracted from I Petrella *The future of liberation theology: an argument and manifesto* (2004);

C Ake 'The unique case of African democracy' (1993) 69(2) *International Affairs* 239; G Mansuri & V Rao *Localizing development: does participation work?* (2013) 21.
26 S Paul 'Community participation in development projects' World Bank discussion papers (1987) 2.
27 As previously stated, 54.
28 Arnstein (n 21) 216.
29 Smith 1998 (n 21) 197.
30 As previously stated, 198.
31 Cornwall 2008 (n 24) 270.
32 The Brookings Institution & University of Bern Project on Internal Displacement 'Moving beyond rhetoric: consultation and participation with populations displaced by conflict or natural disasters' (2008) 4.
33 IM Sinclair *The Vienna Convention on the Law of Treaties* (1984) 128.
34 The Kampala Convention (n 1), art 11(1).
35 IASC Framework on durable solutions for internally displaced persons (2010) A1 www.unhcr.org/50f94cd49.pdf (accessed 24 May 2020).
36 L Juma 'Protection of development-induced internally displaced persons under the African Charter: the case of the Endorois community of northern Kenya' (2013) 46 *Comparative and International Law of Southern Africa* 211, 224.
37 Declaration on the Right to Development, adopted by the UN General Assembly, Resolution 41/128, UN Doc A/RES/41/128 (4 December 1986) (Development Declaration), art 2(3).
38 A Griffiths 'Between paradigms: differing perspectives on justice in Molepolole, Botswana' (1996) 36 *Journal of Legal Pluralism* 195, 197–200.
39 KC Sharma 'Role of traditional structures in local governance for local development: the case of Botswana' Paper for the Community Empowerment & Social Inclusion Programme, World Bank Institute (undated) https://europa.eu/capacity4dev/public-pub.sector-reform-decentralisation/document/sharma-kc-n-d-role-traditional-structures-local-governance-local-development-case-botswana (accessed 21 February 2020).
40 K Tronvoll *Mai Weini, a highland village in Eritrea: a study of the people, their livelihood, and land tenure during times of turbulence* (1998) 277; KT Reda 'Dynamics in pastoral resource management and conflict in the Borana rangelands of southern Ethiopia' (2016) 25(1) *African Security Review* 31; W Negari 'Indigenous knowledge for good governance and development: unleashing the wisdom of the Gada system' (2018) *Amity Journal of Management* 13.
41 UN Economic Commission for Africa 'Relevance of African traditional institutions of governance' (2007) 3 http://repository.uneca.org/bitstream/handle/10855/3086/bib.%2025702_I.pdf?sequence=1 (accessed 22 February 2020); ZT Sirna 'Ethiopia: when the gadaa democracy rules in the federal state: bridging indigenous institutions of governance to modern democracy' Master of Philosophy in indigenous studies, faculty of humanities, social sciences and education, University of Tromsø (2012) 32.
42 R Bereketeab 'Conceptualizing civil society in Africa: the case of Eritrea' (2009) 6 www.diva-portal.org/smash/get/diva2:325466/FULLTEXT02.pdf 6 (accessed 22 February 2020).
43 B Schwimmer 'Akan lineage organisation' (1995) www.umanitoba.ca/faculties/arts/anthropology/tutor/case_studies/akan/lineage.html (accessed 22 February 2020).
44 SJ Salm & T Falola *Culture and customs of Ghana* (2002) 61.
45 D Stewart & C Swanson *Wisdom from Africa: a collection of proverbs* (2005) 10.
46 C Ake 'Rethinking African democracy' (1991) 2(1) *Journal of Democracy* 32, 34.
47 International Covenant on Civil and Political Rights, adopted by the UN General Assembly Resolution 2200A (XXI), UN Doc A/6316 (16 December 1966)

(ICCPR), art 19; African Charter on Human and Peoples' Rights, adopted by the Organisation of African Unity, OAU Doc CAB/LEG/67/3 rev 5 (27 June 1981) (the African Charter), art 9.

48 ICCPR (n 47), art 19.

49 M McDonagh 'The right to information in international human rights law' (2013) *Human Rights Law Review* 5.

50 J Steel *Journalism and free speech* (2012) 9.

51 As previously stated.

52 F Schauer *Free speech: a philosophical enquiry* (1982) quoted in Steel (n 50) 16.

53 African Commission on Human and Peoples' Rights *Model Law on Access to Information in Africa* (2013). Mozambique's Right to Information Draft Law, which is currently in the drafting process, contains similar provisions. The Special Rapporteur on Access to Information in June 2014 'undertook an advocacy visit' to Mozambique to sensitise the government on the Model Law on Access to Information in Africa. The government accepted the offer of 'technical assistance' offered by the Special Rapporteur in drafting its legislation. 'Special Rapporteur on Freedom of Expression and Access to Information for Africa undertakes advocacy visits to Mozambique, Ghana and Botswana' https://www.chr.up.ac.za/news-archive/2014/811-special-rapporteur-on-freedom-of-expression-and-access-to-information-for-africa-undertakes-advocacy-visits-to-mozambique-ghana-and-botswana (accessed 24 May 2020).

54 *Model Law on Access to Information in Africa* (n 53).

55 UN General Assembly 'Report of the Special Rapporteur on the promotion and protection of the right to freedom of opinion and expression, Mr Frank La Rue,' *Note by the Secretary-General* UN Doc A/68/362 (4 September 2013) (the Report).

56 As previously stated, para 19.

57 VCLT (n 5), art 31(1).

58 Oxford Dictionaries 'Feasible' https://www.lexico.com/definition/feasible (accessed 24 May 2020).

59 UN Human Rights Council, 'Basic principles and guidelines on development-based evictions and displacement,' *Report of the Special Rapporteur on adequate housing as a component of the right to an adequate standard of living, Mr Miloon Kothari* UN Doc A/HRC/4/18 annex I (5 February 2007) (Kothari Principles), para 40; Organisation for Economic Cooperation and Development 'Guidelines for aid agencies on involuntary displacement and resettlement in development projects' (1992) (OECD Guidelines).

60 OECD Guidelines (n 59) 6.

61 For instance, in the Ugandan Kaweri Coffee Plantation case, the government should have considered this alternative and, as such, empowered peasant farmers rather than displacing them to make way for the Kaweri Coffee Plantation. Asiimwe notes that for a poor country with large peasantry, Uganda needs to channel its agricultural transformation in a practical way and initiate plans 'based upon the most careful examination of its native peasantry.' SP Asiimwe 'Peasantry struggles and agriculture modernisation in Uganda: the failed attempt at agriculture transformation for development' Masters of Arts, Institute of Social Studies, Erasmus University, The Netherlands (2011) 15.

62 Kothari Principles (n 59), para 31.

63 World Wide Fund for Nature 'Dams and freshwater ecosystems – repairing the damage' (2004) www.panda.org/downloads/general_267054ba/damsandmitigation.pdf (accessed 24 May 2020).

64 P Schelle & J Pittock 'Restoring the Kafue flats: a partnership approach to environmental flows in Zambia' (2005) http://assets.panda.org/downloads/restoringkafueflatsschellepittockriversymposium3sept05.pdf (accessed 24 May 2020);

'Kafue Flats, Zambia: preserving biodiversity through water management' www.un.org/esa/sustdev/publications/africa_casestudies/kafue.pdf (accessed 24 May 2020).

65 MM Cernea 'Compensation and investment in resettlement: theory, practice, pitfalls, and needed policy reform' in MM Cernea & HM Mathur (eds) *Can compensation prevent impoverishment? Reforming resettlement through investments and benefit-sharing* (2008) 78 (Cernea 2008a).

66 As previously stated.

67 The Kampala Convention (n 1), art 12.

68 KM Wyman 'The measure of just compensation' (2007) 41(1) *University of California Davis Law Review* 241 252.

69 BA Lee 'Just undercompensation: the idiosyncratic premium of eminent domain' (2013) 113(3) *Columbia Law Review* 593, 595.

70 Wyman (n 68) 254–255.

71 JO Ataguba 'Towards a disturbance-integrated compensation method for land expropriation: a case of Rwanda' Master's Thesis, Faculty of Geo-Information Science and Earth Observation, University of Twente, The Netherlands (2014).

72 Lee (n 69) 595; MM Cernea 'Compensation and benefit sharing: why resettlement policies and practices must be reformed' (2008) 1(1) *Water Science and Engineering* 89, 91 & 118 (Cernea 2008b); Ataguba (n 71) 1.

73 Ataguba (n 71) 8.

74 As previously stated.

75 E Shapiro *et al Modern methods of valuation* (2013) 468.

76 Kothari Principles (n 59), para 60.

77 Cernea 2008a (n 65) 17.

78 Cernea 2008b (n 72) 91.

79 As previously stated, 95–96.

80 An example of such project windfall is the multi-million-dollar oil deal signed by Ethiopia with the Malaysian oil giant, Petronas. In 2013, when the president of Liberia signed a multi-million-dollar contract with Exxon Mobil, the president noted that the deal was to give Liberia an instant cash flow of a minimum amount of about 45 million dollars as signing fee. In 2014, Nigeria awarded oil contracts of about 40 billion dollars to local corporations. 'Ethiopia: major oil exploration deal' *The New Humanitarian* 16 June 2003; 'Liberia: Ellen Signs Agreement' *The News. (Monrovia)* 11 March 2013; E Farge & T Cooks 'Exclusive – Nigeria favours local firms in $40 billion oil contract awards' *Reuters* 22 April 2014.

81 'Ghana's revenues from natural resources increase 400%' *Extractive Industries Transparency Initiative Report* 8 March 2013.

82 'Big increase in oil and gas revenue in Mozambique' *Extractive Industries Transparency Initiative Report* 14 March 2014.

83 J Whaley 'Oil in Nigeria – curse or blessing?' (2008) 5(4) *Geoscience & Technology Explained* www.geoexpro.com/articles/2008/04/oil-in-nigeria-curse-or-blessing (accessed 25 May 2020).

84 Cernea 2008b (n 72) 97.

85 The Kampala Convention (n 1), art 9(2)(k).

86 BW Terwel *et al* 'Public responses to community compensation: the importance of prior consultations with local residents' (2014) 24 *Journal of Community & Applied Social Psychology* 479.

87 As previously stated.

88 For more on the Greater Port Harcourt City Development, see Chapter 2 (specifically, section 2.3.3: Urban renewal).

89 T Morford 'Demolition of Abonnema wharf community and other waterfronts communities: Rivers State Government must end demolition and pay adequate compensation' *Socialist Democracy* 6 July 2012.

90 UN Sub-Commission on the Promotion and Protection of Human Rights *Principles on Housing and Property Restitution for Refugees and Displaced Persons*, final report of the Special Rapporteur, Paulo Sérgio Pinheiro of 28 June 2005 UN Doc E/CN.4/Sub.2/2005/17.
91 Kothari Principles (n 59), para 16.
92 As previously stated.
93 General Comment No 4 on art 11(1): the right to adequate housing, adopted by the UN Committee on Economic, Social and Cultural Rights, UN Doc E/1992/23 (13 December 1991).
94 African Union Model Law for the Implementation of the African Union Convention for the Protection and Assistance of Internally Displaced Persons in Africa (2012) (Kampala Convention Model Law), art 18(7).
95 Kothari Principles (n 59), para 56(e).
96 ILO Convention 107: The Indigenous and Tribal Populations Convention, adopted by the General Conference of the International Labour Organisation (5 June 1957); ILO Convention 169: Indigenous and Tribal Peoples Convention, adopted by the General Conference of the International Labour Organisation (27 June 1989); United Nations Convention on Biological Diversity (5 June 1992); General recommendation 23: rights of indigenous peoples, adopted by the UN Committee on the Elimination of Racial Discrimination, UN Doc A/52/18 annex V (1997); Declaration on the Rights of Indigenous Peoples, adopted by the UN General Assembly Resolution 61/295, UN Doc A/RES/61/295 (13 September 2007); UN Human Rights Council, *Final report of the study on indigenous peoples and the right to participate in decision-making*, report of the Expert Mechanism on the Rights of Indigenous Peoples, UN Doc A/HRC/18/42 (17 August 2011); U Khatri 'Indigenous peoples' right to free, prior, and informed consent in the context of state-sponsored development: the new standard set by Sarayaku v Ecuador and its potential to delegitimize the Belo Monte Dam' (2013) 29(1) *American University International Law Review* 165; J Gilbert *Indigenous Peoples' land rights under international law: from victims to actors* (2006); AK Barume *Land rights of indigenous peoples in Africa* (2014); AK Lehr 'Indigenous peoples' rights and the role of free, prior and informed consent' A Good Practice Note endorsed by the United Nations Global Compact Human Rights and Labour Working Group (20 February 2014); SJ Anaya *Indigenous peoples in international law* (2004); CM Doyle *Indigenous peoples, title to territory, rights and resources: the transformative role of free prior and informed consent* (2015) 18; R Roesch 'The story of a legal transplant: the right to free, prior and informed consent in sub-Saharan Africa' (2016) 16 *African Human Rights Law Journal* 505–531.
97 R Goodland 'Free, prior and informed consent and the World Bank Group' (2004) 4(2) *Sustainable Development Law and Policy* 66, 69.
98 I Kant *Groundwork of the metaphysics of morals: a German–English edition* trans M Gregor & J Timmermann (2011) 101.
99 Kothari Principles (n 59), para 56(e).
100 Guiding Principles (n 11), art 7(3)(c).
101 UN collaborative initiative on Reducing Emissions from Deforestation and Forest Degradation Programme *Guidelines on Free, Prior and Informed Consent* (2013) (UN-REDD Guidelines).
102 As previously stated, 18–19.
103 As previously stated, 18.
104 As previously stated, 18.
105 As previously stated.
106 As previously stated.
107 As previously stated, 19.
108 UN-REDD Guidelines (n 101) 19.

109 As previously stated.
110 UN-REDD Guidelines (n 101) 20.
111 Guiding Principles (n 11), art 7(2)(c); Kothari Principles (n 59), para 56(e).
112 UN Human Rights Council 'Extractive industries and indigenous peoples,' *Report of the Special Rapporteur on the rights of indigenous peoples, Prof James Anaya, submitted pursuant to UN Human Rights Council resolution 6/12 and 15/14, 1 July 2013,* UN Doc. A/HRC/24/41 (1 July 2013) (UN Extractive Industries Report), para 31.
113 Communication 276/2003, *Centre for Minority Rights Development (Kenya) & Minority Rights Group International (on behalf of Endorois Welfare Council) v Kenya* (2009), para 291; *Case of the Saramaka People v Suriname* IACtHR (28 November 2007) (*Saramaka* case), para 134.
114 KN Bojosi 'The African Commission Working Group of Experts on the Rights of Indigenous Communities/Populations: some reflections on its work so far' in S Dersso (ed) *Perspectives on the rights of minorities and indigenous peoples in Africa* (2010) 127.
115 GM Wachira 'Indigenous peoples' rights to land and natural resources' in S Dersso (n 114) 302.
116 As previously stated, 302–303.
117 Guiding Principles (n 11), art 7(2)(c).
118 M Hansungule 'Who owns land in Zimbabwe? In Africa?' (2000) 7(4) *International Journal of Minority and Group Rights* 305, 306.
119 SJ Anaya 'The evolution of the concept of indigenous peoples and its contemporary dimensions' in Dersso (n 114) 23.
120 B Buchan 'The empire of political thought: civilization, savagery and perceptions of indigenous government' (2005) 18(2) *History of the Human Sciences* 1 8–12.
121 As previously stated, 10.
122 JJ Rousseau *Discourse on the origin of inequality* (2007) 96.
123 As previously stated, 33.
124 Anaya (n 119) 23–31.
125 R Wilde 'From trusteeship to self-determination and back again: the role of the Hague regulations in the evolution of international trusteeship, and the framework of rights and duties of occupying powers' (2009) 31(1) *Loyola of Los Angeles International and Comparative Law Review* 85 93–97.
126 As previously stated, 97.
127 Wilde (n 125), 97.
128 General Act of the Conference of Berlin (26 February 1885) art VI.
129 The Covenant of the League of Nations (1919), art 22 (the Covenant).
130 The Covenant (n 129).
131 Anaya (n 119) 32.
132 ILO Convention 107: The Indigenous and Tribal Populations Convention, adopted by the General Conference of the International Labour Organisation (5 June 1957).
133 ILO Convention 169: Indigenous and Tribal Peoples Convention, adopted by the General Conference of the International Labour Organisation (27 June 1989). Only one African state is party to the ILO Convention 169, and that is Central African Republic.
134 F Viljoen 'Reflections on the legal protection of indigenous peoples' rights in Africa' in Dersso (n 114) 76.
135 As previously stated, 77.
136 *Katangese Peoples' Congress v Zaire* (2000) AHRLR 72 (ACHPR 1995).
137 Such evidence includes reports and decisions of the African Commission; national legislations of countries such as Cameroon and Kenya; national court

decisions in countries such as Botswana, Kenya and South Africa; writings of scholars such as Viljoen, Bojosi, Anaya, Pentassuglia, Xanthaki and Dersso. Cameroon Constitution: Law No 96–06 of 18 January 1996 to amend the Constitution of 2 June 1972; Kenya Constitution: The Constitution of Kenya (2010); Botswana: *Sesana & Others v Attorney-General* (2006) AHRLR 183 (BwHC 2006) (*Sesana* case); Kenya: *Lemeiguran & Others v Attorney-General & Others* (2006) AHRLR 281 (KeHC 2006); South Africa: *Alexkor Limited & Another v The Richtersveld Community & Others* (2005) AHRLR 157 (SACC 2003); Report of the African Commission's Working Group on Indigenous Populations/Communities, submitted in accordance with the 'Resolution on the Right of Indigenous Populations/Communities in Africa Adopted by the African Commission on Human and Peoples' Rights at its 28th Ordinary Session (2003); SA Dersso 'Introduction' in Dersso (n 114); 13; Bojosi (n 114) 95; G Pentassuglia 'Indigenous groups and the developing jurisprudence of the African Commission on Human and Peoples' Rights: some reflections' (2010) 3 *UCL Human Rights Review* 150; A Xanthaki 'Indigenous rights in international law over the last 10 years and future developments' (2009) 10(1) *Melbourne Journal of International Law* 27; F Viljoen *International human rights law in Africa* (2012) 228–238.

138 African Commission on Human and Peoples' Rights and International Work Group for Indigenous Affairs 'Indigenous peoples in Africa: the forgotten peoples?' (2006) 15–16 https://www.achpr.org/public/Document/file/Any/achpr_wgip_report_summary_version_eng.pdf (accessed 24 May 2020).

139 African Commission on Human and Peoples' Rights and International Work Group for Indigenous Affairs (n 138), 10–11. In the *African Commission on Human and Peoples' Rights v Republic of Kenya* (*Ogiek* case), the African Court on Human and Peoples' Rights emphasised that 'the relevant factors to consider [for the identification and understanding of the concept of indigenous populations] are the presence of priority in time with respect to the occupation and use of a specific territory; a voluntary perpetuation of cultural distinctiveness, which may include aspects of language, social organisation, religion and spiritual values, modes of production, laws and institutions; self-identification as well as recognition by other groups, or by State authorities that they are a distinct collectivity; and an experience of subjugation, marginalisation, dispossession, exclusion or discrimination, whether or not these conditions persist.' Application No. 006/2012, *African Commission on Human and Peoples' Rights v Republic of Kenya* (2017), para 107; See also *Endorois* case (n 113), para 102.

140 UN Extractive Industries Report (n 112), para 31.

141 *Endorois* case (n 113), para 291; *Saramaka* case (n 113) 134.

142 The Kampala Convention (n 1), art 4(5).

143 *Endorois* case (n 113), para 212.

144 *Ogiek* case (n 139), para 130.

145 As previously stated.

146 As previously stated.

147 As previously stated.

148 UN Committee on the Elimination of Racial Discrimination 'General recommendation 23: rights of indigenous peoples' UN Doc A/52/18 annex V (1997).

149 UN Committee on the Elimination of Racial Discrimination 'Concluding observations of the Committee on the Elimination of Racial Discrimination: Cameroon' UN Doc. CERD/C/CMR/CO/15–18 (30 March 2010).

150 *Sesana* case (n 137), para 117(b).

151 *Endorois* case (n 113), para 219.

152 See *Saramaka* case (n 113), para; 134–158; *Endorois* case (n 113), paras 288–293.

153 *Saramaka* case (n 113), para 155.

154 As previously stated, para 146.
155 As previously stated, para 147.
156 UN General Assembly 'The situation of human rights and fundamental freedoms of indigenous peoples,' *note by the UN Secretary-General*, UN Doc A/59/258 (12 August 2004), paras 18 & 20.
157 S Young *Indigenous peoples, consent and rights: troubling subjects* (2020).
158 This is a much preferred model given the fact that limitation on the rights of indigenous peoples are to be regarded with a much higher threshold. See Sub-paragraph C under Feasible Alternatives in 4.3.1.4. See generally Indigenous peoples' permanent sovereignty over natural resources, final report of the Special Rapporteur, United Nations Working Group on Indigenous Populations, Erica-Irene A. Daes, UN Doc E/CN.4/Sub.2/2004/30 (13 July 2004), para 48 http://www1.umn.edu/humanrts/demo/IndigenousSovereigntyNaturalResources_Daes.pdf (accessed 24 May 2020); *Endorois* case (n 113), para 212.
159 UN Extractive Industries Report (n 112), para 8.
160 C Sobrevila 'The role of indigenous peoples in biodiversity conservation: the natural but often forgotten partners' (2008) 20–21 http://documents.worldbank.org/curated/en/995271468177530126/pdf/443000WP0BOX321onservation01PUBLIC1.pdf (accessed 22 May 2020).
161 JW Clay *et al* 'Indigenous peoples, forestry management and biodiversity conservation' An Analytical Study for the World Bank's Forestry Policy Implementation Review and Strategy Development Framework (2000) 4.
162 Sobrevila (n 160) xii.
163 JG Sprankling 'The global right to property' University of the Pacific–McGeorge School of Law Research Paper (2013) 16.
164 Universal Declaration of Human Rights, adopted by the UN General Assembly Resolution 217 A (III) of 10 December 1948 (UDHR), art 17.
165 J Locke *Two treaties of government* (1689); TRG van Banning *The human right to property* (2001) 3.
166 Sprankling (n 163) 7.
167 Respect for the right of everyone to own property alone as well as in association with others and its contribution to the economic and social development of Member States, adopted by UN General Assembly Resolution 45/98, UN Doc A/RES/45/98 (14 December 1990), para 5.
168 UN Commission on Human Rights 'The right of everyone to own property alone as well as in association with others' *Completed final report submitted by Mr. Luis Valencia Rodríguez, independent Expert*, UN Doc. E/CN.4/1994/19 (25 November 1993), para 475.
169 First Protocol to the European Convention on Human Rights (1952), art 1, 213 UNTS 262; African Charter (n 47), art 14; The American Convention on Human Rights (1969) 1144 UNTS 123, art 21.
170 African Charter (n 47), art 14.
171 As previously stated.
172 *Endorois* case (n 113), paras 218–219.
173 *Media Rights Agenda and Others v Nigeria* (2000) AHRLR 200 (ACHPR 1998), para 72.
174 South Africa: Prescription Act No 68 of 1969.
175 Ghana: Limitation Act 1972, art 10(2); Uganda: Limitation Act Cap 80 1959, secs 5, 11; Tanzania: The Law of Limitation Act Cap 89 1971, sec 33(1); Kenya: Limitation of Actions Act Cap 22 2012, sec 13; *Ann Itumbi Kiseli v James Muriuki Muriithi* (2013) eKLR.
176 *Peter Mwashi & Another v Javan Mwashi & 4 Others* (2006) eKLR.
177 *Mitu-bell Welfare Society v Attorney General & 2 others* (2013) eKLR (*Mitu-bell* case).

178 As previously stated, para 35.
179 As previously stated, para 57.
180 General Comment No 7 on art 11(1): forced evictions, adopted by the UN Committee on Economic, Social and Cultural Rights, UN Doc E/1998/22 (20 May 1997), para 16.
181 General Comment No 7 (n 180), para 16.
182 International Covenant on Economic, Social and Cultural Rights, adopted by the UN General Assembly Resolution 2200A (XXI), UN Doc A/6316 (16 December 1966) (ICESCR), art 2(1).
183 General Comment No 7 (n 180), para 8.
184 As previously stated.
185 As previously stated.
186 General Comment No 3 on art 2(1): the nature of state parties' obligation, adopted by the UN Committee on Economic, Social and Cultural Rights, UN Doc E/1991/23 (14 December 1990).
187 As previously stated, para 10.
188 *Government of the Republic of South Africa v Grootboom* 2000 (11) BCLR 1169 (*Grootboom* case).
189 As previously stated, para 32.
190 As previously stated, para 33.
191 Optional Protocol to the International Covenant on Economic Social and Cultural Rights, adopted by the UN General Assembly Resolution 63/117, UN Doc A/RES/63/117 (10 December 2008), art 8(4).
192 *Grootboom* case (n 188), para 44.
193 S Liebenberg 'South Africa' in M Langford (ed) *Social rights jurisprudence: emerging trends in international and comparative* law (2008) 85.
194 *Grootboom* case (n 188), para 32.
195 See also The Kampala Convention (n 1), art 9(2).
196 BU Khan & MM Rahman *Protection of minorities: regimes, norms and issues in South Asia* (2012) 1.
197 F Capotorti 'Study on the rights of persons belonging to ethnic, religious and linguistic minorities' Special Rapporteur of the Sub-Commission on Prevention of Discrimination and Protection of Minorities (1979) 7.
198 Khan & Rahman (n 196).
199 SA Dersso 'The socio-historical and political processes leading to the emergence and development of norms on minorities' in Dersso (n 114) 67.
200 Y Dinstein 'Collective human rights of peoples and minorities' (1976) 25 *International and Comparative Law Quarterly* 102 112.
201 Khan & Rahman (n 196) 5.
202 General Comment No 23 on art 27: the right of minorities, adopted by UN Human Rights Committee, UN Doc CCPR/C/21/Rev.1/Add.5 (26 April 1994), para 5.2.
203 K Henrard 'Minorities in Africa and the right to equality and non-discrimination' in Dersso (n 114) 238.
204 Office of the UN High Commissioner for Human Rights 'Minority rights: international standards and guidance for implementation' (2010) 4 www.ohchr.org/Documents/Publications/MinorityRights_en.pdf (accessed 24 May 2020).
205 Saami Council 'The difference between minorities and indigenous peoples under international law' (2002).
206 Declaration on the Rights of Persons Belonging to National or Ethnic, Religious and Linguistic Minorities, adopted by the UN General Assembly 47/135 (18 December 1992) (Minorities Declaration).
207 ICCPR (n 47), art 27.

208 Minorities Declaration (n 206), art 2(2).
209 General Comment No 7 (n 180), para 11.
210 Statement by Mr Miloon Kothari, Special Rapporteur on adequate housing as a component of the right to an adequate standard of living, to the World Urban Forum III, Vancouver, Canada (19–23 June 2006).
211 Convention on the Elimination of All Forms of Discrimination against Women (1979) 1249 UNTS 13 (CEDAW), art 2(a).
212 Protocol to the African Charter on Human and Peoples' Rights on the Rights of Women in Africa, adopted by the African Union, OAU Doc CAB/LEG/66.6/ Rev 1 (11 July 2003) (Maputo Protocol).
213 Such training is important to ensure adequate protection for women. The Brookings-LSE Project on Internal Displacement 'Improving the protection of internally displaced women: assessment of progress and challenges' (2014) 9, 11 & 12.
214 Kothari Principles (n 59), para 34.
215 The Kampala Convention (n 1), art 10(2).
216 Kothari Principles (n 59), para 38.
217 As previously stated, para 57.
218 M Lundberg & A Wuermli 'Children and youth in crisis: protecting and promoting human development in times of economic shocks' Directions in Development: Human Development, The World Bank (2012) 4.
219 P Nampungu & D Kasabiiti 'The impact of involuntary resettlement on children: a case study of the international development associated funded Bujagali hydro-power dam: Naminya resettlement area' (2012) https://consultations.worldbank.org/sites/default/files/consultation-template/review-and-update-world-bank-safeguard-policies/submissions/naminyafinalreport.pdf (accessed 24 May 2020).
220 As previously stated, 13–14.
221 Convention on the Rights of the Child (1989) 1577 UNTS 3 (CRC), art 18(2).
222 CRC (n 221) art 3; African Charter on the Rights and Welfare of the Child, adopted by the Organisation of African Unity, OAU Doc CAB/LEG/153/Rev. 2 (11 July 1990), art 4(1).
223 General Comment No 14 on art 3(1): the right of the child to have his or her best interests taken as a primary consideration, adopted by the UN Committee on the Rights of the Child, UN Doc CRC/C/GC/14 (29 May 2013), para 6.
224 CRC (n 221) art 12; African Children's Charter (n 222) art 7; General Comment No 14 (n 223), para 43–45.
225 In line with paragraph 56(b) of the Kothari Principles, the proposed resettlement plan must lead to the realisation of the rights of 'women, children, indigenous peoples and other vulnerable groups.' Kothari Principles (n 59), para 56(b).
226 For an overview of the child rights impact assessment, see: General Comment No 14 (n 223), para 99.
227 R Adeola & F Viljoen 'The right not to be arbitrarily displaced in Africa' (2017) 25(4) *African Journal of International and Comparative Law* 459.
228 Nampungu & Kasabiiti (n 219) 15.
229 MA Stein & JE Lord 'Human rights and humanitarian assistance for refugees and internally displaced persons with disabilities in Africa' in I Grobbelaar-Du Plessis & T van Reenen (eds) *Aspects of disability law in Africa* (2011) 38.
230 E Ngirabakunzi & J Malinga 'The impact of NUSAF II in the lives of persons with disabilities in northern Uganda, a case study of Patiko sub County in Gulu district 2013' 9 https://bankinformationcenter.cdn.prismic.io/bankinformationcenter%2Faeab6d47-3ce2-43cb-aeb5-c22d1775adb7_final-nusafii-report-final.pdf (accessed 24 May 2020).

231 Bank Information Center & Inclusive Development International 'Human rights and the World Bank: case studies from IDA countries' (2013) 4 www.inclusivedevelopment.net/wp-content/uploads/2014/04/IDA-Case-Study-Book-FINAL_10-4-13.pdf (accessed 24 May 2020).
232 Human Rights Watch '*"As if we were not humans": discrimination and violence against women with disabilities in Northern Uganda*' (2014).
233 As previously stated, 34.
234 As previously stated.
235 As previously stated, 5.
236 UN Children's Fund *We the children: meeting the promises of the World Summit for Children* (2001) 91.
237 International Labour Organisation 'Disabled Beggars in Addis Ababa, Ethiopia' Employment Working Paper No 141 (2013) 13.
238 As previously stated; K Fakhri 'In Kabul, children are "rented" out to beggars' *Pajhwok Afghan News* 4 January 2014.
239 E Kigai 'Kenya-Tanzania: Trafficking handicapped children and the economy of misery' *The Africa Report* 29 July 2013 www.theafricareport.com/East-Horn-Africa/kenya-tanzania-trafficking-handicapped-children-and-the-economy-of-misery.html (accessed 24 May 2020).
240 R Reilly 'Disabilities among refugees and conflict-affected populations' (2010) 35 *Forced Migration Review* 8.
241 Nampungu & Kasabiiti (n 219) 12.
242 The Kampala Convention (n 1) art 2(c).
243 UN Convention on the Rights of Persons with Disabilities, adopted by the UN General Assembly Resolution 61/106, UN Doc A/RES/61/106 (13 December 2006) (CRPD); Protocol to the African Charter on Human and Peoples Rights on the Rights of Persons with Disabilities, adopted by the AU Assembly at the 30th Ordinary Session in Addis Ababa, Ethiopia (29 January 2018) (Disability Rights Protocol).
244 Disability Rights Protocol (n 243), art 2.
245 CRPD (n 243), art 29(b).
246 CRPD (n 243), art 6(2).
247 YA Braun '"How can I stay silent?": one woman's struggles for environmental justice in Lesotho' (2008) 10(2) *Journal of International Women's Studies* 5, 8.
248 YA Braun 'Gender, large-scale development, and food insecurity in Lesotho: an analysis of the impact of the Lesotho highlands water project' (2010) 18(3) *Gender and Development* 453, 458; For discussion on the Lesotho Highland Water Project and affected communities, see ML Thamae 'A decade of advocacy for dam-affected communities' in ML Thamae & L Pottinger (eds) *On the wrong side of development: lessons learned from the Lesotho highlands water project* (2006); see also T Scudder 'Assessing the impacts of the LHWP on resettled households and other affected people 1986–2005' in ML Thamae & L Pottinger (eds) *On the wrong side of development: lessons learned from the Lesotho highlands water project* (2006) 39.
249 F Vanclay 'International principles for social impact assessment' (2003) 21(1) *Impact Assessment and Project Appraisal* 5, 8.
250 Interorganisational Committee on Guidelines and Principles for Social Impact Assessment 'Guidelines and principles for social impact assessment' (1995) 15(1) *Environmental Impact Assessment Review* 11.
251 S Navrud and K Magnussen 'Valuing the impacts of natural disasters and the economic benefits of preventing them' in D Guha-Sapir & I Santos (eds) *The economic impact of natural disasters* (2013) 57.
252 ICESCR (n 182), art 11(1).
253 As previously stated, art 6; African Charter (n 47), art 15.

254 ICESCR (n 182), art 12; African Charter (n 47), art 16.
255 Development Declaration (n 37), art 1; African Charter (n 47), art 22.
256 ICESCR (n 182), art 13; CRC (n 221), art 28; African Charter (n 47), art 17(1).
257 ICESCR (n 182), art 15(a); African Charter (n 47), art 17(2); UDHR (n 164), art 27(1).
258 ICESCR (n 182), art 9.
259 C Badgley 'Fishing and the offshore oil industry: a delicate imbalance' *The Center for Public Integrity* 11 January 2012 www.publicintegrity.org/2011/06/10/4859/fishing-and-offshore-oil-industry-delicate-imbalance (accessed 24 May 2020); C Badgley 'West Africa oil boom overlooks tattered environmental safety net' *Ghana Oil Watch* 24 January 2012; G Otto 'Where there is oil; there is spillage' *Modern Ghana* 18 December 2012; T Mutch 'East African oil and gas – proper environmental planning needed to avoid disaster' *African Arguments* 27 September 2012.
260 PC Williams 'The effect of oil companies' activities on the environment, health and development in sub-Saharan Africa: the Niger Delta' text of presentation at the public hearing organised by the European Parliament Committee on Development on environmental degradation and its impact on poverty, Brussels, European Parliament, 29 February 2012; AE Ite *et al* 'Petroleum exploration and production: past and present environmental issues in the Nigeria's Niger Delta' (2013) 1(4) *American Journal of Environmental Protection* 78.
261 European Parliament 'The effects of oil companies' activities on the environment, health and development in sub-Saharan Africa' (2011) 8–21 EXPO/B/DEVE/FWC/2009–01/Lot5/11.
262 JC Ebegbulem *et al* 'Oil exploration and poverty in the Niger Delta region of Nigeria: a critical analysis' (2013) 4(3) *International Journal of Business and Social Science* 279, 282.
263 J Baird 'We don't hear about Africa's oil spills' *Newsweek* 18 July 2010 www.newsweek.com/baird-we-dont-hear-about-africas-oil-spills-74469 (accessed 24 May 2020).
264 ML Ramos 'Angola's oil industry operations' Open Society Initiative for Southern Africa (2012) 29.
265 L Redvers 'Oil-rich Cabinda the poorer for it' *Mail & Guardian* 28 September 2012 http://mg.co.za/article/2012-09-28-00-oil-rich-cabinda-the-poorer-for-it (accessed 24 May 2020).
266 *Socio-Economic Rights and Accountability Project (SERAP) v Nigeria* ECW/CCJ/JUD/18/12.
267 *Social and Economic Rights Action Centre (SERAC) & another v Nigeria* (2001) AHRLR 60 (ACHPR 2001) (*SERAC* case), para 52.
268 Report of the independent expert on the issue of human rights obligations relating to the enjoyment of a safe, clean, healthy and sustainable environment, John H. Knox UN Doc A/HRC/22/43 (24 December 2012), para 42.
269 DR Boyd *The environmental rights revolution: a global study of constitutions, human rights, and the environment* (2012) 151–157; *Gbemre v Shell Petroleum Development Company Nigeria Limited & Others* (2005) AHRLR 151 (NgHC 2005) (*Gbemre* case).
270 *Gbemre* case (n 269), para 5.
271 Principles of Environmental Impact Assessment Best Practice (EIA Principles) (1999) https://www.iaia.org/uploads/pdf/principlesEA_1.pdf (accessed 24 May 2020). The EIA Principles was developed by the International Association for Impact Assessment in cooperation with the Institute of Environmental Assessment, United Kingdom. The EIA Principles have been recognised by the UN Environment Programme. UN Environment Programme *Environmental impact assessment training resource manual, second edition* (2002). World Bank 'Revised

operational policy 4.01: Environmental assessment' (2013) (OP 4.01); African Development Bank Group's Policy on the Environment (2004) 20.

272 EIA Principles (n 271).

273 Institute of Environmental Management & Assessment *Special report – the state of environmental impact assessment practice in the UK* (2011) 18.

274 UN Economic Commission for Europe 'Convention on access to information, public participation in decision-making and access to justice in environmental matters' made in Aarhus, Denmark (25 June 1998), para 9 of Preamble.

275 O Fagbohun 'Mournful remedies, endless conflicts and inconsistencies in Nigeria's quest for environmental governance: rethinking the legal possibilities for sustainability' (2012) 86 www.elri-ng.org/Inaugural%20Paper%20-%20Prof%20Fagbohun%20(NIALS).pdf (accessed 24 May 2020).

276 As previously stated, 82.

277 EIA Principles (n 271).

278 As previously stated.

279 As previously stated; OP 4.01 (n 271), para 8.

280 EIA Principles (n 271).

281 UN Environmental Programme *Environmental impact assessment and strategic environmental assessment: towards an integrated approach* (2004) 43 (UNEP report).

282 EIA Principles (n 271).

283 As previously stated.

284 UNEP report (n 281).

5 Regulating private actors in the prevention of development-induced displacement

5.1 Introduction

Article 10(1) of the AU Convention for the Protection and Assistance of Internally Displaced Persons in Africa (the Kampala Convention) obligate states to 'prevent displacement caused by projects carried out by public or private actors.'[1] In the previous chapter, the obligation in article 10 of the Kampala Convention was examined; however, an aspect of this obligation that was not discussed relates to private actors. This is the focus of this chapter.

This chapter begins with a discussion on corporate responsibility in international law. This discussion is significant in view of the debate as to whether corporations can be held responsible under international law and whether it is legitimate to assert that corporations should be accountable to the society since, as Friedman asserts, the 'social responsibility of business is to increase its profit.'[2]

5.2 Corporate responsibility under international law

At the heart of the discussion on international law is the concept of responsibility.[3] Pellet describes this concept as 'the inevitable regulatory mechanism' through which tensions that may arise from the exercise of sovereignty among states are managed.[4]

As states were solely regarded as subjects of international law, they were the only entities that could incur responsibility under this system.[5] This traditional approach was legitimised in the Peace of Westphalia signed in 1648[6] and affirmed in the writings of scholars such as Anzilotti.[7]

But in the Advisory Opinion of the International Court of Justice (ICJ) in the case concerning the *Reparation for Injuries Suffered in the Service of the United Nations*, the ICJ took a progressive position on the idea of subjects of international law, extending its applicability to international organisations.[8] The ICJ emphasised that the UN was an international legal person in view of the fact that 'its [m]embers, by entrusting certain functions to it, with the attendant duties and responsibilities, have clothed it with the competence required to enable those functions to be effectively discharged.'[9] The ICJ equally emphasised that subjects of law may not necessarily be 'identical in their nature or in the extent of their rights.'[10] Moving beyond the traditional view of states as subjects, the ICJ's position suggests that an expansion of the doctrine is essential in order to align with developments in international law since 'throughout its history the development of international law has been influenced by the requirements of international life.'[11]

Over time, the pertinent question has become: does the concept of responsibility under international law also apply to non-state actors, such as individuals and corporations? With regards to individuals, scholars like Lauterpacht, Kelsen and Shaw have argued in the affirmative. Lauterpacht argues that individuals, for instance, have duties under laws of war and the international prohibition of piracy.[12] Kelsen argues that international law, being a 'regulation of human conduct,'[13] must be understood as conferring rights, duties and responsibilities not solely on states but also on human beings.[14] From a normative perspective, the most visible application of the concept of responsibility to individuals is in the field of international criminal law.

With regards to corporations, there are emerging trends.But at present, the most visible mechanisms for accountability are within national legal systems. Although the effectiveness of these systems is a concern.[15] But with the growing awareness of the impact of corporate activities in the 20th century, there have calls for corporate conscientiousness among various stakeholders at various levels of governance. This has notably featured in the context of social expectations encased in the idea of corporate social responsibility (CSR).[16]

5.3 The emergence of corporate social responsibility

The central thrust of CSR is the need for corporations to behave reasonably in accordance with certain social standards that it voluntarily adopts.[17] The history of CSR can be traced back to the 19th century with the wave of industrialisation and the emergence of corporations as significant institutions in society.[18]

Although Bowen coined the phrase 'corporate social responsibility' in 1953, the ideology had existed before this time in the works of scholars, such as Tead and Metcalf, who argued that the role of businesses in societies should be reconsidered in light of societal realities.[19] In 1920, Tead and Metcalf observed that the conflict between corporations and societies through the former's practices had brought 'disappointments, fears and hates; and these have in turn brought unhappiness.'[20] They argued that the practices of corporations had 'to be judged in terms of their effect on human beings.'[21] Prior to the 1920s, however, similar arguments had arisen. Thoreau and Rockefeller had rebutted the idea that corporations could not be said to have a conscience. In 1849, Thoreau argued that although it is said that a corporation had no conscience, 'a corporation of conscientious men is a corporation with a conscience.'[22] In 1919, Rockefeller Jr was of the view that[23]

> the day has passed when the conception of industry as chiefly a revenue producing process can be maintained. To cling to such a conception is only to arouse antagonisms and to court trouble. In the light of the present, every thoughtful man must concede that the purpose of industry is quite as much as the advancement of social well-being as the accumulation of wealth.

A decade after Rockefeller Jr's assertion, Donham observed that corporations were yet to come to terms with their social significance.[24] Hence, he argued that businessmen had to 'develop and enforce a group conscience . . . which will hold not only the individual but the whole group to both personal and group responsibility for relations with the . . . community.'[25] In 1932, Dodd took a similar stance, arguing that there was a building trend that not only do corporations have responsibilities towards society but that those in charge of these corporations should 'voluntarily and without waiting for legal compulsion manage it in such a way as to fulfil those responsibilities.'[26]

In his seminal work of 1953, Bowen expressed that the question which needs to be answered is: 'what responsibilities to society may businessmen reasonably be expected to assume?'[27] In practice and in academic writings on CSR, this question has held a significant place[28] and scholars like Carroll have argued that '[f]or a definition of social responsibility to fully address the entire range of obligations business has to society, it must embody the economic, legal, ethical, and discretionary categories of business.'[29] Bowen asserts that businesses have an obligation to 'pursue those policies, to make those decisions, or to follow those lines of action which are desirable in terms of the objectives and values of . . . society.'[30] Between the 1950s and 1970s, there was a wide consensus that businesses had to assume certain responsibilities and contribute to the society[31] as their 'continued vitality . . . was premised upon their vigorous acceptance of socio-human responsibilities along with socio-economic responsibilities.'[32]

However, scholars like Levitt in 1958 and Friedman in 1962 felt differently. Levitt argued that '[t]here is nothing mysterious about the social responsibility syndrome. It does not reflect change in businessmen's nature or the decay of self-interest.'[33] He argued instead that businesses should focus on profits and not delve into welfare, which is the function of the government.[34] Moreover, Friedman argued that the view that corporations should be socially responsible is 'a fundamental misconception of the character and nature of a free economy.'[35] According to Friedman[36]

> [i]n . . . an economy, there is one and only one social responsibility of business – to use its resources and engage in activities designed to increase its profit so long as it stays within the rules of the game, which is to say, engage in open and free competition, without deception or fraud.

However, in the late 1960s,[37] there were growing attractions for CSR.[38] From this period to the 1970s, several authors made expositions on what CSR should entail.[39] In 1967, Walton argued that CSR should entail a close relationship between corporations and society.[40] Taking a similar view, Sethi argued that CSR infers the compatibility of corporate behaviour with 'prevailing social norms, values, and expectations of performance.'[41] Though the concept holds a central idea of mutual relationship between the corporation and society, an agreement on its normative content has been daunting.[42] This may be attributed to the proliferations of theories on its normative underpinnings,[43] the complexities of society and socially varied perceptions, and the emphasis on voluntariness, which has always underpinned the discourse on CSR.[44] As a consequence, there has been an abundance of guidelines, codes and voluntary standards developed by corporations which makes it unclear whether CSR is a relevant idea or – as Levitt observes – 'a [p]hilistinic form of self-flattery.'[45]

In more recent times, advocates concerned about corporate violations – wanting to avoid this term – have drawn a distinction between CSR and corporate accountability.[46] Unlike CSR, corporate accountability demands that corporations are to be held liable for breach of legal norms.[47] Hence, while CSR requires corporations to develop and abide by voluntary guidelines, corporate accountability contemplates legal consequences in event of non-compliance.[48]

The evolving shift towards corporate accountability reveals a growing trend that corporations cannot be perceived as mere objects of international law in view of the shifting roles of power between states and corporations precipitated by globalisation and privatisation.[49] This trend may further be justified in light of the underlying values of international law as reflected in the UN Charter.[50] In the preamble to the UN Charter, the values of peace and international cooperation in resolving problems relating to social, economic, humanitarian and cultural issues are emphasised.[51] And since states are not the sole architects of some of these common global concerns, it has been argued that the idea of responsibility should be broadened in keeping with the 'requirements of international life.'[52] In addition, if international law affords corporations certain rights, such as the right to bring a claim against a state for violations of investment agreements,[53] then international law should impose duties; hence, corporations cannot be perceived as mere objects of international law with no legal responsibility. The discussion on corporate regulations over the past couple of years in the international community has lent credence to this viewpoint.

5.4 The discussions on corporate responsibility under international law

The discussion on corporate regulation in international law emerged in 1972. In that year, the UN Economic and Social Council (ECOSOC) passed a resolution requesting the UN Secretary-General to engage a group of eminent persons 'to study the role of multinational corporations and their impact on the process of development . . . and also their implications for international relations.'[54] This resolution was prompted by the government of Chile on account of a 1972 report by the *Washington Post* that the International Telegraph and Telephone Corporation – a US-based corporation which owned about 60% share of Chile's telephone company – was plotting a coup against the Marxist idealist Salvador Allende with the support of the US government.[55] Following ECOSOC's resolution, a Group of Eminent Persons (Group) was appointed. In its 1974 report, the Group observed that[56]

> national and especially international institutions do not deal adequately with the various ways in which multinational corporations can use their power in a manner which may run counter to the needs of the societies in which they operate.

Requesting the 'continuing involvement'[57] of ECOSOC in the issue of corporate accountability, the Group further requested that a specific body be set up to assist with ensuring that this involvement was actualised. In light of this recommendation, the UN Commission on Transnational Corporations (UNCTC) was established[58] to serve as a focal point within the UN on issues regarding transnational corporate activities and to provide a platform of engagement among states, organisations and corporations.[59] In addition, the UNCTC was to develop certain recommendations for ECOSOC's approval which would serve as a code of conduct for states and corporations.[60] It was to equally explore the probability of creating a legally binding treaty for states on corporations.[61] Following its formation, the UNCTC began negotiations on developing a code of conduct for regulating corporate activities.[62] While developing states wanted a binding instrument, the idea was opposed by some developed states who maintained that voluntary guidelines should be maintained.[63] After nearly two decades of negotiations, the draft code was eventually set aside in 1992 due to different views on the minimum benchmark for regulating corporations.[64] In 1994, the UNCTC was integrated into the United Nations Conference on Trade and Development following a resolution by ECOSOC.[65]

But while the draft code was being negotiated at the global level, on 21 June 1976, member states of the Organisation for Economic Cooperation and Development (OECD) adopted a Declaration on International Investment and Multinational Enterprises.[66] The OECD Declaration was a 'policy commitment by adhering governments to provide an open and transparent environment for international investment and encourage the positive contribution multinational enterprises can make to economic and social progress.'[67] Significantly, the OECD Declaration was comprised of a set of guidelines on corporate activities, known as the OECD Guidelines on Multinational Enterprises.[68] In its 2011 revision, the OECD Guidelines incorporates a new chapter on human rights,[69] requiring enterprises to 'respect the internationally recognised human rights of those affected by their activities.'[70] Though the Guidelines are non-binding, as clearly expressed in the first paragraph of its foreword,[71] they have had some notable impacts on corporate activities.[72]

Following the OECD Declaration in 1976, the International Labour Organisation (ILO) adopted a Tripartite Declaration of Principles concerning Multinational Enterprises and Social Policy in 1977 (Tripartite Declaration).[73] The Tripartite Declaration was the 'first effort' at corporate regulation by the international community,[74] done at a time when the UNCTC draft code was being negotiated. Aside from being an initiative at the international level, the Tripartite Declaration is wider in scope in that, unlike the OECD Guidelines, it extends to employers and employees' unions.[75] It equally recognises international standards such as the Universal Declaration of Human Rights (UDHR) 'and the corresponding international covenants,'[76] and requires all parties to conform to these standards.[77]

In 1999, Kofi Annan introduced a third significant initiative towards corporate regulation during the World Economic Forum in Davos, Switzerland.[78] In his speech to business leaders, Annan noted that without the involvement of businesses in upholding universal values such as human rights, labour and environmental standards, such 'universal values will remain little more than fine words.'[79] Annan called for 'a global compact of shared values and principles, which will give a human face to the global market.'[80] The Global Compact (The Compact) was created in 2000 and instantly became a reference point for initiatives on corporate responsibility with 'close to 7,000 business and more than 3,000 nonbusiness participants in nearly 140 countries.'[81] Although not binding, the Compact traverses some norms in human rights, environment, labour and anti-corruption laws as contained in international instruments[82] through a set of ten principles on these areas.[83]

Prior to the meeting in Davos, the Sub-Commission on the Promotion and Protection of Human Rights (the Sub-Commission) – an arm of the UN Commission on Human Rights (CHR) – established a sessional Working Group on the Working Methods and Activities of Transnational Corporations (the Working Group) in August 1998.[84] The Working Group, which was to be comprised of not more than five members of the Sub-Commission, was mandated to investigate and report on the impact of corporate activities on the enjoyment of civil, political, social, economic and cultural rights.[85]

Over a period of five years, the Working Group developed a set of Draft UN Norms on the Responsibilities of Transnational Corporations and Other Business Enterprises with Regard to Human Rights (the Norms), which it submitted to the Sub-Commission.[86] In 2003, the Sub-Commission adopted the Norms; however, the CHR did not take further action on it.[87]

In the same year the Norms were adopted by the Sub-Commission, a set of principles for enhancing transparency in the extractive industries was developed at the first Extractive Industries Plenary Conference (Plenary Conference) held in Lancaster, London.[88] The Plenary Conference was attended by 140 delegates representing 70 governments, corporations and civil society organisations.[89] Addressing the Plenary Conference, Tony Blair called for transparency in the extractive industries, as he had done in 2002 at the World Summit on Sustainable Development in Johannesburg.[90] Blair noted how history had 'shown that the discovery and exploitation of . . . highly prized resources. . . [do] not automatically translate into economic growth and sustainable development.'[91] In various studies on oil-rich countries like Venezuela, Nigeria and Angola, scholars like Karl, Stiglitz, Sachs and Warner have demonstrated this fact.[92] In the late 20th and early 21st century, civil society organisations increasingly began to call for transparency in the extractive industries through campaigns requiring corporations in this sector to publish what they pay and demanding governments to publish what they earn.[93]

These efforts culminated in the creation of the Extractive Industries Transparency Initiative (EITI) Principle at the Plenary Conference held in 2003. The EITI Principles reflect 12 principles which serve as the cornerstone for enhancing transparency.[94] Though financial disclosure by states and corporations has become standard procedure through the EITI, the need for more concrete measures has been expressed.[95]

In 2005, the CHR requested the UN Secretary-General to 'appoint a special representative on the issue of human rights and transnational corporations.'[96] Among other duties, the special representative was to 'identify and clarify standards of corporate responsibility and accountability for transnational corporations and other business enterprises with regard to human rights.'[97] In the same year, the UN Secretary-General appointed John Ruggie, who '[i]n his first interim report of 2006. . . rather than reviewing the UN Norms, adopted a radical criticism of them.'[98] López notes that '[i]n the end, he decided to put them aside and start everything anew.'[99] Over a period of six years and 47 international consultations in different continents, the United Nations developed the 'Protect, Respect and Remedy' Framework for Business and Human Rights (the Ruggie Principles).[100] The Ruggie Principles were unanimously endorsed by the UN Human Rights Council.[101]

The Ruggie Principles rest on three pillars: the state responsibility to *protect* human rights, corporate responsibility to *respect* human rights and access to remedies in the event of rights violations.[102] These principles, which Ruggie describes as 'principled pragmatism,'[103] have received wide acclaim from corporations as 'a lasting beacon for business entities,'[104] and from states as 'guidance that will contribute to enhancing standards and practices with regard to business and human rights.'[105] However, it has equally been criticised as 'setting a lower bar than international human rights standards,'[106] 'as woefully inadequate'[107] and as 'a missed opportunity to clarify central legal principles on the application of the international human rights regime to corporations.'[108] Deva argues that '[t]aking human rights seriously would require, among others, the evolution of a legally binding international instrument that imposes direct obligations on non-state actors.'[109] López argues that 'they [the Ruggie Principles] do not close the original and long-running debate about corporate human rights obligations.'[110]

In 2011, the UN Human Rights Council adopted two significant resolutions on the issue of a binding treaty. The first resolution, sponsored by Norway and supported by 21 other countries, called on the Working Group on Business and Human Rights to 'launch an inclusive and transparent consultative process with states in 2015. . . to explore . . . the benefits and limitations of a legally binding instrument.'[111] The second resolution, sponsored by Ecuador and South Africa, called for the establishment of 'an open-ended intergovernmental working group on a legally binding instrument on transnational corporations and other business enterprises with respect to human rights, the mandate of which shall be to elaborate an international legally binding instrument to regulate, in international human rights law, the activities of transnational corporations and other business enterprises.'[112] This resolution, supported by 20 states and opposed by 14 states with 13 states abstaining from voting,[113] has been described by Ruggie as a 'case of dysfunction redux.'[114] Ruggie argues that there is need for 'treaty supporters, states and NGOs, to recognize that no treaty of any kind will emerge in the near future.'[115] Pending the entry into force of a binding treaty, the Ruggie Principles remain a global authoritative statement on corporate human rights responsibility. Within the African region, this instrument has inspired an attempt towards developing a regional framework on business and human rights.[116]

5.4.1 Observations from the discussions on corporate responsibility

In light of the discussion in the previous section, two observations can be made. First, there is consensus that normative and institutional measures that ensure accountability are needed beyond voluntary codes adopted by corporations. Second, there is an emerging consensus that corporations should observe international law and be held accountable.[117] The Kampala Convention emphasises the obligation of states to ensure accountability of non-state actors including businesses.[118] This is reinforced by the obligation of the state to protect human rights.[119] In *Velásquez-Rodríguez v Honduras*, the Inter-American Court of Human Rights emphasised that a wrong act in violation of human rights which is not directly attributable to a state can invoke the responsibility of that state, where the state fails to exercise due diligence in preventing violation or ensuring accountability for such violation.[120] In the *NGO Forum* case, the African Commission equally emphasised that a state will incur responsibility for acts of private actors where it fails to exercise due diligence.[121] In *Opuz v Turkey*, the European Court of Human Rights inferred that the due diligence obligation requires a state to take specific measures commensurate with the need to protect human rights against violations.[122] Moreover, in the *SERAC* case, the African Commission emphasised that this requires the establishment and preservation of an 'atmosphere or framework by an effective interplay of laws and regulations.'[123] Having clear regulations that establish the responsibility of these actors is imperative in ensuring accountability. In the context of DID, a regulatory standard may be developed at the national level or at the regional level by the Conference of State Parties to the Kampala Convention. Developing a standard at the regional level is useful in ensuring commonality of standard among state parties to the Kampala Convention, significantly in light of article 2(c) which emphasises the need for 'solidarity, cooperation, promotion of durable solutions and mutual support between the states parties in order to combat displacement and address its consequences.'[124] This common regulatory standard should detail the corporate responsibility to respect the provisions of the Kampala Convention, in particular as it relates to DID.[125]

5.5 Conclusion

The need to ensure that corporations are accountable in situations where their operations have adverse human rights impacts has gained significant traction over the last decades. The emergence of the Ruggie Principles is a significant win in that these, for the first time, set out the responsibility of corporations to respect human rights. Moreover, it emphasises the duty on states to ensure corporate accountability given the presence of an existing duty under international human rights law to protect individuals within their territory. In the context of internal displacement, the Kampala Convention reinforces this obligation, requiring states to ensure accountability of non-state actors including businesses. In regulating corporations, this chapter emphasises that it is pertinent for states to adopt a regulatory standard. To ensure uniformity of standards among state parties to the Kampala Convention, a common regulatory standard may be developed by the Conference of State Parties to the Kampala Convention.

Notes

1 African Union Convention for the Protection and Assistance of Internally Displaced Persons in Africa, adopted at the Special Summit of the African Union Heads of States and Government in Kampala, Uganda (19–23 October 2009) (the Kampala Convention), art 10. Cross-referencing is to endnotes in this chapter.

2 M Friedman 'The social responsibility of business is to increase its profit' *The New York Times* 13 September 1970.

3 A Pellet 'The definition of responsibility in international law' in J Crawford *et al* (eds) *The Law of International Responsibility* (2010) 3.

4 As previously stated, 4.

5 As previously stated, 6; H Lauterpacht 'The subjects of international law' in A Bianchi (ed) *Non-state actors and international law* (2009) 3; *See also* Draft Articles on State Responsibility for Internationally Wrongful Acts, adopted by the International Law Commission at its 53rd session (2001) (ILC Draft Articles). The notion of responsibility of a state arises where there is a breach of an international obligation contained in a treaty or an agreement that is imputable to the state. A joint reading of articles 1 and 2 of the ILC Draft Articles emphasises this notion. The International Court of Justice (ICJ) has, in its decisions, also given weight to this notion. In the *Case concerning United States diplomatic and consular staff in Tehran (United States of America v Iran)*, the ICJ found that Iran incurred responsibility towards the United States by its continuous breaches of the treaty obligations. In the *Case Concerning Military and Paramilitary Activities in and against Nicaragua (Nicaragua v United States of America) (Merits)*, the ICJ found that the support given by the United States to the *Contras*, an armed group in Nicaragua, was in breach of the principle of non-intervention in article 2(4) of the United Nations Charter, and, as such, responsibility arises. Central to the notion of state responsibility – deducible from these cases and the provision of the Draft Articles – is the concept of 'attribution' of an internationally wrongful act to a state. In the Draft Articles, a state can only incur responsibility for (1) acts of its organs (art 4), (2) acts of persons or entities empowered by the laws of the state to exercise governmental authority (art 5), (3) acts of organs placed at the disposal of the state (art 6), (4) acts of persons or entities exercising governmental authority even though such acts exceeds governmental authority or instructions (art 7), (5) acts of persons or entities acting on the instruction of the state (art 8), (6) acts of persons or entities exercising governmental authority even though without state official authority (art 9), (7) acts of an insurrectional movement which takes over power in a state (art 10) and (8) acts which it acknowledges and adopts as its own (art 11). I Brownlie *Principles of public international law* (1990) 435; J Crawford *The International Law Commission's articles on state responsibility: introduction, text and commentaries* (2002) 81; J Dugard *International law: a South African perspective* (2011) 269; *The case concerning military and paramilitary activities in and against Nicaragua (Nicaragua v United States of America) (Merits)* ICJ (27 June 1986) (1986) ICJ Reports 14, para 242; *Case concerning United States diplomatic and consular staff in Tehran (United States of America v Iran)* (Judgement) ICJ (24 May 1980) ICJ Reports 3, para 90.

6 G Boas *Public international law: contemporary principles and perspectives* (2012) 156.

7 G Nolte 'From Dionisio Anzilotti to Roberto Ago: the classical international law of state responsibility and the traditional primacy of a bilateral conception of inter-state relations' (2002) 13(5) *European Journal of International Law* 1083 1087.

8 *Reparation for Injuries Suffered in the Service of the United Nations* ICJ Reports (Judgement) ICJ (11 April 1949) ICJ Reports 174.

9 As previously stated, 179.

10 As previously stated, 178.

11 As previously stated.

12 Lauterpacht (n 5) 8; A Clapham *Human rights obligations of non-state actors* (2006) 72.

13 H Kelsen *Principles of international law* (1952) 97.
14 As previously stated.
15 I Bantekas 'Corporate social responsibility in international law' (2004) 22 *Boston University International Law Journal* 309.
16 For an overview of the discourse see: DK David 'Greetings by Dean David to the incoming class' 14 February 1946 Baker Library (Archive), Harvard Business School; M Nehme & CKG Wee 'Tracing the historical development of corporate social responsibility and corporate social reporting' (2008) 15 *James Cook University Law Review* 129–168; PL Cochran 'The evolution of corporate social responsibility' (2007) 50 *Business Horizons* 449–454; B Spector '"Business responsibilities in a divided world": the Cold War roots of the corporate social responsibility movement' (2008) 9(2) *Enterprise & Society* 314 316–328; AB Carroll & KM Shabana 'The business case for corporate social responsibility: a review of concepts, research and practice' (2010) 12(1) *International Journal of Management Reviews* 85 86–88.
17 See S Brammer *et al* 'Corporate social responsibility and institutional theory: new perspectives on private governance' (2012) 10(1) *Socio-Economic Review* 3 5.
18 G Cheney *et al* 'Overview' in S May *et al* (eds) *The debate over corporate social responsibility* (2007) 4.
19 O Tead & HC Metcalf *Personnel administration: its principles and practice* (1920).
20 As previously stated, 513.
21 As previously stated, 21.
22 HD Thoreau *Civil disobedience (resistance to civil government) 1849* in HD Thoreau *Civil disobedience* (2013).
23 JD Rockefeller Jr. 'Representation in industry,' Annals, American Academy of Political and Social Sciences (January 1919) 168 quoted in Tead & Metcalf (n 19) 515.
24 Speech by WB Donham Dean of Harvard Business School at the North-Western University (1929). Donham asserts that 'Business started long centuries before the dawn of history, but business as we now know it is new – new in its broadening scope, new in its social significance. Business has not learned how to handle these changes, nor does it recognize the magnitude of its responsibilities for the future of civilization.' Quoted in U Singh 'Corporate social responsibility and challenges ahead' *Lexology* 30 November 2012 www.lexology.com/library/detail.aspx?g=b22d13e7-1640-413b-9832-8a4d5454e8ab (accessed 25 May 2020).
25 WB Donham 'Business ethics – a general survey' (1929) 7 *Harvard Business Review* 385 quoted in G Flynn & PH Werhane 'Introduction' in G Flynn (ed) *Leadership and business ethics* (2008) 1–2.
26 M Dodd 'For whom are corporate managers trustees' (1932) 45(7) *Harvard Law Review* 1153–1154.
27 H Bowen *Social responsibilities of the businessman* (1953) xi quoted in SAGE Publications *SAGE brief guide to corporate social responsibility* (2012) 3; AB Carroll 'A history of corporate social responsibility: concepts and practices' in A Crane *et al* (eds) *The Oxford handbook of corporate social responsibility* (2008) 25.
28 SAGE Publications (n 27).
29 AB Carroll 'A three-dimensional conceptual model of corporate performance' (1979) 4(4) *Academy of Management Review* 497 499.
30 Bowen (n 27) quoted in RC Moura-Leite & RC Padgett 'Historical background of corporate social responsibility' (2011) 7(4) *Social Responsibility Journal* 528 529–530.
31 For further discussion, see: F Abrams 'Management's responsibilities in a complex world' (1951) 29(3) *Harvard Business Review* 29; Bowen (n 27); D Keith

'Can business afford to ignore social responsibilities?' (1960) 1 *California Management Review* 70; Nehme & Wee (n 16) 145–153; Carroll (n 27) 24–34; A Okoye 'Theorising corporate social responsibility as an essentially contested concept: is a definition necessary?' (2009) 89 *Journal of Business Ethics* 613.

32 Keith (n 31) 74.

33 T Levitt 'The dangers of social responsibility' 1958 *Harvard Business Review* 41, 43.

34 As previously stated, 49. Levitt argued that '[w]ith none of the corrosive distractions and costly bureaucracies that now serve the pious cause of welfare, politics, society, and putting up a pleasant front, with none of these draining its vitality, management can shoot for the economic moon.'

35 M Friedman *Capitalism and freedom: fortieth anniversary edition* (2009) 133.

36 As previously stated.

37 Nehme & Wee (n 16) 146.

38 As previously stated.

39 Moura-Leite & Padgett (n 30) 531; NK Kakabadse 'Corporate social responsibility and stakeholder approach: a conceptual review' (2005) 1(4) *International Journal of Business Governance and Ethics* 277 281.

40 CC Walton *Corporate Social Responsibilities* (1967) 18 quoted in A Crane *et al* 'The corporate social responsibility agenda' in Crane *et al* (n 27) 27.

41 SP Sethi 'Dimensions of corporate social performance: an analytical framework' (1975) 17(3) *California Management Review* 58, 62.

42 Okoye (n 31) 614.

43 For a discourse on these theories see: D Melé 'Social responsibility theories' in Crane *et al* (n 27) 47–82.

44 R Mushkat 'Corporate social responsibility, international law, and business economics: convergence and divergences' 12 *Oregon Review of International Law* 55, 66.

45 Levitt (n 33) 41.

46 Clapham (n 12) 195.

47 S Marshall & K MacDonald 'What is corporate accountability' (n.d.) https://pdfs.semanticscholar.org/39be/af6cf61c55a02d7596a0d92118fe49cbc6ec.pdf (accessed 25 May 2020).

48 Clapham (n 12) 195.

49 K Nowrot 'New approaches to the international legal personality of multinational corporations: towards a rebuttable of normative responsibilities' 2, 3, 14 https://esil-sedi.eu/wp-content/uploads/2018/04/Nowrot.pdf (accessed 25 May 2020).

50 Charter of the United Nations 1945 1 UNTS XVL (the UN Charter).

51 Nowrot (n 49) 7–12.

52 As previously stated.

53 *Tullow Uganda Operations PTY Ltd v Republic of Uganda,* International Centre for Settlement of Investment Disputes No. ARB/12/34 (2012); T Butagira 'Tullow sues government in new tax dispute' *The Sunday Monitor (Uganda)* 17 December 2012.

54 The Economic and Social Council Resolution 1721 (LIII), 2 July 1972.

55 J Anderson 'Memos bare ITT try for Chile coup' (Washington Merry-Go-Round) *The Washington Post* 21 March 1972; J Anderson & L Whitten 'Ugly truth about Chile' (Washington Merry-Go-Round) *Kingman Daily Miner and Mohave County Miner Viewpoint* 27 October 1975.; L Segerlund 'Thirty years of corporate social responsibility within the UN: from codes of conduct to norms' Paper presented at the 6th Pan-European Conference on International Relations, Turin, Italy (12–15 September 2007).

56 UN Economic and Social Council, 'The impact of multinational corporations on the development process and on international relations,' *Report of the Group*

of Eminent Persons to Study the Role of Multinational Corporations on Development and on International Relations, UN Doc E/5500/Add.1 (Part 1) (24 May 1974) (Report of Group of Eminent Persons), 811.

57 As previously stated, 793.

58 TH Moran 'The United Nations and transnational corporations: a review and a perspective' (2009) 18(2) *Transnational Corporations* 91, 92; K Hamdani & L Ruffing *United Nations Centre on Transnational Corporations: corporate conduct and the public interest* (2015) 80–81.

59 Report of Group of Eminent Persons (n 56), 795.

60 As previously stated.

61 As previously stated.

62 Bantekas (n 15) 318.

63 Moran (n 58) 92–93.

64 Bantekas (n 15); Moran (n 58).

65 Integration of the Commission on Transnational Corporations into the institutional machinery of the UN Conference on Trade and Development, adopted by the UN Economic and Social Council Resolution 1994/1 (14 July 1994); Integration of the Commission on Transnational Corporations into the institutional machinery of the UN Conference on Trade and Development, adopted by the UN General Assembly Resolution 49/130, UN Doc A/RES/49/130 (19 December 1994); Statement on Item 4(b): realisation of the economic, social and cultural rights, joint written NGO statement, received by the UN Secretary-General, UN E/CN.4/Sub.2/2000/NGO/16 (1 August 2000).

66 DJ Plaine 'The OECD Guidelines for Multinational Enterprises' (1977) 11(2) *International Lawyer* 339.

67 Organisation for Economic Cooperation and Development 'OECD Declaration and Decisions on International Investment and Multinational Enterprises' (1976) (OECD Declaration).

68 Plaine (n 66).

69 Organisation for Economic Cooperation and Development 'OECD Guidelines for Multinational Enterprises' (2011), chap IV: human rights (OECD Guidelines); Organisation for Economic Cooperation and Development 'New OECD guidelines to protect human rights and social development' *OECD Directorate for Financial and Enterprise Affairs* 25 May 2011.

70 OECD Guidelines (n 69), chap II: general policies, para 2.

71 Clapham (n 12) 202; the first paragraph of the OECD Guidelines reads: 'The OECD Guidelines for Multinational Enterprises are recommendations addressed by governments to multinational enterprises operating in or from adhering countries. They provide non-binding principles and standards for responsible business conduct in a global context consistent with applicable laws and internationally recognised standards.' Quoted from OECD Guidelines (n 69), Foreword.

72 For an overview of some of these impacts see: Clapham (n 12) 208–211.

73 Tripartite Declaration of Principles concerning Multinational Enterprises and Social Policy, adopted by the Governing Council of the International Labour Office at its 204th Session in Geneva, Switzerland (1977). The Tripartite Declaration has been amended twice, first in November 2000 and in March 2006. JL Černič 'Corporate responsibility for human rights: analysing the ILO Tripartite declaration of principles concerning multinational enterprises and social policy' (2009) 1 *Miskolc Journal of International Law* 24, 26.

74 O Amao *Corporate social responsibility, human rights and the law: multinational corporations in developing countries* (2011) 28.

75 PT Muchlinksi *Multinational enterprises and the law* (2007) 476.

76 Tripartite Declaration (n 73), para 8.

77 As previously stated; BA Andreassen 'Development and the human rights responsibilities of non-state actors' in BA Andreassen & SP Mark (eds) *Development as a human right: legal, political and economic dimensions* (2010) 163–164. In referencing human rights standards, the Tripartite Declaration recognises the significance of human rights in enhancing labour standards. It equally recognises the role of multinationals in making 'important contribution . . . to the enjoyment of basic human rights' globally.' Tripartite Declaration (n 73), para 1.

78 Secretary-General proposes global compact on human rights, labour, environment, in address to World Economic Forum in Davos, Switzerland on 31 January 1999, UN Doc SG/SM/6881 (1 February 1999).

79 As previously stated.

80 As previously stated.

81 A Rasche 'The United Nations and transnational corporations' in JT Lawrence & PW Beamish (eds) *Globally responsible leadership: managing according to the UN Global Compact* (2013) 33.

82 Universal Declaration of Human Rights, adopted by the UN General Assembly Resolution 217 A(III) of 10 December 1948 (UDHR); Rio Declaration on Environment and Development, adopted at the UN Conference on Environment and Development, Rio de Janeiro, Brazil on 3–14 June 1992 (A/CONF 151/26 I); ILO Declaration on Fundamental Principles and Rights at Work, adopted at the 86th International Labour Conference (18 June 1998); UN Convention against Corruption, adopted by UN General Assembly Resolution 58/4, UN Doc A/58/422 (31 October 2003); UN Global Compact 'The ten principles' www.unglobalcompact.org/AboutTheGC/TheTenPrinciples/index.html (accessed 25 May 2020).

83 Principles 1 and 2 encourage businesses to respect human rights and ensure that they are not involved in human rights abuses. Principles 3, 4, 5 and 6 relate to labour standards. They require businesses to uphold freedom of association, and abolish all forced labour and discrimination in relation to work. Principles 7, 8 and 9 relate to the environment. These principles require businesses to be guided by the precautionary principle, promote environmental sustainability and support technologies that ensure the protection of the environment. Principle 10 enjoins businesses to work against corrupt practices. See UN Global Compact (n 82).

84 UN Commission on Human Rights *The relationship between the enjoyment of economic, social and cultural rights and the right to development, and the working methods and activities of transnational corporations*, Report of the Sub-Commission on Prevention of Discrimination and Protection of Minorities on its 50th Session, UN Doc E/CN.4/Sub.2/1998/45 (20 August 1998), 31.

85 As previously stated, 31–32.

86 Norms on the Responsibilities of Transnational Corporations and Other Business Enterprises with regard to Human Rights, UN Doc E/CN.4/Sub.2/2003/12/Rev.2 (2003) (the Norms); UN Sub-Commission on the Promotion and Protection of Human Rights *Economic, social and cultural rights: Mr Alfonso Martinez, Mr Guissé, Mr Kartashkin, Mr Park and Mr Weissbrodt: draft resolution*, 7 August 2003, UN Doc. E/CN.4/Sub.2/2003/L.8; see D Weissbrodt & M Kruger 'Norms on the responsibilities of transnational corporations and other business enterprises with regard to human rights' 97 *American Journal of International Law* (2003) 901.

87 DM Chirwa 'State responsibility for human rights' in MA Baderin & M Ssenyonjo (eds) *International human rights law: six decades after the UDHR and beyond* (2010) 409.

88 Department of International Development, United Kingdom 'Report of the Extractive Industries Transparency Initiative (EITI) London Conference, 17 June 2003' (2007); EITI International Secretariat 'The EITI standard' (2013); C Short 'The development of the extractive industries transparency initiative' (2014) *Journal of World Energy Law and Business* 1 2.

89 Extractive Industries Transparency Initiative (EITI) London Conference 17 June 2003: Final Attendance List https://webarchive.nationalarchives.gov.uk/20070701122619/http://www.dfid.gov.uk/pubs/files/eitidraftreportattendance.pdf (accessed 25 May 2020).

90 Speech by Tony Blair, UK Prime Minister at the Extractive Industries Transparency Initiative Conference, London, 17 June 2003 (Speech by Tony Blair); G Hilson & R Maconachie ' "Good governance" and the extractive industries in sub-Saharan Africa' (2008) 30(1) *Mineral Processing & Extractive Metallurgy Review* 52, 53.

91 Speech by Tony Blair (n 90).

92 TL Karl *The paradox of plenty: oil booms and petro-states* (1997); JD Sachs & AM Warner 'Natural resource abundance and economic growth' Working Paper 5398, National Bureau of Economic Research (NBER) Working Paper Series, Cambridge, Massachusetts (1995); JE Stiglitz 'Making natural resources into a blessing rather than a curse' in S Tsalik & A Schiffrin (eds) *Covering oil: a reporter's guide to energy and development* (2005) 13–19; N Shaxson 'Nigeria's extractive industries transparency initiative: just a glorious audit?' Chatham House (2009) 1.

93 Global Witness *A crude awakening: the role of oil and banking industries in Angola's civil war and the plunder of state assets* (1999); Short (n 88) 2; Publish What You Pay https://www.pwyp.org (accessed 25 May 2020); 'History of the EITI' (undated) http://eiti.org/eiti/history (accessed 25 May 2020).

94 EITI International Secretariat (n 88) 9.

95 Human Rights Watch *A new accountability agenda: human rights and extractive industries transparency initiative* (2013) 12.

96 UN Commission on Human Rights, Human rights and transnational corporations and other business enterprises, adopted by the UN Commission on Human Rights Resolution 2005/69, UN Doc E/CN.4/RES/2005/69 (20 April 2005).

97 As previously stated, para 1(a); T Thabane 'Weak extraterritorial remedies: the Achilles heel of Ruggie's "Protect, Respect and Remedy" framework and guiding principles' (2014) 14 *African Human Rights Law Journal* 43, 46.

98 C López 'The "Ruggie Process": from legal obligations to corporate social responsibility' in S Deva & D Bilchitz *Human rights obligations of business: beyond the corporate responsibility to respect?* (2013) 62.

99 As previously stated, 62.

100 UN Human Rights Council 'Guiding Principles on Business and Human Rights: Implementing the United Nations "Protect, Respect and Remedy" Framework' *Report of the Special Representative of the Secretary-General on the issue of human rights and transnational corporations and other business enterprises, John Ruggie* UN Doc A/HRC/17/31 (21 March 2011) (Ruggie Principles).

101 As previously stated; Human rights and transnational corporations and other business enterprises, adopted by the UN Human Rights Council Resolution 17/4, UN Doc A/HRC/RES/17/4 (6 July 2011) (Resolution 17/4); 'UN Human Rights Council endorses principles to ensure businesses respect human rights' *UN News* 16 June 2011.

102 Ruggie Principles (n 100).

103 UN Commission on Human Rights *Promotion and protection of human rights: interim report of the Special Representative to the Secretary-General on the issue of*

human rights and transnational corporations and other business enterprises UN Doc E/CN.4/2006/97 (22 February 2006) 70–81; J Ruggie 'UN Guiding Principles for Business and Human Rights' *The Harvard Law School Forum on Corporate Governance and Financial Regulation* 9 April 2011.

104 'Business and human rights: interview with John Ruggie' *Business Ethics* 30 October 2011.

105 Human rights and transnational corporations and other business enterprises, adopted by the UN Human Rights Council Resolution 17, UN Doc A/HRC/17/L.17/Rev.1 (15 June 2011), para 4.

106 C Albin-Lackey 'Without rules: a failed approach to corporate accountability' (2013) 4 www.hrw.org/sites/default/files/related_material/business.pdf (accessed 25 May 2020).

107 As previously stated.

108 J Kaufmann 'Ruggie's guiding principles fail to address major questions of obligations and accountability' *Earth Rights International* 5 April 2011.

109 S Deva 'Treating human rights lightly: a critique of the consensus rhetoric and the language employed by the Guiding Principles' in Deva & Bilchitz (n 98) 103.

110 López (n 98) 77.

111 Human rights and transnational corporations and other business enterprises, adopted by the UN Human Rights Council Resolution 26, UN Doc A/HRC/26/L.1 (23 June 2014), para 8.

112 UN Human Rights Council 'Elaboration of an international legally binding instrument on transnational corporations and other business enterprises with respect to human rights' UN Doc A/HRC/26/L.22/Rev.1 (25 June 2014).

113 International Justice Resource Center 'In controversial landmark resolution, Human Rights Council takes first step toward treaty on transnational corporations' human rights obligations' (2015) www.ijrcenter.org/2014/07/15/in-controversial-landmark-resolution-human-rights-council-takes-first-step-toward-treaty-on-transnational-corporations-human-rights-obligations/ (accessed 25 May 2020).

114 J Ruggie 'The past as prologue? A moment of truth for UN business and human rights treaty' *Institute for Human Rights and Business (Commentary)* 8 July 2014.

115 As previously stated.

116 O Bamidele 'AU set on making African businesses more responsive to human rights' *Premium Times* 24 March 2017.

117 E Oshionebo *Regulating transnational corporations in domestic & international regimes* (2009) 145–151; Nowrot (n 49) 7–12.

118 Kampala Convention (n 1), art 3(1)(h) & (i).

119 *Social and Economic Rights Action Centre (SERAC) & Another v Nigeria* (2001) AHRLR 60 (ACHPR 2001) (*SERAC* case), para 46; *Zimbabwe Human Rights NGO Forum v Zimbabwe* (2006) AHRLR 128 (ACHPR 2006) (*NGO Forum* case), para 143.

120 *Velásquez-Rodríguez v Honduras* IACtHR (29 July 1988) Ser C. No 4, para 172.

121 *NGO Forum* case (n 119) 143.

122 *Opuz v Turkey* ECHR (9 June 2009) Application No 33401/02, para 148–149.

123 *SERAC* case (n 119) 46.

124 The Kampala Convention (n 1), art 2(c).

125 For a discussion on this, see R Adeola 'The responsibility of businesses to prevent development-induced displacement in Africa' (2017) 17 *African Human Rights Law Journal* 244, 254.

6 Conclusion and recommendations

6.1 Conclusion

Development-induced displacement is a significant root cause of internal displacement in Africa. However, it is one of the least discussed. This book addresses the gap in the literature leveraging on the provision of the African Union Convention for the Protection and Assistance of Internally Displaced Persons (the Kampala Convention).[1] The Kampala Convention was adopted in 2009 at the Special Summit of African Union Heads of States and Government held in Kampala, Uganda. On 6 December 2012, it entered into force. Through the lens of article 10 of the Kampala Convention, this book examines how a balance can be struck between the imperative of development projects and the rights of persons likely to be displaced. A summary of the main arguments in this book is advanced in this chapter.

6.1.1 Principle – article 10

Article 10 of the Kampala Convention provides that 'states parties shall, as much as possible, prevent displacement caused by projects carried out by public or private actors.'[2] Explicit from the provision of the Kampala Convention is the prevention of arbitrary displacement. Article 3(1) of the Kampala Convention require states to '[r]efrain from, prohibit and prevent arbitrary displacement of populations.'[3] In line with article 4(4) of the Kampala Convention, '[a]ll persons have a right to be protected against arbitrary displacement.'[4] While an understanding of the notion of 'arbitrary' displacement is integral to comprehending the scope of obligation, this is not explicitly defined in the Kampala Convention. In the *United States of America v Italy*,[5] the International Court of Justice (ICJ) offered a useful guidance on the idea of 'arbitrary' as being more than 'unlawfulness,' which 'may well be relevant to an argument that. . . [an act] was also arbitrary.'[6] Beyond legality, however, the notion of arbitrary implies 'a wilful disregard of due process.'[7] Within this context, there are two aspects of arbitrary displacement. First, the root cause of internal displacement must be lawful or permissible under international law. Second, due process requirements must be followed. There are three dimensions of the due process requirement: general, group-based and cause-specific guarantees. Within the context of cause-specific guarantees, the provisions of article 10(2) and 10(3) of the Kampala Convention are integral to DID.

6.1.2 Participation – article 10(2)

Article 10(2) of the Kampala Convention provides that 'states parties shall ensure that the stakeholders concerned will explore feasible alternatives, with full information and consultation of persons likely to be displaced by projects.'[8] In line with international standards, stakeholders in article 10(2) include individuals, communities, corporate bodies and institutions connected with the implementation of a project, including those that are bound to be negatively and positively affected.

Consultations cannot be conceived as a means of legitimising previously made decisions; rather, consultation must be understood as a means through which persons likely to be displaced are engaged in discussions on feasible alternatives to the project sought to be implemented. On the content of information, every vital piece on the development project – including details on the environmental and social impacts, other details that will assist persons likely to be displaced in exploring feasible alternatives, state policies and corporate guidelines on how to address the concerns of those likely to be displaced – must be provided.

Six feasible alternatives are discussed in this book. These feasible alternatives are (1) the possibility of not implementing the project in order to avoid displacement, (2) the possibility of implementing the project in a different location where people will not be affected, (3) the possibility of implementing the project in collaboration with persons likely to be displaced, (4) strategies for minimising displacements, (5) the possibility of negotiating a lease to protect against loss of ownership of land and properties where projects are for a duration and (6) voluntary compensation with investment in development. However, it is imperative that an external review mechanism exists to sanction the actions of public or private actors and to ensure compliance with the Kampala Convention and other relevant international standards including human rights. Also, access to justice must be protected and the jurisdiction of courts to determine matters relating to the process, for instance, the adequacy of compensation, must not be restricted.

Different categories of persons likely to be displaced by development projects should also be identified, inclusive among which are indigenous peoples, property rights holders, squatters, minorities, women, children and persons with disabilities. The specific needs of these categories of persons must also be integrated into socio-economic and environmental impact assessments required under article 10(3) of the Kampala Convention.[9]

6.1.3 Prior impact assessments – article 10(3)

Article 10(3) of the Kampala Convention provides that '[s]tates parties shall carry out a socio-economic and environmental impact assessment of a proposed development project prior to undertaking such a project.'[10]

In assessing environmental impacts, there are 14 basic notions and ten operational standards on environmental impact assessments – developed by the International Association for Impact Assessment (IAIA) and recognised by the UN Environment Programme. In light of the basic principles, environmental impact assessments must be '(a) purposive (b) rigorous (c) practical (d) relevant (e) cost-effective (f) efficient (g) focused (h) adaptive (i) participatory (j) inter-disciplinary (k) credible (l) integrated (m) transparent (n) systematic.'[11]

With regards to socio-economic impact assessments, it is argued that reference should be made to socio-economic rights as a benchmark for this assessment. In this regard, the rights to an adequate standard of living, right to work, health, development, education, culture and social security should be considered.

Aside from the regulation of public actors, article 10(1) of the Kampala Convention also extends to private actors. The next section examines this aspect.

6.1.4 Private actors

The discourse on corporate accountability under international law has, in the past decades, been characterised by demands for concrete standards beyond voluntary corporate social standards. In 2011, the UN 'Protect, Respect and Remedy' Framework for Business and Human Rights (Ruggie Principles)[12] was adopted by the UN Human Rights Council. The Ruggie Principles rest on three pillars: the state duty to protect human rights, corporate responsibility to respect human rights and access to remedies in event of rights violations.

As subjects of international law, states have the primary duty to protect populations within their territories. There is also a due diligence obligation on states to ensure that corporations are regulated in order to prevent human rights violations. In the context of internal displacement, articles 3(h) and (i) of the Kampala Convention require states to ensure that corporations are held accountable for acts and activities that result in arbitrary displacements.[13] In the context of DID, article 10(1) of the Kampala Convention mandate states to 'prevent displacement caused by projects carried out by . . . private actors.'[14] In realising this obligation, states should adopt a regulatory standard. To ensure commonality, this standard may be developed at the level of the Conference of State Parties to the Kampala Convention.

6.2 Recommendations

While states have the primary obligation to ensure compliance with the Kampala Convention, institutions beyond the state are also imperative in advancing compliance. This section focuses on two pertinent institutions: the Conference of State Parties to the Kampala Convention (the Conference) and the African Commission. This book recommends that the Conference should establish a working group on the issue of DID through which compliance with the obligation in the Kampala Convention may be amplified. As the primary regional institution saddled with the protection and promotion of human rights, the African Commission should (1) develop a General Comment on article 10 of the Kampala Convention, (2) conduct missions to countries where development projects are to be implemented and (3) revise the Guidelines on State Reporting so as to ensure that states report on their obligation under the Kampala Convention. These recommendations are discussed in the following sections.

6.2.1 The Conference should establish a working group on development-induced displacement

In article 14(1) of the Kampala Convention, the Conference is saddled with the mandate 'to monitor and review the implementation of the objectives of this Convention.'[15] The first Conference was held in April 2017 in Harare, Zimbabwe.[16] At the event, a Plan of Action was adopted to translate the norms in the Kampala Convention to concrete actions.[17] The Conference was operationalised 'as a mechanism for fostering cooperation and solidarity among State Parties in the implementation of the Convention'[18] and, in doing so, it sets out the modalities for the furtherance of the treaty. One of the ways through which the Conference may advance the implementation of article 10 of the Kampala Convention is through the establishment of a working group on DID. Such thematic working groups have emerged in the context of other treaties that establish Conferences. For instance, under the United Nations Convention against Corruption,[19] there at two thematic working groups on Prevention and Asset Recovery.[20] These working groups provide advice and assistance on the specific thematic area in furtherance of the implementation of the instrument. Through a specific working group on DID, states can collectively address the issue, share good practices and also set out guidance on sustainable solutions. Through this working group, standard-setting may also be enhanced, for instance, with respect to private actors.

6.2.2 The African Commission should adopt a General Comment on article 10 of the Kampala Convention

In interpreting specific treaty provisions, General Comments are valuable.[21] These comments are used to advance clarification on specific treaty concepts,[22] outline the extent of state obligations[23] and provide insight on issues not explicitly covered by treaty provisions.[24] Though non-binding,[25] General Comments offer concise blueprints, integral to understanding the content of treaties. At national level, these comments have featured in judicial expositions. For instance, in the *Mitu-bell* case, the High Court of Kenya (HCK) applied General Comment No 7 of the CESCR in defining the obligations of Kenya in situations of displacement.[26] Echoing the language of the General Comment, the HCK stated that 'the right to housing . . . is violated when evictions and demolitions, as in the current case [*Mitu-bell* case] are carried out, leaving citizens homeless.'[27]

In 2012, the African Commission adopted its first General Comment elaborating on the provisions of article 14(1)(d) and (e) of the Protocol to the African Charter on Human and Peoples' Rights on the Rights of Women in Africa.[28] In the preface to the General Comment, the African Commission highlighted two significant functions of its General Comment; namely, that it serves to 'respond to a need to articulate the specific measures to be taken by [s]tate [p]arties in order to fulfil their obligations'[29] and that it serves to 'provide a set of international standards . . . towards . . . effective implementation.'[30] The African Commission further noted that[31]

> [i]n the absence of this guidance, there is a risk not only of non-compliance . . . with . . . relevant international standards, but also of violations of . . . human rights . . . through inaction and ignorance.

In ensuring that the provisions of the Kampala Convention are met, this book recommends that the African Commission adopts a General Comment elaborating on article 10 of the Kampala Convention. The following is a draft General Comment, which the African Commission may consider.

A. Introduction

The Kampala Convention is the first continental binding treaty on internal displacement. Adopted by the African Union Heads of States and Government (AU Assembly), the Kampala Convention advances the regional dialogue on internal displacement. On the whole, the Kampala Convention seeks to prevent arbitrary displacement and obligate states to protect the rights of all persons against arbitrary displacement. It further obligate states to respect the human rights obligations that flow from the obligation to prevent arbitrary displacement.

In article 10 of the Kampala Convention, states are required to prevent displacement caused by projects that are implemented by public or private actors. The recognition of this form of displacement is indeed significant considering the scale of displacements caused by development projects across the continent. In article 10(1) of the Kampala Convention, states are obligated to 'as much as possible, prevent displacement caused by projects carried out by public or private actors.'[32] Although the Kampala Convention does not define the term 'as much as possible,' its emphasis on the need for states to prevent arbitrary displacement presupposes that its provision must be read in light of what constitutes 'arbitrary' displacement. This General Comment clarifies the obligation in article 10 of the Kampala Convention, stating explicitly what the obligation entails.

B. Principle

Article 10(1) of the Kampala Convention seeks to strike a balance between the imperative of development and the rights of persons likely to be displaced. In striking this balance, states must be mindful of the need to prevent arbitrary displacement. While the African Commission appreciates the fact that states exercise discretion in determining their national developmental policies, the African Commission seeks to reaffirm that it is important for states to respect their international human rights obligations and, as such, DID must not render rights illusory. States must protect the right not to be arbitrarily displaced. While situations of DID may be permissible, it is important that prior impact assessments are conducted in line with the requirement of article 10(3) of the Kampala Convention in order to ascertain the socio-economic and environmental effects of development projects. Further, feasible alternatives should be explored in consultation with persons likely to be displaced in line with article 10(2) of the Kampala Convention.

C. Participation

Article 10(2) of the Kampala Convention require states to 'ensure that the stakeholders concerned . . . explore feasible alternatives, with full information and consultation of persons likely to be displaced by projects.'[33] In ensuring the sustainability of development projects and in protecting the rights of persons likely to be displaced, the African Commission emphasises that this obligation should be met.

The African Commission notes that the term 'stakeholders' is capable of various meanings. However, within the context of this provision, the African Commission emphasises that stakeholders in the implementation of a development project are individuals, communities, corporate bodies and institutions connected with the implementation of a project, including those that are bound to be affected.

The African Commission further stresses that consultation in this provision must not be considered as a means of legitimising already-made decisions; rather, consultation must be a means through which stakeholders, including persons likely to be displaced, are actively engaged in the decision-making on the feasible alternatives to the proposed project. The African Commission emphasises that such understanding of consultation is consistent with international standards on participatory development and are in line with traditional African values integral to the fabric of many societies across the continent.

The African Commission further clarifies that the term 'full information' in the provision is four-pronged. First, all information requested with regards to the development project must be provided to persons likely to be displaced. Second, information with regards to the likely environmental and socio-economic impacts of the development project on the rights of these persons or communities should be provided. Third, information on state policies and corporate guidelines on how the concerns of these persons or communities will be addressed are to be provided. Fourth, since the primary objective of the consultation process in article 10(2) of the Kampala Convention is to explore feasible alternatives, all other information relevant to this process must be provided.

Prior to the implementation of a development project, the African Commission stresses that six feasible alternatives must be considered. First, the possibility of not implementing the project at all should be given due consideration. Second, the possibility of implementing the project in another location where individuals and communities will not be affected should be taken into account. Third, the alternative of implementing the project in collaboration with the individuals and communities should be considered. Fourth, strategies for minimising displacements should be given due consideration. Fifth, lease agreements should be negotiated as an alternative in situations where projects are for a limited period of time so as to prevent loss of ownership rights. But in circumstances where these alternatives are not feasible, voluntary compensation should be given priority coupled with investment in development. The African Commission further stresses that the Free Prior and Informed Consent (FPIC) of persons likely to be displaced should be sought. With respect to indigenous peoples, the African Commission stresses that states must ensure that the FPIC of these peoples are obtained where the project sought to be implemented will have a major impact on them. States should ensure that an external review mechanism exist to check the actions of public and private actors and ensure compliance with the Kampala Convention and other relevant international standards including human rights. Further, access to justice must be protected. The jurisdiction of national courts to determine matters relating to the process must also not be restricted.

D. Prior impact assessments

Article 10(3) of the Kampala Convention require states to 'carry out a socio-economic and environmental impact assessment of a proposed development project prior to undertaking such a project.'[34] Information on the likely socio-economic and environmental impacts of a development project is important in considering feasible alternatives in line with article 10(2) and in ensuring that the rights of persons likely to be displaced are protected.

The African Commission emphasises that the impact of projects on the socio-economic rights of those likely to be displaced must be duly considered. In carrying out these assessments, the African Commission stresses that states must ensure that the impact of the project on the rights to adequate standard of living, work, health, development, education, culture and social security are considered. In carrying out environmental impact assessments, the African Commission stresses that states must comply with international standards on environmental impact assessments, including the Principles of Environmental Impact Assessment Best Practice (EIA Principles).[35] In line with the EIA Principles, states must ensure that the environmental assessment process is thorough and participatory.[36] In carrying out an environmental impact assessment, the African Commission emphasises that states must equally be mindful of the right to a satisfactory environment guaranteed under article 24 of the African Charter.

In sum, the African Commission strongly encourages states to take targeted steps and, in particular, legislative, administrative and judicial measures to ensure that the provision of article 10 of the Kampala Convention is observed.

E. Private actors

The African Commission further seeks to highlight that the obligation in article 10(1) of the Kampala Convention require states to regulate private actors. In view of this fact, the African Commission stresses that states should promote corporate due diligence and ensure that regulatory measures are set in place in line with global standards and notably the UN 'Protect, Respect and Remedy' Framework for Business and Human Rights. The African Commission further emphasises that states should urge corporations to incorporate corporate due diligence in their policy statements and respect the international human rights obligations of states in which they operate, including the provision of article 10 of the Kampala Convention.

6.2.3 The African Commission should revise its reporting guidelines

The Kampala Convention mandate states to report on measures taken in furtherance of the obligations in the treaty when reporting to the African Commission,[37] in line with article 62 of the African Charter.[38] However, the African Commission's reporting guidelines do not offer explicit guidance on the specific content of this requirement. The African Commission's reporting guidelines also do not mention internally displaced persons as a specific group requiring protection. In addressing this gap, a revision of the state reporting guidelines is imperative. As such, the African Commission should explicitly provide guidance to states in reporting on measures taken to prevent arbitrary displacement within the context of the Kampala Convention, including article 10.

6.2.4 The African Commission should conduct missions

In ensuring that the obligation in article 10 of the Kampala Convention is realised, it is recommended that the African Commission should conduct missions to states where development projects are sought to be implemented.[39] These missions should be aimed at engaging in constructive dialogues with relevant stakeholders on protecting the rights of communities likely to be affected by development projects,[40] and promote the Kampala Convention.[41] During these missions, the African Commission should discuss realising the obligation in article 10 of the Kampala Convention with relevant stakeholders. The African Commission should also meet with affected communities, document their concerns and engage with states on ensuring that the concerns are addressed.

6.3 Concluding remarks

As at February 2020, 31 states have ratified the Kampala Convention.[42] At the continental level, the instrument has gained significant traction. Indeed, its impacts have become visible at various levels of governance. However, there is a need for explicit guidance on specific obligations, notably in fostering implementation. Within the context of DID, this book elaborates guidance. Overall, this book examines how a balance may be struck between the imperative of development and the rights of persons likely to be displaced. Further research is needed specifically on the application of this obligation at national level. Moreover, there is also a need for research on various categories of displaced persons in the DID context, particularly in relation to impact assessments. Also, data is an imperative to draw attention to this issue and provide information on the prevalence of this concern in order to effectively influence policy formation.

Notes

1 African Union Convention for the Protection and Assistance of Internally Displaced Persons in Africa, adopted at the Special Summit of the African Union Heads of States and Government in Kampala, Uganda (19–23 October 2009) (Kampala Convention). Cross-referencing is to endnotes in this chapter.
2 The Kampala Convention (n 1), art 10(1).
3 The Kampala Convention (n 1), art 3(1).
4 As previously stated, art 4(4).

5 *Elettronica Sicula S.p.A. (ELSI) (United States of America v Italy)* (Judgement) (1989) (*ELSI* case) ICJ Rep 15.
6 *ELSI* case (n 5), para 124.
7 *ELSI* case (n 5), para 128.
8 The Kampala Convention (n 1) art 10(2).
9 The Kampala Convention (n 1) art 10(3).
10 As previously stated.
11 Principles of Environmental Impact Assessment Best Practice (EIA Principles) (1999) https://www.iaia.org/uploads/pdf/principlesEA_1.pdf (accessed May 2020).
12 UN Human Rights Council *Report of the Special Representative of the Secretary-General on the Issue of Human Rights and Transnational Corporations and Other Business Enterprises, John Ruggie* UN Doc A/HRC/17/31 (21 March 2011) (Ruggie Principles).
13 The Kampala Convention (n 1), art 3(h) & (i).
14 As previously stated, art 10(1).
15 The Kampala Convention (n 1), art 14(1).
16 '1st meeting of the conference of states parties to the Kampala Convention' *African Union (Press Releases)* 3 April 2017.
17 The Plan of Action seeks to '(a) Pursue the vision of the AU in addressing the forced displacement on the Continent, (b) Consolidate and create synergy with on-going initiatives to address the phenomenon of forced displacement on the Continent, (c) Serve as an implementation and accountability framework of collective efforts in reducing internal displacement on the Continent, (d) Set broad targets, benchmarks and indicators of achievement in the implementation of the Kampala Convention within the context of the AU long-term vision, (e) Devise means to facilitate coordination, follow-up, reporting and monitoring mechanisms to ensure timely and effective implementation of the Kampala Convention and various strategies aimed at dealing with internal displacement, (f) Provide a structured platform for interactions between States parties, the AU and RECs and its partners in dealing with internal displacement on the Continent.' Conference of State Parties *Harare Plan of Action for the Implementation of the Kampala Convention (2017–2022)* (2017) IV–V.
18 Conference of State Parties (n 17) IV.
19 UN Convention against Corruption, adopted by UN General Assembly Resolution 58/4, UN Doc A/58/422 (31 October 2003).
20 Resolution 1/4: Establishment of an intergovernmental working group on asset recovery, adopted by the Conference of the State Parties to the UN Convention against Corruption, UN Doc CAC/COSP/2006/12 (10–14 December 2006); Resolution 3/2: Preventive measures, adopted by the Conference of the State Parties to the UN Convention Against Corruption, UN Doc CAC/COSP/2009/15 (9–13 November 2009).
21 I Bantekas & L Oette *International human rights law and practice* (2020) 211–214.
22 See General Comment No 14 on art 3(1): the right of the child to have his or her best interests taken as a primary consideration, adopted by the UN Committee on the Rights of the Child, UN Doc CRC/C/GC/14 (29 May 2013).
23 See General Comment No 31: the nature of the general legal obligation imposed on states parties to the Covenant, adopted by the UN Human Rights Committee, UN Doc CCPR/C/21/Rev.1/Add.13 (26 May 2004).
24 See UN Committee on the Elimination of Racial Discrimination 'General recommendation 23: rights of indigenous peoples' UN Doc A/52/18 annex V (1997).
25 Bantekas & Oette (n 21) 213.
26 *Mitu-bell Welfare Society v Attorney General & 2 Others* (2013) eKLR (*Mitu-bell* case); General Comment No 7 on art 11(1): forced evictions, adopted by the

UN Committee on Economic, Social and Cultural Rights, UN Doc E/1998/22 (20 May 1997).

27 As previously stated.

28 General Comments on article 14(1)(d) and (e) of the Protocol to the African Charter on Human and Peoples' Rights on the Rights of Women in Africa (2012).

29 As previously stated.

30 As previously stated.

31 As previously stated.

32 The Kampala Convention (n 1), art 10(1).

33 The Kampala Convention (n 1), art 10(2).

34 The Kampala Convention (n 1), art 10(3).

35 EIA Principles (n 11).

36 As previously stated.

37 The Kampala Convention (n 1), art 14(4).

38 Article 62(1) of the African Charter provides that 'Each party shall undertake to submit every two years, from the date the present Charter comes into force, a report on the legislative or other measures taken with a view to giving effect to the rights and freedoms recognized and guaranteed by the present Charter.' See African Charter on Human and Peoples' Rights, adopted by the Organisation of African Unity, OAU Doc CAB/LEG/67/3 rev 5 (27 June 1981) (African Charter), art 62.

39 African Charter (n 38), art 45.

40 For instance, the African Commission may visit the Democratic Republic of Congo ahead of the planned Inga dam III to ensure that those that are likely to be affected are provided adequate protection. See M Mwenda 'Inga 3, the world's largest dam will displace tens of thousands in DR Congo' *Life Gate (News)* 23 January 2017.

41 See African Charter (n 38), art 45.

42 Angola, Benin, Burkina Faso, Cameroon, Central African Republic, Chad, Côte d'Ivoire, Congo, Djibouti, Equatorial Guinea, Eswatini, Ethiopia, Gabon, Gambia, Guinea-Bissau, Lesotho, Liberia, Malawi, Mali, Mauritania, Niger, Nigeria, Rwanda, Sahrawi Arab Democratic Republic, Sierra Leone, Somalia, South Sudan, Togo, Uganda, Zambia and Zimbabwe. African Union 'List of countries which have signed, ratified/acceded to the African Union Convention for the Protection and Assistance of Internally Displaced Persons in Africa (Kampala Convention)' (2019); 'UNHCR welcomes Somalia's ratification of the Kampala Convention' *UN Refugee Agency* 27 November 2019; 'UNHCR welcomes Ethiopia's ratification of the Kampala Convention' *UN Refugee Agency* 14 February 2020.

Bibliography

Books

Abebe, A (2016) *The emerging law of forced displacement in Africa: development and implementation of the Kampala Convention on internal displacement* London: Routledge.

Amao, O (2011) *Corporate social responsibility, human rights and the law: multinational corporations in developing countries* London: Routledge.

Anaya, SJ (2004) *Indigenous peoples in international law* Oxford: Oxford University Press.

Anugwom, EE (2019) *The Boko Haram insurgence in Nigeria: perspectives from within* Cham: Palgrave Macmillan/Springer Nature.

Bantekas, I & Oette, L (2020) *International human rights law and practice* Cambridge: Cambridge University Press.

Barume, AK (2010) *Land rights of indigenous peoples in Africa* Copenhagen: International Work Group for Indigenous Affairs.

Bellamy, AJ (2015) *The responsibility to protect: a defense* Oxford: Oxford University Press.

Bereketeab, R (2019) *The Ethiopia-Eritrea rapprochement: peace and stability in the horn of Africa* Uppsala: The Nordic Africa Institute.

Boas, G (2012) *Public international law: contemporary principles and perspectives* Gloucester: Edward Elgar Publishing.

Bowen, H (1953) *Social responsibilities of the businessman* New York: Harper.

Boyd, DR (2012) *The environmental rights revolution: a global study of constitutions, human rights, and the environment* British Columbia: University of British Columbia Press.

Breau, S (2016) *The responsibility to protect and international law: an emerging paradigm shift* Oxford University Press.

Brownlie, I (1990) *Principles of public international law* Oxford: Oxford University Press.

Cantor, DJ (2018) *Returns of internally displaced persons during armed conflict: international law and its application in Columbia* Leiden: Brill Nijhoff.

Cernea, MM (ed) (1999) *The economics of involuntary resettlement: questions and challenges* Washington DC: World Bank Publications.

Clapham, A (2006) *Human rights obligations of non-state actors* Oxford: Oxford University Press.

Cohen, RG & Deng, FM (1998) *Masses in flight: the global crisis of internal displacement* Washington DC: The Brookings Institution Press.

Crawford, J (2002) *The International Law Commission's articles on state responsibility: introduction, text and commentaries* Cambridge: Cambridge University Press.

Diamond, L, Linz, J & Lipset, SM (eds) (1988) *Democracy in developing countries, volume 2* Colorado: Lynne Rienner Publishers.

Doyle, CM (2015) *Indigenous peoples, title to territory, rights and resources: the transformative role of free prior and informed consent* London: Routledge.

Dugard, J (2011) *International law: a South African perspective* Cape Town: Juta & Co Ltd.

Dunn, ID (2012) *The right to development and international economic law: legal and moral dimensions* Oxford: Hart Publishing.

Emerson, SA (2014) *The battle for Mozambique: the Frelimo-Renamo struggle, 1977–1992* West Midlands: Helion and Company Ltd.

Fahim, HM (1981) *Dams, people and development: the Aswan High Dam Case* Oxford: Pergamon Press.

Friedman, M (2009) *Capitalism and freedom: fortieth anniversary edition* Chicago: University of Chicago Press.

Gilbert, J (2006) *Indigenous peoples' land rights under international law: from victims to actors* Leiden: Brill Nijhoff.

Hamdani, K & Ruffing, L (2015) *United Nations Centre on Transnational Corporations: corporate conduct and the public interest* London: Routledge.

Hansen, SJ (2013) *Al-Shabaab in Somalia: the history and ideology of an Islamist group, 2005–2012* Oxford: Oxford University Press.

Ikuenobe, P (2006) *Philosophical perspectives on communalism and morality in African traditions* Maryland: Lexington Books.

Joseph, D & Maruf, H (2018) *Inside Al-Shabaab: the secret history of Al-Qaeda's most powerful ally* Bloomington: Indiana University Press.

Kant, I (2011) *Groundwork of the metaphysics of morals: a German – English edition* trans M Gregor & J Timmermann Cambridge: Cambridge University Press.

Karl, TL (1997) *The paradox of plenty: oil booms and petro-states* Berkeley, CA: University of California.

Kelsen, H (1952) *Principles of international law* Clark, NJ: The Lawbook Exchange Ltd.

Khan, BU & Rahman, MM (2012) *Protection of minorities: regimes, norms and issues in South Asia* Newcastle Upon Tyne: Cambridge Scholars Publishing.

Kleine-Ahlbrandt, ST (2004) *The protection gap in the international protection of internally displaced persons: the case of Rwanda* Geneva: The Graduate Institute of International Studies.

Korn, DA (1999) *Exodus within borders: an introduction to the crisis of internal displacement* Washington, DC: Brookings Institution Press.

Kuwali, D (2011) *The responsibility to protect: implementation of article 4(h) intervention* Leiden: Martinus Nijhoff.

Locke, J (1689) *Two treaties of government.*

Mansuri, G & Rao, V (2013) *Localizing development: does participation work?* Washington, DC: World Bank Publications.

Maru, MT (2014) *The Kampala Convention and its contribution to international law: legal analyses and interpretations of the African Union Convention for the Protection and Assistance of Internally Displaced Persons* The Hague: Eleven International Publishing.

Muchlinksi, PT (2007) *Multinational enterprises and the law* Oxford: Oxford University Press.

Newton, M & May, L (2014) *Proportionality in international law* Oxford: Oxford University Press.

Oliver-Smith, A (2010) *Defying displacement: grassroots resistance and critique of development* Texas: University of Texas Press.

Oluduro, O (2014) *Oil exploitation and human rights violations in Nigeria's oil producing communities* Cambridge: Intensentia.

Orchard, P (2019) *Protecting the internally displaced: rhetoric and reality* London: Routledge.

Oshionebo, E (2009) *Regulating transnational corporations in domestic & international regimes: an African case study* Toronto: University of Toronto Press.

Ouguergouz, F (2003) *The African Charter of Human and People's Rights: a comprehensive agenda for human dignity and sustainable democracy in Africa* The Hague: Martinus Nijhoff Publishers.

Penz, P, Drydyk, J & Bose, PS (2011) *Displacement by development: ethics, rights and responsibilities* Cambridge: Cambridge University Press.

Petrella, I (2004) *The future of liberation theology: an argument and manifesto* Surrey: Ashgate Publishing.

Phuong, C (2005) *The international protection of internally displaced persons* Cambridge: Cambridge University Press.

Rousseau, JJ (2007) *Discourse on the origin of inequality* Minneapolis, MN: Filiquarian Publishing, LLC.

SAGE Publications (2012) *SAGE brief guide to corporate social responsibility* Thousand Oaks, CA: SAGE Publications.

Salm, SJ & Falola, T (2002) *Culture and customs of Ghana* Westport, CT: Greenwood Publishing Group.

Sayaka, FC (2012) *The origins of war in Mozambique: a history of unity and division* Tokyo: Ochanomizu Shobo Co Ltd.

Schauer, F (1982) *Free speech: a philosophical enquiry* Cambridge: Cambridge University Press.

Scudder, T (2005) *The future of large dams: dealing with social, environmental, institutional and political costs* London: Earthscan Publications.

Shapiro, E, Mackmin, D & Sams, G (2013) *Modern methods of valuation* London: Routledge.

Sinclair, IM (1984) *The Vienna Convention on the Law of Treaties* Manchester: Manchester University Press.

Smith, BC (2007) *Good governance and development* Basingstoke/New York: Palgrave Macmillan.

Steel, J (2012) *Journalism and free speech* London: Routledge.

Stewart, D & Swanson, C (2005) *Wisdom from Africa: a collection of proverbs* Cape Town: Struik Publishers.

Szablowski, D (2007) *Transnational law and local struggles: mining, communities and the World Bank* Oxford: Hart Publishing.

Tead, O & Metcalf, HC (1920) *Personnel administration: its principles and practice* New York: McGraw-Hill Book Company Inc.

Thoreau, HD (2013) *Civil disobedience (resistance to civil government) 1849* in Thoreau, HD Civil disobedience Wisconsin: Cricket House Books, LLC.

Thurston, B (2018) *Boko Haram: the history of an African jihadist movement* Princeton: Princeton University Press.

Tronvoll, K (1998) *Mai Weini, a highland village in Eritrea: a study of the people, their livelihood, and land tenure during times of turbulence* Eritrea, NJ: The Red Sea Press Inc.

van Banning, TRG (2001) *The human right to property* Antwerp: Intersentia.

Viljoen, F (2012) *International human rights law in Africa* Oxford: Oxford University Press.

Walton, CC (1967) *Corporate Social Responsibilities* Belmont, CA: Wadsworth Publishing.

Weiss, TG & Korn, DA (2006) *Internal displacement: conceptualization and its consequences* London: Routledge.

Young, S (2020) *Indigenous peoples, consent and rights: troubling subjects* London: Routledge.

Chapters in books

Adeola, R (2018) 'The African Union Model Law on Internally Displaced Persons: a critique' in Shyllon, L (ed) *The Model Law on Access to Information for Africa and other regional instruments: soft law and human rights in Africa* Pretoria: Pretoria University Law Press.

Adepoju, A (1995) 'The politics of international migration in post-colonial Africa' in Cohen, R (ed) *The Cambridge survey of world migration* Cambridge: Cambridge University Press.

Adrien, SM (2007) 'The DRC case study: the impact of the "Carbon Sinks of Ibi-Batéké Project" on the indigenous pygmies of the Democratic Republic of Congo' in Abhainn, M, Bernard, KM & Grey, S (eds) *Indigenous peoples and climate change: vulnerabilities, adaptation and responses to mechanisms of the Kyoto Protocol: a collection of case studies* Chiang Mai: The International Alliance of Indigenous and Tribal Peoples of the Tropical Forests.

Anaya, SJ (2010) 'The evolution of the concept of indigenous peoples and its contemporary dimensions' in Dersso, S (ed) *Perspectives on the rights of minorities and indigenous peoples in Africa* Pretoria: Pretoria University Law Press.

Andreassen, BA (2010) 'Development and the human rights responsibilities of non-state actors' in Andreassen, BA & Mark, SP (eds) *Development as a human right: legal, political and economic dimensions* Antwerp/Oxford/Portland: Intensentia.

Barutciski, M (2006) 'International law and development-induced displacement and resettlement' in De Wet, C (ed) *Development-induced displacements: problems, policies and people* Oxford: Berghahn Books.

Bojosi, KN (2010) 'The African Commission Working Group of Experts on the Rights of Indigenous Communities/Populations: some reflections on its work so far' in Dersso, S (ed) *Perspectives on the rights of minorities and indigenous peoples in Africa* Pretoria: Pretoria University Law Press.

Carroll, AB (2008) 'A history of corporate social responsibility: concepts and practices' in Crane, A, McWilliams, A, Matten, D, Moon, J & Siegel, DS (eds) *The Oxford handbook of corporate social responsibility* Oxford: Oxford University Press.

Cernea, MM (1996) 'Understanding and preventing impoverishment from displacement: reflections on the state of knowledge' in McDowell, C (ed) *Understanding impoverishment: the consequences of development-induced displacement* Oxford: Berghahn Books.

Cernea, MM (2008) 'Compensation and investment in resettlement: theory, practice, pitfalls, and needed policy reform' in Cernea, MM & Mathur, HM (eds) *Can compensation prevent impoverishment? Reforming resettlement through investments and benefit-sharing* Oxford: Oxford University Press.

Cernea, MM & McDowell, C (2000) 'Reconstructing resettlers' and refugees' livelihood' in Cernea, MM & McDowell, C (eds) *Risks and reconstruction: experiences of resettlers and refugees* Washington DC: World Bank Publications.

Cheney, G, Roper, J & May, S (2007) 'Overview' in May, S, Cheney, G & Roper, J (eds) *The debate over corporate social responsibility* Oxford: Oxford University Press.

Chimni, BS (2010) 'International financial institutions and international law: a third world perspective' in Bradlow, DD & Hunter, DB (eds) *International financial institutions and international law* Alphen aan den Rijn: Kluwer Law International.

Chirwa, DM (2010) 'State responsibility for human rights' in Baderin, MA & Ssenyonjo, M (eds) *International human rights law: six decades after the UDHR and beyond* Surrey: Ashgate Publishing.

Clark, D & Hunter, D (2001) 'The World Bank Inspection Panel – amplifying citizen voices for sustainable development' in Alfredsson, G & Ring, R (eds) *The Inspection Panel of the World Bank: a different complaints procedure* The Hague: Martinus Nijhoff Publishers.

Crane, A, McWilliams, A, Matten, D, Moon, J & Siegel, DS (2008) 'The corporate social responsibility agenda' in Crane, A, McWilliams, A, Matten, D, Moon, J & Siegel, DS (eds) *The Oxford handbook of corporate social responsibility* Oxford: Oxford University Press.

Dersso, SA (2010) 'Introduction' in Dersso, S (ed) *Perspectives on the rights of minorities and indigenous peoples in Africa* Pretoria: Pretoria University Law Press.

Dersso, SA (2010) 'The socio-historical and political processes leading to the emergence and development of norms on minorities' in Dersso, S (ed) *Perspectives on the rights of minorities and indigenous peoples in Africa* Pretoria: Pretoria University Law Press.

Deva, S (2013) 'Treating human rights lightly: a critique of the consensus rhetoric and the language employed by the Guiding Principles' in Deva, S & Bilchitz, D (eds) *Human rights obligations of business: beyond the corporate responsibility to respect* Cambridge: Cambridge University Press.

Deva, S & Bilchitz, D (2013) 'The human rights obligations of business: a critical framework for the future' in Deva, S & Bilchitz, D (eds) *Human rights obligations of business: beyond the corporate responsibility to respect* Cambridge: Cambridge University Press.

De Wet, C (2006) 'Risk, complexity and local initiatives in forced resettlement outcomes' in De Wet, C (ed) *Development-induced displacements: problems, policies and people* Oxford: Berghahn Books.

Dieng, A (1987) 'Background to and growth of the right to development: the role of law and lawyers in development' in Nobel, P (ed) *Refugees and development in Africa* Uppsala: Scandinavian Institute of African Studies.

Downing, T & Garcia-Downing, C (2009) 'Routine and dissonant cultures: a theory about the psycho-socio-cultural disruptions of involuntary displacement and the ways to mitigate them without inflicting even more damage' in Oliver-Smith, A (ed) *Development and Dispossession: The anthropology of displacement and resettlement* New Mexico: School for Advanced Research Press.

El Jack, A (2007) 'Gendered implications: development-induced displacement in Sudan' in Vandergeest, P, Idahosa, P & Bose, PS (eds) *Development's displacements: ecologies, economics, and cultures at risk* British Columbia: University of British Columbia Press.

Flynn, G & Werhane, PH (2008) 'Introduction' in Flynn, G (ed) *Leadership and business ethics* Dordrecht: Springer.

Henrard, K (2010) 'Minorities in Africa and the right to equality and non-discrimination' in Dersso, S (ed) *Perspectives on the rights of minorities and indigenous peoples in Africa* Pretoria: Pretoria University Law Press.

Lauterpacht, H (2009) 'The subjects of international law' in Bianchi, A (ed) *Non-state actors and international law* Surrey: Ashgate Publishing.

Liebenberg, S (2008) 'South Africa' in Langford, M (ed) *Social rights jurisprudence: emerging trends in international and comparative* law Cambridge: Cambridge University Press.

López, C (2013) 'The "Ruggie Process": from legal obligations to corporate social responsibility' in Deva, S & Bilchitz, D (eds) *Human rights obligations of business: beyond the corporate responsibility to respect* Cambridge: Cambridge University Press.

Melé, D (2008) 'Social responsibility theories' in Crane, A, McWilliams, A, Matten, D, Moon, J & Siegel, DS (eds) *The Oxford handbook of corporate social responsibility* Oxford: Oxford University Press.

Mooney, ED (2010) 'Something old, something new, something borrowed . . . something blue? The protection potential of a marriage of concepts between R2P and IDP protection' in Davies, SE & Glanville, L (eds) *Protecting the displaced: deepening the responsibility to protect* Leiden: Martinus Nijhoff.

Narayan, P (2015) 'Patterns in arbitrariness: resettlement experiences of the unrecognized urban poor in Chennai' in Satiroglu, I & Choi, N (eds) *Development-induced displacement and resettlement: new perspectives on persisting problems* London: Routledge.

Navrud, S & Magnussen, K (2013) 'Valuing the impacts of natural disasters and the economic benefits of preventing them' in D Guha-Sapir & I Santos (eds) *The economic impact of natural disasters* Oxford: Oxford University Press.

Oduwole, O (2015) 'Africa's contribution to the advancement of the right to development in international law' in Jalloh, CC & Elias, O (eds) *Shielding humanity: essays in international law in honour of Judge Abdul G Koroma* Leiden: Brill Nijhoff.

Oliver-Smith, A (2005) 'Applied anthropology and development-induced displacement and resettlement' in Kedia, S & van Willigen, J (eds) *Applied anthropology: domains of application* Westport, CT: Greenwood Publishing Group.

Pellet, A (2010) 'The definition of responsibility in international law' in Crawford, J, Pellet, A & Olleson, S (eds) *The Law of International Responsibility* Oxford: Oxford University Press.

Rasche, A (2013) 'The United Nations and transnational corporations' in Lawrence, JT & Beamish, PW (eds) *Globally responsible leadership: managing according to the UN Global Compact* California: SAGE Publications.

Rowe, P (2010) 'The application of international humanitarian law to attacks on education in armed conflict' in United Nations Educational, Scientific and Cultural Organization (ed) *Protecting education from attack: a state-of-the-art review* Paris: United Nations Educational, Scientific and Cultural Organization.

Scudder, T (2006) 'Assessing the impacts of the LHWP on resettled households and other affected people 1986–2005' in Thamae, ML & Pottinger, L (eds) *On the wrong side of development: lessons learned from the Lesotho highlands water project* Maseru: Transformation Resource Centre.

Spieldoch, A & Murphy, S (2009) 'Agricultural land acquisitions: implications for food security and poverty alleviation' in Kugelman, M & Levenstein, SL (eds)

Land grab? The race for the world's farmland Washington DC: Woodrow Wilson International Center for Scholars.
Stein, MA & Lord, JE (2011) 'Human rights and humanitarian assistance for refugees and internally displaced persons with disabilities in Africa' in Grobbelaar-Du Plessis, I & van Reenen, T (eds) *Aspects of disability law in Africa* Pretoria: Pretoria University Law Press.
Stiglitz, JE (2005) 'Making natural resources into a blessing rather than a curse' in Tsalik, S & Schiffrin, A (eds) *Covering oil: a reporter's guide to energy and development* New York: Revenue Watch, Open Society Initiative.
Tamakloe, MA (1994) 'Long-term impacts of resettlement: the Akosombo dam experience' in CC Cook (ed) *Involuntary resettlement in Africa: selected papers from a conference on environment and settlement issues in Africa* Washington DC: World Bank Publications.
Thamae, ML (2006) 'A decade of advocacy for dam-affected communities' in Thamae, ML & Pottinger, L (eds) *On the wrong side of development: lessons learned from the Lesotho highlands water project* Maseru: Transformation Resource Centre.
Viljoen, F (2010) 'Reflections on the legal protection of indigenous peoples' rights in Africa' in Dersso, S (ed) *Perspectives on the rights of minorities and indigenous peoples in Africa* Pretoria: Pretoria University Law Press.
Wachira, GM (2010) 'Indigenous peoples' rights to land and natural resources' in Dersso, S (ed) *Perspectives on the rights of minorities and indigenous peoples in Africa* Pretoria: Pretoria University Law Press.
Weitzberg, K (2016) 'Rethinking the *Shifta War* fifty years after independence: myth, memory, and marginalization' in Kithinji, MM, Koster, MM & Rotich, JP (eds) *Kenya after 50: reconfiguring historical, political, and policy milestones* New York: Palgrave Macmillan.
Wouters, J & Ryngaert, C (2005) 'Good governance: lessons from international organizations' in Curtin, DM & Wessel, RA (eds) *Good governance and the European Union: reflections on concepts, institutions and substance* Antwerp: Intersentia.

Journal articles

Abbott, KW & Snidal, D 'Hard and soft law in international governance' (2000) 54(3) *International Organization* 421.
Abebe, AM 'Legal and institutional dimensions of protecting and assisting internally displaced persons in Africa' (2009) 22(2) *Journal of Refugee Studies* 155.
Abebe, AM 'The African Union convention on internally displaced persons: its codification background, scope and enforcement challenges' (2010) 29(3) *Refugee Survey Quarterly* 28.
Abrams, F 'Management's responsibilities in a complex world' (1951) 29(3) *Harvard Business Review* 29.
Adeola, R 'The right not to be arbitrarily displaced under the United Nations Guiding Principles on Internal Displacement' (2016) 1 *African Human Rights Law Journal* 83, 84.
Adeola, R 'The legal protection of development-induced displaced persons in Africa' (2017) 10(1) *African Journal of Legal Studies* 91
Adeola, R 'The responsibility of businesses to prevent development-induced displacement in Africa' (2017) 17 *African Human Rights Law Journal* 244.
Adeola, R 'The Kampala Convention and the right not to be arbitrarily displaced' (2018) 59 *Forced Migration Review* 15.

Adeola, R 'The impact of the African Union Convention on the Protection and Assistance of Internally Displaced Person in Africa' (2019) 19 *African Human Rights Law Journal* 591.

Adeola, R & Viljoen, F 'The right not to be arbitrarily displaced in Africa' (2017) 25(4) *African Journal of International and Comparative Law* 459.

Agbaje, EBA 'Modernisation, urban renewal and the social cost of development' (2013) 4(10) *Mediterranean Journal of Social Sciences* 318.

Agha, M 'Nubia still exists: on the utility of the nostalgic space' (2019) 8(1) *Humanities* 24.

Ake, C 'African democracy' (1991) 2(1) *Journal of Democracy* 32.

Ake, C 'Rethinking African democracy' (1991) 2(1) *Journal of Democracy* 32.

Ake, C 'The unique case of African democracy' (1993) 69(2) *International Affairs* 239.

Arnstein, SR 'A ladder of citizen's participation' (1969) 35(4) *Journal of the American Institute of Planners* 216.

Askouri, AK 'The Merowe dam: controversy and displacement in Sudan' (2004) 21 *Forced Migration Review* 56.

Bailey, L 'Out of Africa: toward regional solutions for internal displacement' (2014) 39(1) *Brooklyn Journal of International Law* 353.

Bantekas, I 'Corporate social responsibility in international law' (2004) 22 *Boston University International Law Journal* 309.

Beyani, C 'Recent developments: the elaboration of a legal framework for the protection of internally displaced persons in Africa' (2006) 50(2) *Journal of African Law* 187.

Brammer, S, Jackson, G & Matten, D 'Corporate social responsibility and institutional theory: new perspectives on private governance' (2012) 10(1) *Socio-Economic Review* 3.

Braun, YA '"How can I stay silent?": one woman's struggles for environmental justice in Lesotho' (2008) 10(2) *Journal of International Women's Studies* 5.

Braun, YA 'Gender, large-scale development, and food insecurity in Lesotho: an analysis of the impact of the Lesotho highlands water project' (2010) 18(3) *Gender and Development* 453.

Buchan, B 'The empire of political thought: civilization, savagery and perceptions of indigenous government' (2005) 18(2) *History of the Human Sciences* 1.

Carroll, AB 'A three-dimensional conceptual model of corporate performance' (1979) 4(4) *Academy of Management Review* 497.

Carroll, AB & Shabana, KM 'The business case for corporate social responsibility: a review of concepts, research and practice' (2010) 12(1) *International Journal of Management Reviews* 85.

Casalin, D 'The Guiding Principles in international human rights courts' (2018) 59 *Forced Migration Review: Twenty Years of the Guiding Principles on Internal Displacement* 42.

Cernea, MM 'The risks and reconstruction model for resettling displaced populations' 25(10) *World Development* (1997) 1569.

Cernea, MM 'Risks, safeguards and reconstruction: a model for population displacement and resettlement' (2000) 35(41) *Economic & Political Weekly* 3659.

Cernea, MM 'Compensation and benefit sharing: why resettlement policies and practices must be reformed' (2008) 1(1) *Water Science and Engineering* 89.

Cernea, MM & Schmidt-Soltau, K 'The end of forcible displacements? Conservation must not impoverish people' (2003) 12 *Policy Matters* 42.

Černič, JL 'Corporate responsibility for human rights: analysing the ILO Tripartite declaration of principles concerning multinational enterprises and social policy' (2009) 1 *Miskolc Journal of International Law* 24.

Chinkin, CM 'The challenge of soft law: development and change in international law' (1989) 38 *International and Comparative Law Quarterly* 850.

Cleaver, F 'Paradoxes of participation: questioning participatory approaches to development' (1999) 11 *Journal of International Development* 597.

Cochran, PL 'The evolution of corporate social responsibility' (2007) 50 *Business Horizons* 449.

Cohen, R 'The guiding principles on internal displacement: an innovation in international standard setting' (2004) 10 *Global Governance* 459.

Cornwall, A 'Historical perspectives on participation in development' (2006) 44(1) *Commonwealth & Comparative Politics* 62.

Cornwall, A 'Unpacking "participation": models, meanings and practices' (2008) 43(3) *Community Development Journal* 269.

Deng, FM 'The global challenge of internal displacement' (2001) 5(1) *Washington University Journal of Law and Policy* 141.

Deng, FM 'From "sovereignty as responsibility" to the "responsibility to protect"' (2010) 2 *Global Responsibility to Protect* 353.

Dieng, A 'Protecting internally displaced: the value of the Kampala Convention as a regional example' (2017) 99(904) *International Review of the Red Cross* 263.

Dinstein, Y 'Collective human rights of peoples and minorities' (1976) 25 *International and Comparative Law Quarterly* 102.

Dodd, M 'For whom are corporate managers trustees' (1932) 45(7) *Harvard Law Review* 1153.

Donaldson, T & Preston, LE 'The stakeholder theory of the corporation: concepts, evidence, and implications' (1995) 20(1) *Academy of Management Review* 65.

Donham, WB 'Business ethics – a general survey' (1929) 7 *Harvard Business Review* 385.

Donnelly, J 'In search of the unicorn: the jurisprudence and politics of the right to development' (1985) 15 *California Western International Law Journal* 473.

D'Orsi, C 'Strengths and weaknesses in the protection of the internally displaced persons in Sub-Saharan Africa' (2012) 28(1) *Connecticut Journal of International Law* 73.

Dwivedi, R 'Models and methods in development-induced displacement' (2002) 33(4) *Development and Change* 709.

Ebegbulem, JC, Ekpe, D & Adejumo, TO 'Oil exploration and poverty in the Niger Delta region of Nigeria: a critical analysis' (2013) 4(3) *International Journal of Business and Social Science* 279.

Fahim, HM 'Community-heath aspects of Nubian resettlement in Egypt' (1979) 55–56 *Kroeber Anthropological Society Papers* 81.

Gellert, PK & Lynch, BD 'Mega-projects as displacements' (2004) 55(175) *International Social Science Journal* 15.

Goodland, R 'Free, prior and informed consent and the World Bank Group' (2004) 4(2) *Sustainable Development Law and Policy* 66.

Griffiths, A 'Between paradigms: differing perspectives on justice in Molepolole, Botswana' (1996) 36 *Journal of Legal Pluralism* 195.

Grnchalla-Wesierski, T 'A framework for understanding "soft law"' (1984) *McGill Law Journal* 29.

Groth, L 'Engendering protection: an analysis of the 2009 Kampala Convention and its provision for internally displaced women' (2011) 23(2) *International Journal of Refugee Law* 1.

Guistiniani, FZ 'New hopes and challenges for the protection of IDPs in Africa: the Kampala Convention for the Protection and Assistance of Internally Displaced Persons in Africa' (2011) 39(2) *Denver Journal of International Law and Policy* 347.

Guzman, AT & Meyer, TL 'International soft law' (2010) 2 *Journal of Legal Analysis* 171.

Gyau-Boakye, P 'Environmental impacts of the Akosombo dam and effects of climate change on the lake levels' (2001) 3(1) *Environment, Development and Sustainability* 25.

Hansungule, M 'Who owns land in Zimbabwe? In Africa?' (2000) 7(4) *International Journal of Minority and Group Rights* 305.

Hickey, S & Mohan, G 'Relocating participation within a radical politics of development' (2005) 36(2) *Development and Change* 237.

Hilson, G & Maconachie, R ' "Good governance" and the extractive industries in sub-Saharan Africa' (2008) 30(1) *Mineral Processing & Extractive Metallurgy Review* 52.

Interorganisational Committee on Guidelines and Principles for Social Impact Assessment 'Guidelines and principles for social impact assessment' (1995) 15(1) *Environmental Impact Assessment Review* 11.

Ite, AE, Ibok, UJ, Ite, MU & Petters, SW 'Petroleum Exploration and production: past and present environmental issues in the Nigeria's Niger Delta' (2013) 1(4) *American Journal of Environmental Protection* 78.

Joestan, J 'Nasser's daring dream: the Aswan High Dam' (1960) 16(2) *The World Today* 55.

Johnson, LB, Howell, JP & Evered, KT ' "Where nothing was before": (re)producing population and place in Ghana's Volta River Project' (2015) 32(2) *Journal of Cultural Geography* 195.

Juma, L 'Protection of development-induced internally displaced persons under the African Charter: the case of the Endorois community of northern Kenya' (2013) 46 *Comparative and International Law of Southern Africa* 211.

Kakabadse, NK 'Corporate social responsibility and stakeholder approach: a conceptual review' (2005) 1(4) *International Journal of Business Governance and Ethics* 277.

Kamga, SAD 'The right to development in the African human rights system: the *Endorois* case' (2011) 23 *De Jure* 381.

Kamungi, P 'Beyond good intentions: implementing the Kampala Convention' (2010) 34 *Forced Migration Review* 53.

Keith, D 'Can business afford to ignore social responsibilities?' (1960) 1 *California Management Review* 70.

Khatri, U 'Indigenous peoples' right to free, prior, and informed consent in the context of state-sponsored development: the new standard set by Sarayaku v; Ecuador and its potential to delegitimize the Belo Monte Dam' (2013) 29(1) *American University International Law Review* 165.

Kidane, W 'Managing forced. Displacement by law in Africa: the role of the new African Union IDPs Convention' (2011) 44(1) *Vanderbilt Journal of Transnational. Law* 1.

Kiwanuka, RN 'The meaning of "people" in the African charter on human and peoples' rights' (1988) 82(1) *American Journal of International Law* 82.

Lee, BA 'Just undercompensation: the idiosyncratic premium of eminent domain' (2013) 113(3) *Columbia Law Review* 593.

Levitt, T 'The dangers of social responsibility' 1958 *Harvard Business Review* 41.

Lucas, K 'The Inspection Panel of the World Bank: an effective extrajudicial complaint mechanism?' (2015) 6 *World Bank Review* 531.

Madebwe, C, Mabedwe, V & Mavusa, S 'Involuntary displacement and resettlement to make way for diamond mining: the case of Chiadzwa villagers in Marange, Zimbabwe' (2011) 1(10) *Journal of Research in Peace, Gender and Development* 292.

M'Baye, K 'Le droit au développement comme droit de l'homme' (1972) 5 *Revue des droits de l'homme* 505.

McDonagh, M 'The right to information in international human rights law' (2013) *Human Rights Law Review* 5.

Moran, TH 'The United Nations and transnational corporations: a review and a perspective' (2009) 18(2) *Transnational Corporations* 91.

Moura-Leite, RC & Padgett, RC 'Historical background of corporate social responsibility' (2011) 7(4) *Social Responsibility Journal* 528.

Mteki, N, Murayama, T & Nishikizawa, S 'Social impacts induced by a development project in Tanzania: a case of airport expansion' (2017) 35(4) *Impact Assessment and Project Appraisal* 272.

Mushkat, R 'Corporate social responsibility, international law, and business economics: convergence and divergences' 12 *Oregon Review of International Law* 55.

Negari, W 'Indigenous knowledge for good governance and development: unleashing the wisdom of the Gada system' (2018) *Amity Journal of Management* 13.

Nehme, M & Wee, CKG 'Tracing the historical development of corporate social responsibility and corporate social reporting' (2008) 15 *James Cook University Law Review* 129.

Nicolai, J 'Operation Marambatsvina: a crime against humanity under the Rome statute?' 21(5) *American University International Law Review* 813.

Nolte, G 'From Dionisio Anzilotti to Roberto Ago: the classical international law of state responsibility and the traditional primacy of a bilateral conception of inter-state relations' (2002) 13(5) *European Journal of International Law* 1083.

Oakley, P 'The concept of participation in development' (1991) 20 *Landscape and Urban Planning* 115.

Obiadi, BN, Onochie, AO & Uduak, PU 'Where is home for the Abuja, Nigeria urban poor' (2019) 8(1) *Mgbakoigba, Journal of African Studies* 50.

Okoye, A 'Theorising corporate social responsibility as an essentially contested concept: is a definition necessary?' (2009) 89 *Journal of Business Ethics* 613.

Olsson, IA 'Four competing approaches to international soft law' (2013) 58 *Scandinavian Study in Law* 177.

Orchid, P 'Protection of internally displaced persons: soft law as a norm-generating mechanism' (2010) 36 *Review of International Studies* 281, 286–287.

Otunnu, O 'Factors affecting the treatment of Kenyan-Somalis and Somali refugees in Kenya: a historical overview' (1992) 12(5) *Refuge* 21.

Pentassuglia, G 'Indigenous groups and the developing jurisprudence of the African Commission on Human and Peoples' Rights: some reflections' (2010) 3 *UCL Human Rights Review* 150.

Pettersson, B 'Development-induced displacement: internal affair or international human rights issue?' (2002) 12 *Forced Migration Review* 16.

Plaine, DJ 'The OECD Guidelines for Multinational Enterprises' (1977) 11(2) *International Lawyer* 339.

Price, S 'Prologue: victims or partners? The social perspective in development-induced displacement and resettlement' (2009) 10(4) *The Asia Pacific Journal of Anthropology* 266.

Reda, KT 'Dynamics in pastoral resource management and conflict in the Borana rangelands of southern Ethiopia' (2016) 25(1) *African Security Review* 31.

Reilly, R 'Disabilities among refugees and conflict-affected populations' (2010) 35 *Forced Migration Review* 8.

Richter, R 'International Conference on the Plight of Refugees, Returnees and Displaced Persons in Southern Africa (SARRED), Oslo, 22–24 August 1988' (1989) 2(2) *Journal of Refugee Studies* 284.

Ridderbos, K 'The Kampala Convention and obligations of armed groups' (2011) 37 *Forced Migration Review* 36.

Rockefeller, JD Jr. 'Representation in industry' (January 1919) *Annals, American Academy of Political and Social Sciences.*

Roesch, R 'The story of a legal transplant: the right to free, prior and informed consent in sub-Saharan Africa' (2016) 16 *African Human Rights Law Journal* 505.

Schabas, WA 'The omission of the right to property in the international covenants' (1991) *Hague Yearbook of International Law* 135.

Sethi, SP 'Dimensions of corporate social performance: an analytical framework' (1975) 17(3) *California Management Review* 58.

Shaffer, GC & Pollack, MA 'Hard vs. soft law: alternatives, complements, and antagonists in international governance' (2010) 94 *Minnesota Law Review* 706.

Short, C 'The development of the extractive industries transparency initiative' (2014) *Journal of World Energy Law and Business* 1.

Smith, BC 'Participation without power: subterfuge or development?' (1998) 33(3) *Community Development Journal* 197.

Spector, B ' "Business responsibilities in a divided world": the cold war roots of the corporate social responsibility movement' (2008) 9(2) *Enterprise & Society* 314.

Stavropoulou, M 'The Kampala Convention and protection from arbitrary displacement' (2010) 36 *Forced Migration Review* 62.

Stiglitz, JE 'Participation and development: perspectives from the comprehensive development paradigm' (2002) 6(2) *Review of Development Economics* 163.

Terwel, BW, Koudenberg, FA & Ter Mors, E. 'Public responses to community compensation: the importance of prior consultations with local residents' (2014) 24 *Journal of Community & Applied Social Psychology* 479.

Thabane, T 'Weak extraterritorial remedies: the Achilles heel of Ruggie's "Protect, Respect and Remedy" framework and Guiding Principles' (2014) 14(1) *African Human Rights Law Journal* 43.

Vanclay, F 'International principles for social impact assessment' (2003) 21(1) *Impact Assessment and Project Appraisal* 5.

Weissbrodt, D & Kruger, M 'Norms on the responsibilities of transnational corporations and other business enterprises with regard to human rights' (2003) 97 *American Journal of International Law* 901.

Wilde, R 'From trusteeship to self-determination and back again: the role of the Hague regulations in the evolution of international trusteeship, and the framework of rights and duties of occupying powers' (2009) 31(1) *Loyola of Los Angeles International and Comparative Law Review* 85.

Wyman, KM 'The measure of just compensation' (2007) 41(1) *University of California Davis Law Review* 241.

Xanthaki, A 'Indigenous rights in international law over the last 10 years and future developments' (2009) 10(1) *Melbourne Journal of International Law* 27.

Reports/theses/Internet sources

African Commission on Human and Peoples' Rights and International Work Group for Indigenous Affairs 'Indigenous peoples in Africa: the forgotten peoples?' (2006) https://www.achpr.org/public/Document/file/Any/achpr_wgip_report_summary_version_eng.pdf (accessed 24 May 2020).

African Development Bank (AfDB) *Handbook on stakeholder consultation and participation in ADB operations* (2001).

'African Union addressing the challenge of forced displacement in Africa' Conference Background Paper, Special Summit on Refugees, Returnees and Displaced Persons in Africa held in Addis Ababa, Ethiopia (5–11 November 2008).

Albin-Lackey, C 'Without rules: a failed approach to corporate accountability' (2013) www.hrw.org/sites/default/files/related_material/business.pdf (accessed 25 May 2020).

AMC Mining Consultants (Canada) Ltd 'Technical report Sabodala gold project, Senegal, West Africa: prepared for Teranga Gold Corporation' (2012)

Amnesty International *"Just move them" forced evictions in Port Harcourt, Nigeria* (2010).

Amnesty International 'Public statement: state of housing rights and forced evictions in Africa: African Commission on Human and Peoples' Rights during its 50th ordinary session, to be held in Banjul, The Gambia (24 October – 7 November 2011) www.refworld.org/pdfid/4eba7e912.pdf (accessed 21 May 2020).

Amnesty International *Nigeria: forced eviction of Abonnema wharf waterfront: "Pack and Go!"* (2012).

Amnesty International *Mining and human rights protection in Senegal: closing the gaps in protection* (2014).

Amnesty International *Coerced and denied: forced marriages and barriers to contraception in Burkina Faso* (2016).

Amnesty International *"We are not animals to be hunted or sold" Violence and discrimination against people with albinism in Malawi* (2016).

AU Economic, Social and Cultural Council 'Making the Kampala Convention work for IDPs: Guide for civil society on supporting the ratification and implementation of the Convention for the Protection and Assistance of Internally Displaced Persons in Africa' (2010).

AU Executive Council, fifth ordinary session 25 June – 3 July 2004, Addis Ababa, Ethiopia, Decision on the meeting of experts on the review of OAU/AU treaties, Doc EX/CL/95 (V).

AU Executive Council, fifth ordinary session 25 June – 3 July 2004, Addis Ababa, Ethiopia, Decision on the Situation of Refugees, Returnees and Displaced Persons, Doc EX. CL/108 (V).

AU Executive Council, ninth ordinary session, 25–29 June 2006, Banjul, the Gambia, Decision on the situation of refugees, returnees and displaced persons, Doc EX.CL/254 (IX).

AU Executive Council, ninth ordinary session, 25–29 June 2006, Banjul, the Gambia, Decision on the ministerial conference on refugees, returnees and internally displaced persons, Doc EX.CL/259 (IX).

Bank Information Center & Inclusive Development International 'Human rights and the World Bank: case studies from IDA countries' (2013) www.inclusivedevelopment.net/wp-content/uploads/2014/04/IDA-Case-Study-Book-FINAL_10-4-13.pdf (accessed 24 May 2020).

Bereketeab, R 'Conceptualizing civil society in Africa: the case of Eritrea' (2009) www.diva-portal.org/smash/get/diva2:325466/FULLTEXT02.pdf 6 (accessed 22 February 2020).

Capotorti, F 'Study on the rights of persons belonging to ethnic, religious and linguistic minorities' Special Rapporteur of the Sub-Commission on Prevention of Discrimination and Protection of Minorities (1979).

Centre on Housing Rights and Evictions *The human right to adequate housing: chronology of United Nations activity* (2000).

Clay, JW, Alcorn, JB & Butler, JR 'Indigenous peoples, forestry management and biodiversity conservation' An Analytical Study for the World Bank's Forestry Policy Implementation Review and Strategy Development Framework (2000).

Cohen, R 'UN human rights bodies should deal with the internally displaced' presented at a meeting for delegates to the UN Commission on Human Rights by the Quaker United Nations Office and the World Council of Churches (7 February 1990).

Committee on Economic, Social and Cultural Rights, *Concluding observations on the second periodic report of Honduras*, UN Doc E/C.12/HND/CO/2 (11 July 2016).

Committee on Economic, Social and Cultural Rights, *Concluding observations on the fourth and fifth periodic report of Angola*, UN Doc E/C.12/AGO/CO/2 (15 July 2016).

Committee on Economic, Social and Cultural Rights, *Concluding observations on the second periodic report of Lebanon*, UN Doc E/C.12/LBN/CO/2 (24 October 2016).

Concluding observations of the UN Human Rights Committee: Kenya, adopted by the UN Human Rights Committee, UN Doc CCPR/CO/83/KEN (29 April 2005), para 22.

Darko, D, Kpessa-Whyte, M, Obuobie, E, Siakwah, P, Torto, O & Tsikata, D 'The context and politics of decision making on large dams in Ghana: an overview' Future Dams Working Paper 002 (2019).

David, DK 'Greetings by Dean David to the incoming class' 14 February 1946 Baker Library (Archive), Harvard Business School.

Department of International Development, United Kingdom 'Report of the Extractive Industries Transparency Initiative (EITI) London Conference, 17 June 2003' (2007).

Dersso, S 'Peoples' rights under the African charter on human and peoples' rights: much ado about nothing' SAIFAC Research Papers Series No 6.

EITI International Secretariat 'The EITI standard' (2013).

European Investment Bank *The EIB statement of environmental and social principles and standards* (2009).

European Parliament 'The effects of oil companies' activities on the environment, health and development in sub-Saharan Africa' (2011) 8–21 EXPO/B/DEVE/FWC/2009–01/Lot5/11.

'Explanatory note on the African Union Convention on the Protection and Assistance of Internally Displaced Persons in Africa (Kampala Convention).'

Extractive Industries Transparency Initiative (EITI) London conference 17 June 2003: Final attendance list https://webarchive.nationalarchives.gov.uk/20070701122619/http://www.dfid.gov.uk/pubs/files/eitidraftreportattendance.pdf (accessed 25 May 2020).

Fagbohun, O 'Mournful remedies, endless conflicts and inconsistencies in Nigeria's quest for environmental governance: rethinking the legal possibilities for sustainability' (2012) www.elri-ng.org/Inaugural%20Paper%20-%20Prof%20Fagbohun%20(NIALS).pdf (accessed 24 May 2020).

FIAN International 'Coffee to go – with a taste of eviction' A Film from: Michael Enger (2012)

'Forced displacement, citizenship and statelessness in Africa: report of a civil society consultation on African Union mechanisms and the protection of refugees, internally displaced persons and citizenship rights' (2009).

'Foreign land investments in developing countries – contribution or threat to sustainable development?' (Swedish FAO Committee Publication Series No 7, 2010).

Global Witness *A crude awakening: the role of oil and banking industries in Angola's civil war and the plunder of state assets* (1999).

Greater Port Harcourt City Development Authority 'The Authority' http://www.gph-city.com/about/authority.php (accessed 21 May 2020).

Human rights and transnational corporations and other business enterprises, adopted by the UN Human Rights Council Resolution 17, UN Doc A/HRC/17/L.17/Rev.1 (15 June 2011).

Human rights and transnational corporations and other business enterprises, adopted by the UN Human Rights Council Resolution 26, UN Doc A/HRC/26/L.1 (23 June 2014).

'Human rights protection for internally displaced persons' an international conference convened by the Refugee Policy Group (24–25 June 1991).

Human Rights Watch *Zimbabwe: evicted and forsaken: internally displaced persons in the aftermath of Operation Marambatsvina* (2005).

Human Rights Watch *A new accountability agenda: human rights and extractive industries transparency initiative* (2013).

Human Rights Watch '*"As if we were not humans": discrimination and violence against women with disabilities in Northern Uganda*' (2014).

IASC Framework on durable solutions for internally displaced persons (2010) A1 www.unhcr.org/50f94cd49.pdf (accessed 24 May 2020).

'Implementation of the African Union Convention for the Protection and Assistance of Internally Displaced Persons (IDPs) 2009 (The Kampala Convention)' Speech delivered by Chaloka Beyani at the first ministerial meeting of the Economic Community of West African States (ECOWAS) on internally displaced Persons in Abuja, Nigeria (7 July 2011).

Inclusive Development International et al *Reforming the World Bank Policy on Involuntary Resettlement* (Submission to the World Bank safeguards review, April 2013).

Indigenous peoples' permanent sovereignty over natural resources, final report of the Special Rapporteur, United Nations Working Group on Indigenous Populations, Erica-Irene A. Daes, UN Doc E/CN.4/Sub.2/2004/30 (13 July 2004) http://www1.umn.edu/humanrts/demo/IndigenousSovereigntyNaturalResources_Daes.pdf (accessed 24 May 2020).

Institute of Environmental Management & Assessment *Special report – the state of environmental impact assessment practice in the UK* (2011) 18.
Integration of the Commission on Transnational Corporations into the institutional machinery of the UN Conference on Trade and Development, adopted by the UN Economic and Social Council Resolution 1994/1 (14 July 1994).
Integration of the Commission on Transnational Corporations into the institutional machinery of the UN Conference on Trade and Development, adopted by the UN General Assembly Resolution 49/130, UN Doc A/RES/49/130 (19 December 1994).
Internal Displacement Monitoring Centre (2019) *Africa report on internal displacement* Geneva: Internal Displacement Monitoring Centre.
Internally Displaced Persons, adopted by UN Commission on Human Rights Resolution 1991/25, UN Doc. E/CN.4/RES/1991/25 (5 March 1991).
Internally Displaced Persons, adopted by the UN Commission on Human Rights Resolution 1992/73, UN Doc. E/CN.4/RES/1992/73 (5 March 1992).
International Committee of the Red Cross 'How is the term "armed conflict" defined in international humanitarian law?' (Opinion paper, March 2008).
International Conference on the Plight of Refugees, Returnees and Displaced Persons in Southern Africa, adopted by the UN General Assembly Resolution 42/106, UN Doc A/RES/42/106 (7 December 1987).
International Conference on the Plight of refugees, Returnees and Displaced persons in Southern Africa, adopted by UN General Assembly Resolution 43/116, UN Doc A/RES/43/116 (8 December 1988).
International Justice Resource Center 'In controversial landmark resolution, Human Rights Council takes first step toward treaty on transnational corporations' human rights obligations' (2015) www.ijrcenter.org/2014/07/15/in-controversial-landmark-resolution-human-rights-council-takes-first-step-toward-treaty-on-transnational-corporations-human-rights-obligations/ (accessed 25 May 2020).
International Labour Organisation 'Disabled Beggars in Addis Ababa, Ethiopia' Employment Working Paper No 141 (2013).
International Refugee Rights Initiative 'Comparison of the Kampala Convention and the IDP Protocol of the Great Lakes Pact' (2014).
Kachika, T 'Land grabbing in Africa: a review of the impacts and the possible policy responses' (2010) www.oxfamblogs.org/eastafrica/wp-content/uploads/2010/11/Land-Grabbing-in-Africa.-Final.pdf (accessed 2 March 2020).
Kälin, W 'How hard is soft law? The Guiding Principles on Internal Displacement and the need for a normative framework' Brookings/CUNY Project on Internal Displacement (19 December 2001).
Kaufmann, J 'Ruggie's guiding principles fail to address major questions of obligations and accountability' *Earth Rights International* 5 April 2011.
'Lagos state government displaced the people of Makoko community' *CNN iReport* 19 July 2012.
Large-scale land acquisitions and leases: a set of core principles and measures to address the human rights challenge, Mr. Olivier De Schutter, Special Rapporteur on the Right to Food (11 June 2009).
Lundberg, M & Wuermli, A (2012) *Children and Youth in crisis: protecting and promoting human development in times of economic shocks. Directions in development: human development* Washington, DC: The World Bank.

Marshall, S & MacDonald, K 'What is corporate accountability' (n.d.) https://pdfs.semanticscholar.org/39be/af6cf61c55a02d7596a0d92118fe49cbc6ec.pdf (accessed 25 May 2020).

Ministry of Finance, Planning and Economic Development (Kampala) 'Uganda's poverty eradication action plan: summary and main objectives' Poverty Reduction Strategy Paper (2000).

Nampungu, P & Kasabiiti, D 'The impact of involuntary resettlement on children: a case study of the international development associated funded Bujagali hydropower dam: Naminya resettlement area' (2012) https://consultations.worldbank.org/sites/default/files/consultation-template/review-and-update-world-bank-safeguard-policies/submissions/naminyafinalreport.pdf (accessed 24 May 2020).

Ngirabakunzi, E & Malinga, J 'The impact of NUSAF II in the lives of persons with disabilities in northern Uganda, a case study of Patiko sub County in Gulu district 2013' https://bankinformationcenter.cdn.prismic.io/bankinformationcenter%2Faeab6d47-3ce2-43cb-aeb5-c22d1775adb7_final-nusafii-report-final.pdf (accessed 24 May 2020).

Ngunshi, BR (2011) *Breast ironing . . . a harmful practice that has been silenced for too long* Bamenda: Gender Empowerment and Development.

'Nigeria: Two years after Njemanze community was demolished – Nigerians need a housing policy that respects human rights' *Amnesty International (Joint Public Statement)* 26 August 2011.

Norms on the Responsibilities of Transnational Corporations and Other Business Enterprises with regard to Human Rights, UN Doc E/CN.4/Sub.2/2003/12/Rev.2 (2003).

Nowrot, K 'New approaches to the international legal personality of multinational corporations: towards a rebuttable of normative responsibilities' https://esil-sedi.eu/wp-content/uploads/2018/04/Nowrot.pdf (accessed 25 May 2020).

Office of the UN High Commissioner for Human Rights 'Minority rights: international standards and guidance for implementation' (2010) www.ohchr.org/Documents/Publications/MinorityRights_en.pdf (accessed 24 May 2020).

'On the occasion of the commemoration of the entry into force of the African Union Convention for the Protection and Assistance of Internally Displaced Persons in Africa (the Kampala Convention)' Statement made by Chaloka Beyani in Addis Ababa, Ethiopia (6 December 2012).

Oslo Declaration and Plan of Action on the Plight of Refugees, Returnees and Displaced persons in Southern Africa, adopted at the International Conference on the Plight of Refugees, Returnees and Displaced Persons in Southern Africa, held at Oslo, Norway (22–24 August 1988).

Paul, S 'Community participation in development projects' World Bank discussion papers (1987).

Principles of Environmental Impact Assessment Best Practice (1999) https://www.iaia.org/uploads/pdf/principlesEA_1.pdf (accessed 24 May 2020)

Ramos, ML 'Angola's oil industry operations' Open Society Initiative for Southern Africa (2012).

Refugees, Displaced Persons and Returnees, UN Economic and Social Council Resolution 1990/78, UN Doc E/RES/1990/78 (27 July 1990).

Remarks by the Secretary of State (George C Marshall Jr) at Harvard University (5 June 1947) (Marshall Plan Speech).

Report of the African Commission's Working Group on Indigenous Populations/ Communities, submitted in accordance with the 'Resolution on the Right of Indigenous Populations/Communities in Africa Adopted by the African Commission on Human and Peoples' Rights at its 28th Ordinary Session (2003).

Report of the Fact Finding Mission to Zimbabwe to assess the scope and impact of Operation Marambatsvina by the UN Special Envoy on Human Settlements Issues in Zimbabwe: Mrs. Anna Kajumulo Tibaijuka (2005)

Report of the independent expert on the issue of human rights obligations relating to the enjoyment of a safe, clean, healthy and sustainable environment, John H. Knox UN Doc A/HRC/22/43 (24 December 2012).

Republic of Uganda 'Plan for Modernisation of agriculture: eradicating poverty in Uganda' https://semuwemba.files.wordpress.com/2010/03/uga-plan-for-modernisation-of-agriculture.pdf (accessed 19 February 2020).

Respect for the right of everyone to own property alone as well as in association with others and its contribution to the economic and social development of Member States, adopted by UN General Assembly Resolution 45/98, UN Doc A/ RES/45/98 (14 December 1990).

Ruggie, J 'The past as prologue? A moment of truth for UN business and human rights treaty' *Institute for Human Rights and Business (Commentary)* 8 July 2014.

Ruggie, J 'UN Guiding Principles for Business and Human Rights' *The Harvard Law School Forum on Corporate Governance and Financial Regulation* 9 April 2011.

Saami Council 'The difference between minorities and indigenous peoples under international law' (2002).

Sachs, JD & Warner, AM 'Natural resource abundance and economic growth' Working Paper 5398, National Bureau of Economic Research (NBER) Working Paper Series, Cambridge, Massachusetts (1995).

Schwimmer, B 'Akan lineage organisation' (1995) www.umanitoba.ca/faculties/ arts/anthropology/tutor/case_studies/akan/lineage.html (accessed 22 February 2020).

Secretary-General proposes global compact on human rights, labour, environment, in address to World Economic Forum in Davos, Switzerland on 31 January 1999, UN Doc SG/SM/6881 (1 February 1999).

Segerlund, L 'Thirty years of corporate social responsibility within the UN: from codes of conduct to norms' Paper presented at the 6th Pan-European Conference on International Relations, Turin, Italy (12–15 September 2007).

Sharma, KC 'Role of traditional structures in local governance for local development: the case of Botswana' Paper for the Community Empowerment & Social Inclusion Programme, World Bank Institute (undated) https://europa.eu/ capacity4dev/public-pub.sector-reform-decentralisation/document/sharma-kc-n-d-role-traditional-structures-local-governance-local-development-case-botswana (accessed 21 February 2020).

Shaxson, N 'Nigeria's extractive industries transparency initiative: just a glorious audit?' Chatham House (2009).

Singh, U *'Corporate social responsibility and challenges ahead' Lexology* 30 November 2012 www.lexology.com/library/detail.aspx?g=b22d13e7-1640-413b-9832-8a4d5454e8ab (accessed 25 May 2020).

Sobrevila, C 'The role of indigenous peoples in biodiversity conservation: the natural but often forgotten partners' (2008) http://documents.worldbank.org/

curated/en/995271468177530126/pdf/443000WP0BOX321onservation01PUBLIC1.pdf (accessed 22 May 2020).

Speech by Tony Blair, UK Prime Minister at the Extractive Industries Transparency Initiative Conference, London, 17 June 2003.

Speech by WB Donham, Dean of Harvard Business School at the North-Western University (1929).

Speech by Dr Kwame Nkrumah of Ghana on the Volta River Project (25 March 1963).

Sprankling, JG 'The global right to property' University of the Pacific – McGeorge School of Law Research Paper (2013).

Statement by Mr Miloon Kothari, Special Rapporteur on adequate housing as a component of the right to an adequate standard of living, to the World Urban Forrum III, Vancouver, Canada (19–23 June 2006).

Statement by the United Nations Independent Expert on the enjoyment of human rights by persons with albinism, Ms. Ikponwosa Ero, upon conclusion of her official visit to Malawi (18 to 29 April 2016) www.ohchr.org/EN/NewsEvents/Pages/DisplayNews.aspx?NewsID=19903&LangID=E (accessed 21 May 2020).

Statement on Item 4(b): realisation of the economic, social and cultural rights, Joint written NGO statement, received by the UN Secretary-General, UN E/CN.4/Sub.2/2000/NGO/16 (1 August 2000).

Tapscott, R 'Understanding breast "ironing": a study of the methods, motivations, and outcomes of breast flattening practices in Cameroon' Feinstein International Center, Tufts University (2012) http://fic.tufts.edu/assets/Understanding-breast-flattening.pdf (accessed 21 May 2020).

Tarnoff, C 'The Marshall Plan: design, accomplishments, and significance' Congressional Research Service (CRS) Report (18 January 2018).

Terminski, B 'The concept of human security as a tool for analysing the consequences of development-induced displacement and resettlement' (2012).

The Brookings Institution & University of Bern Project on Internal Displacement 'Moving beyond rhetoric: consultation and participation with populations displaced by conflict or natural disasters' (2008).

The Brookings-LSE Project on Internal Displacement 'Improving the protection of internally displaced women: assessment of progress and challenges' (2014).

The Economic and Social Council Resolution 1721 (LIII), 2 July 1972.

'The global farmland grab in 2016: how big, how bad?' *GRAIN* 14 June 2016.

UN Committee on Economic, Social and Cultural Rights, *Concluding observations on the fourth periodic report of Morocco,* UN Doc E/C.12/MAR/CO/4 (22 October 2015).

UN Commission on Human Rights 'Annex: Comprehensive study prepared by Mr Francis Deng, Representative of the Secretary-General on the human rights issues related to internally displaced persons, submitted pursuant to Commission on Human Rights resolution 1992/73' *Note by the Secretary-General,* UN Doc. E/CN.4/1993/35 (21 January 1993).

UN Commission on Human Rights, Addendum, 'Guiding Principles on Internal Displacement' *Report of the Representative of the Secretary-General, Mr. Francis M. Deng, submitted pursuant to Commission on Human Rights resolution 1997/39,* UN Doc. E/CN.4/1998/53/Add.2 (11 February 1998).

UN Commission on Human Rights *The relationship between the enjoyment of economic, social and cultural rights and the right to development, and the working methods and activities of transnational corporations*, Report of the Sub-Commission on Prevention of Discrimination and Protection of Minorities on its fiftieth session, UN Doc E/CN.4/Sub.2/1998/45 (20 August 1998).

UN Commission on Human Rights 'The right of everyone to own property alone as well as in association with others' *Completed final report submitted by Mr. Luis Valencia Rodríguez, independent Expert*, UN Doc. E/CN.4/1994/19 (25 November 1993).

UN Commission on Human Rights, 'Internally displaced persons' *Report of the Representative of the Secretary-General, Francis M. Deng, submitted pursuant to Commission on Human Rights resolutions 1993/95 and 1994/68*, UN Doc. E/CN.4/1995/50 (2 February 1995).

UN Commission on Human Rights 'Internally displaced persons: compilation and analysis of legal norms' *Report of the Representative of the Secretary-General, Mr Francis M Deng submitted pursuant to the UN Commission on Human Rights resolution 1995/*57, UN Doc. E/CN.4/1996/52/Add.2 (5 December 1995).

UN Commission on Human Rights, Human rights and transnational corporations and other business enterprises, adopted by the UN Commission on Human Rights Resolution 2005/69, UN Doc E/CN.4/RES/2005/69 (20 April 2005).

UN Commission on Human Rights *Promotion and protection of human rights: interim report of the Special Representative to the Secretary-General on the issue of human rights and transnational corporations and other business enterprises*, UN Doc E/CN.4/2006/97 (22 February 2006).

UN Committee on the Elimination of Racial Discrimination 'Concluding observations of the Committee on the Elimination of Racial Discrimination: Cameroon' UN Doc. CERD/C/CMR/CO/15–18 (30 March 2010).

UN Children's Fund *We the children: meeting the promises of the World Summit for Children* (2001).

Under the Same Sun *Reported attacks of persons with albinism* (2016)

UN Economic and Social Council, Addendum, 'Annex: Report on refugees, displaced persons and returnees, prepared by Mr. Jacques Cuénod, Consultant,' *Note by the Secretary-General*, UN Doc. E/1991/109/Add.1 (27 June 1991).

UN Economic and Social Council, 'The impact of multinational corporations on the development process and on international relations,' *report of the Group of Eminent Persons to Study the Role of Multinational Corporations on Development and on International Relations*, UN Doc E/5500/Add.1 (Part 1) (24 May 1974).

UN Economic Commission for Africa 'Relevance of African traditional institutions of governance' (2007) 3 http://repository.uneca.org/bitstream/handle/10855/3086/bib.%2025702_I.pdf?sequence=1 (accessed 22 February 2020).

UN Environment Programme *Environmental impact assessment training resource manual, second edition* (2002).

UN Environmental Programme *Environmental impact assessment and strategic environmental assessment: towards an integrated approach* (2004).

UN General Assembly *Provisional summary record of the two hundred and fifty-seventh meeting held at Lake Success, New York, on Tuesday, 8 November 1949, at 3 p.m.* (9 November 1949).

UN General Assembly *International Conference on the Plight of Refugees, Returnees and Displaced Persons in Southern Africa: Report of the UN Secretary-General*, UN Doc A/43/717 (19 October 1988).

UN General Assembly 'The situation of human rights and fundamental freedoms of indigenous peoples,' *note by the UN Secretary-General*, UN Doc A/59/258 (12 August 2004).

UN General Assembly 'Report of the Special Rapporteur on the promotion and protection of the right to freedom of opinion and expression, Mr Frank La Rue' *Note by the Secretary-General,* UN Doc A/68/362 (4 September 2013).

UN General Assembly 'Enjoyment of human rights by persons with albinism,' prepared by Ms Ikponwosa Ero, UN Special Rapporteur on the enjoyment of human rights by persons with albinism' *Note by the Secretary-General,* UN Doc A/71/255 (29 July 2016).

UN Global Compact 'The ten principles' www.unglobalcompact.org/AboutTheGC/TheTenPrinciples/index.html (accessed 25 May 2020).

UN Human Rights Council 'Guiding Principles on Business and Human Rights: Implementing the United Nations "Protect, Respect and Remedy" Framework' *Report of the Special Representative of the Secretary-General on the issue of human rights and transnational corporations and other business enterprises, John Ruggie,* UN Doc A/HRC/17/31 (21 March 2011).

UN Human Rights Council *Report of the Special Representative of the Secretary-General on the issue of human rights and transnational corporations and other business enterprises, John Ruggie,* UN Doc A/HRC/17/31 (21 March 2011) (Ruggie Principles).

UN Human Rights Council 'Extractive industries and indigenous peoples,' *Report of the Special Rapporteur on the rights of indigenous peoples, Prof James Anaya, submitted pursuant to UN Human Rights Council resolution 6/12 and 15/14, 1 July 2013,* UN Doc. A/HRC/24/41 (1 July 2013).

UN Human Rights Council 'Elaboration of an international legally binding instrument on transnational corporations and other business enterprises with respect to human rights' UN Doc A/HRC/26/L.22/Rev.1 (25 June 2014).

UN Sub-Commission on the Promotion and Protection of Human Rights *Economic, social and cultural rights: Mr Alfonso Martinez, Mr Guissé, Mr Kartashkin, Mr Park and Mr Weissbrodt: draft resolution,* 7 August 2003, UN Doc. E/CN.4/Sub.2/2003/L.8.

UN Sub-Commission on the Promotion and Protection of Human Rights *Principles on Housing and Property Restitution for Refugees and Displaced Persons,* final report of the Special Rapporteur, Paulo Sérgio Pinheiro of 28 June 2005 UN Doc E/CN.4/Sub.2/2005/17.

'Urgent action (bad news): Nigeria. Thousands forcibly evicted in Port Harcourt' *Amnesty International* (20 August 2012).

Vinciguerra, V 'How the Daewoo attempted land acquisition contributed to Madagascar's political crisis in 2009' Paper presented at the International Conference on Global Land Grabbing, 6–8 April 2011.

Williams, PC 'The effect of oil companies' activities on the environment, health and development in sub-Saharan Africa: the Niger Delta' text of presentation at the public hearing organised by the European Parliament Committee on Development on Environmental degradation and its impact on poverty, Brussels, European Parliament, 29 February 2012.

Woddis, J 'Ghana's changing economy' (1964) www.sahistory.org.za/sites/default/files/archive-files4/Acn1764.0001.9976.000.017.Apr1964.4.pdf (accessed 16 February 2020).

World Bank *The World Bank participation sourcebook* (1996).

World Bank (2003) *Accountability at the World Bank: the Inspection Panel 10 year on* Washington DC: World Bank Publications.

World Bank (2018) *Groundswell: preparing for internal climate migration* Washington DC: World Bank Publications.

News

Abbas, R 'Sudan: no clear studies on impact of Merowe Dam' *Inter Press Service* 2 January 2012.
Adegbite, A 'The tragic end of Makoko' *The Guardian (Nigeria)* 22 July 2012.
African Union 'List of countries which have signed, ratified/acceded to the African Union Convention for the Protection and Assistance of Internally Displaced Persons in Africa (Kampala Convention)' (2019).
Ahemba, T 'Nigeria evicted 800,000 Abuja residents: report' *Reuters* 15 May 2008.
Akujobi, A 'RSG defends Abonnema wharf demolition' *The Tide* 29 June 2012.
'Amnesty International condemn forced evictions in Abonnema Wharf' *Vanguard* 6 July 2012.
Anderson, J 'Memos bare ITT try for Chile coup' (Washington Merry-Go-Round) *The Washington Post* 21 March 1972.
Anderson, J & Whitten, L 'Ugly truth about Chile' (Washington Merry-Go-Round) *Kingman Daily Miner and Mohave County Miner Viewpoint* 27 October 1975.
Badgley, C 'Fishing and the offshore oil industry: a delicate imbalance' *The Center for Public Integrity* 11 January 2012 www.publicintegrity.org/2011/06/10/4859/fishing-and-offshore-oil-industry-delicate-imbalance (accessed 24 May 2020).
Badgley, C 'West Africa oil boom overlooks tattered environmental safety net' *Ghana Oil Watch* 24 January 2012.
Baird, J 'We don't hear about Africa's oil spills' *Newsweek* 18 July 2010 www.newsweek.com/baird-we-dont-hear-about-africas-oil-spills-74469 (accessed 24 May 2020).
Bamidele, O 'AU set on making African businesses more responsive to human rights' *Premium Times* 24 March 2017.
'Bandits displace 4,030 persons in Niger – NSEMA' *The Guardian* 3 February 2020.
'Big increase in oil and gas revenue in Mozambique' *Extractive Industries Transparency Initiative Report* 14 March 2014.
Biteye, M '70% of Africans make a living through agriculture, and technology could transform their world' *World Economic Forum (News)* 6 May 2016.
'Business and human rights: interview with John Ruggie' *Business Ethics* 30 October 2011.
Butagira, T 'Tullow sues government in new tax dispute' *The Sunday Monitor (Uganda)* 17 December 2012.
Cherian, J 'Grabbing Africa' *Frontline* 20 April 2010.
'Conclusion of the Inspection Panel Toolkit Review' *The World Bank (Factsheet)* 9 March 2020.
'Court orders halt to Tarkwa Bay waterfront evictions' *The Guardian (Nigeria)* 31 January 2020.
'East Africa reels from deadly floods in extreme weather' *News24* 2 November 2019.
'Ethiopia: major oil exploration deal' *The New Humanitarian* 16 June 2003.
Fakhri, K 'In Kabul, children are "rented" out to beggars' *Pajhwok Afghan News* 4 January 2014.
Farge, E & Cooks, T 'Exclusive – Nigeria favours local firms in $40 billion oil contract awards' *Reuters* 22 April 2014.
'Fresh battled on port Harcourt's waterfronts' *Daily Trust* 6 November 2010.
Friedman, M 'The social responsibility of business is to increase its profit' *The New York Times* 13 September 1970.

'Ghana's revenues from natural resources increase 400%' *Extractive Industries Transparency Initiative Report* 8 March 2013.
'Guinea: South Africa's Anglo-Gold Ashanti accused of wrongful eviction of villagers' *West Africa Democracy Radio* 2 February 2017.
Head, B 'Deal brings many jobs, but at what price?' *The Guardian (UK)* 22 November 2008.
'History of the EITI' (undated) http://eiti.org/eiti/history (accessed 25 May 2020).
Ike, IJ and Esiebo, A '"They came while we were asleep": Lagos residents tell of brutal evictions' *The Guardian (UK)* 31 May 2017.
'In Malawi, people with albinism face "total extinction" – UN rights expert' *UN News Centre* 29 April 2016.
Jelimo, R 'Nandi girl walks 50km to flee forced marriage' *The Standard Media* 22 June 2015.
Jibrell, F 'Pastoralism in Somalia: a lifestyle under threat' https://afrikansarvi.fi/issue1/15-artikkeli/41-pastoralism-in-somalia-a-lifestyle-under-threat (accessed 16 February 2020).
Jonathan, O 'Tears as soldiers evict Tarkwa Bay residents from home' *Premium Times (Nigeria)* 21 January 2020.
'Kafue Flats, Zambia: preserving biodiversity through water management' www.un.org/esa/sustdev/publications/africa_casestudies/kafue.pdf (accessed 24 May 2020).
'Kenya post-election violence displaces over 100,000 children – UNICEF' *UN News* 17 January 2008.
Kigai, E 'Kenya-Tanzania: Trafficking handicapped children and the economy of misery' *The Africa Report* 29 July 2013 www.theafricareport.com/East-Horn-Africa/kenya-tanzania-trafficking-handicapped-children-and-the-economy-of-misery.html (accessed 24 May 2020).
'Land leased to secure crops for South Korea' *Financial Times* 18 November 2008.
'Liberia: Ellen Signs Agreement' *The News. (Monrovia)* 11 March 2013.
'Madagascar scraps Daewoo farm deal' *Financial Times* 18 March 2009.
'Many rendered homeless as Navy evicts residents from Tarkwa Bay' *Punch* 21 January 2020.
Masava, M 'Mitumba slum dwellers evicted, land fenced off' *The Star* 9 January 2012.
McKie, R 'Global heating to inflict more droughts on Africa as well as floods' *The Guardian* 16 June 2019.
'Million squatters face eviction' *News24* 24 May 2005.
'Ministry prioritizes communities displaced by Volta Lake Project' *Citi 97.3 FM* 2 February 2018.
Morka, F 'Abonnema wharf community demolished by the Rivers State Government in flagrant disregard of judicial process' *Social and Economic Rights Action Center (SERAC)* 29 June 2012.
Morford, T 'Demolition of Abonnema wharf community and other waterfronts communities: Rivers State Government must end demolition and pay adequate compensation' *Socialist Democracy* 6 July 2012.
Morford, T 'Demolition of Abonnema and other water front communities (2)' *Vanguard* 27 August 2012.
Mutch, T 'East African oil and gas – proper environmental planning needed to avoid disaster' *African Arguments* 27 September 2012.

Mwenda, M 'Inga 3, the world's largest dam will displace tens of thousands in DR Congo' *Life Gate (News)* 23 January 2017.

' "New Suez Canal" construction displaces over 2,000 people in Egypt' *Middle East Eye* 13 February 2015.

'Nigeria court orders halt to Lagos waterfront evictions' *News24* 30 January 2020.

Obia, V 'SERAC condemns demolition of Abonnema' *This Day Live* 01 July 2012.

Odula, T 'East African albinos flee murder, dismemberment' *The Toronto Star* 29 November 2009.

Olawoyin, O 'Displaced Otodo-Gbame residents protest in Lagos' *Premium Times (Nigeria)* 15 November 2017.

Oseni, AL 'Mega city projects leave slum dwellers with uncertain future' *Premium Times* 31 May 2013.

Otto, G 'Where there is oil; there is spillage' *Modern Ghana* 18 December 2012.

'Police displace thousands in Nigeria's Otodo-Gbame slum' *Al Jazeera* 18 March 2017.

Publish What You Pay https://www.pwyp.org (accessed 25 May 2020).

Redvers, L 'Oil-rich Cabinda the poorer for it' *Mail & Guardian* 28 September 2012 http://mg.co.za/article/2012-09-28-00-oil-rich-cabinda-the-poorer-for-it (accessed 24 May 2020).

'Report: scores of albinos in hiding after attacks' *CNN* 29 November 2009.

Schelle, P & Pittock, J 'Restoring the Kafue flats: a partnership approach to environmental flows in Zambia' (2005) http://assets.panda.org/downloads/restoringkafueflatsschellepittockriversymposium3sept05.pdf (accessed 24 May 2020).

Sessou, E 'Ijora-Badia proposed 1008 housing project: govt can't be trusted on the project' *Vanguard* 9 March 2013.

Sessou, E 'The untold story of Badia as 40,000 displaced persons groan in pain' *Vanguard* 2 March 2013.

Silverstein, K 'For Southern Africa, climate change is real as prolonged droughts are creating food shortages' *Forbes* 7 November 2019.

'Special Rapporteur on Freedom of Expression and Access to Information for Africa undertakes advocacy visits to Mozambique, Ghana and Botswana' https://www.chr.up.ac.za/news-archive/2014/811-special-rapporteur-on-freedom-of-expression-and-access-to-information-for-africa-undertakes-advocacy-visits-to-mozambique-ghana-and-botswana (accessed 24 May 2020).

Stebbins, C 'African land grab threatens food security: study' *Reuters* 27 July 2011.

'Tarkwa Bay residents storm Alausa, protest forceful eviction' *Channels Television* 28 January 2020.

'The Kenyan girls who fled their families to escape FGM' *BBC News (Africa)* 14 July 2016.

Underwood, A 'The sudden end of the Ethiopia-Eritrea war, explained' *Vox* 31 July 2018.

'UNHCR welcomes Ethiopia's ratification of the Kampala Convention' *UN Refugee Agency* 14 February 2020.

'UNHCR welcomes Somalia's ratification of the Kampala Convention' *UN Refugee Agency* 27 November 2019.

'UN Human Rights Council endorses principles to ensure businesses respect human rights' *UN News* 16 June 2011.

Vellvé, R & Rakotondrainibe, M 'The Daewoo-Madagascar land grab: ten years on' *Reuters* 16 November 2018.

Washington, R 'How Africa will be affected by climate change' *BBC (News)* 15 December 2019.

Whaley, J 'Oil in Nigeria – curse or blessing?' (2008) 5(4) *Geoscience & Technology Explained* www.geoexpro.com/articles/2008/04/oil-in-nigeria-curse-or-blessing (accessed 25 May 2020).

'What is the LAPSSET Corridor Program' www.lapsset.go.ke/#1461328856794-2dee9bba-e774 (accessed 19 February 2020).

'World Bank enhances its accountability' *The World Bank (Press Release)* 9 March 2020.

World Wide Fund for Nature 'Dams and freshwater ecosystems – repairing the damage' (2004) www.panda.org/downloads/general_267054ba/damsandmitigation.pdf (accessed 24 May 2020).

'Zimbabwe "forced child evictions": Amnesty' *Times Live* 5 October 2011.

Cases

Alexkor Limited & Another v The Richtersveld Community & Others (2005) AHRLR 157 (SACC 2003).

Amann v Switzerland ECHR (16 February 2000).

Ann Itumbi Kiseli v James Muriuki Muriithi (2013) eKLR.

Application No. 006/2012, *African Commission on Human and Peoples' Rights v Republic of Kenya* (2017).

The case concerning military and paramilitary activities in and against Nicaragua (Nicaragua v United States of America) (Merits) ICJ (27 June 1986) (1986) ICJ Reports 14.

Case concerning United States diplomatic and consular staff in Tehran (United States of America v Iran) (Judgement) ICJ (24 May 1980) ICJ Reports 3.

Case of the Saramaka People v Suriname IACtHR (28 November 2007).

Communication 276/2003, *Centre for Minority Rights Development (Kenya) & Minority Rights Group International on behalf of Endorois Welfare Council v Kenya* (2009).

Constitutional Rights Project & Others v Nigeria (2000) AHRLR 227 (ACHPR 1999).

Coster v The United Kingdom (2001) 33 EHRR 479.

Elettronica Sicula S.p.A. (ELSI) (United States of America v Italy) (Judgement) (1989) (*ELSI* case) ICJ Rep 15.

Gbemre v Shell Petroleum Development Company Nigeria Limited & Others (2005) AHRLR 151 (NgHC 2005).

Government of the Republic of South Africa v Grootboom 2000 (11) BCLR 1169.

Handyside v United Kingdom (1976) ECHR 5.

Incal v Turkey (1998) ECHR 48.

Jim George & Others v The Executive Governor of Rivers States & Others (2011) (PHC/2286/2009).

Katangese Peoples' Congress v Zaire (2000) AHRLR 72 (ACHPR 1995).

Kimel v Argentina IACtHR (2 May 2008).

Lemeiguran & Others v Attorney-General & Others (2006) AHRLR 281 (KeHC 2006).

Malone v the United Kingdom (2 August 1984).

Media Rights Agenda and Others v Nigeria (2000) AHRLR 200 (ACHPR 1998).

Mitu-bell Welfare Society v Attorney General & 2 Others (2013) eKLR.

Modder East Squatters and Another v Modderklip Boerdery (Pty) Ltd, President of the Republic of South African and Others v Modderklip Boerdery (Pty) Ltd (2004) ZASCA 47.

Nana Kofi Karikari & 44 Others v Ghanaian Australian Goldfields (GAG) Ltd (2007) Suit No LS.34/97.

Occupiers of 51 Olivia Road, Berea Township, and 197 Main Street, Johannesburg v City of Johannesburg & Others (2008) ZACC 1.

Opuz v Turkey ECHR (9 June 2009) Application No 33401/02.
Peter Mwashi & Another v Javan Mwashi & 4 Others (2006) eKLR.
Reparation for Injuries Suffered in the Service of the United Nations ICJ Reports (Judgement) ICJ (11 April 1949) ICJ Reports 174.
Rotaru v Romania (4 May 2000).
Sesana & Others v Attorney-General (2006) AHRLR 183 (BwHC 2006).
Social and Economic Rights Action Centre (SERAC) & Another v Nigeria (2001) AHRLR 60 (ACHPR 2001).
Socio-Economic Rights and Accountability Project (SERAP) v Nigeria ECW/CCJ/JUD/18/12.
Sudan Human Rights Organisation & Another v Sudan (2009) AHRLR 153 (ACHPR 2009).
Tswelopele Non-Profit Organisation and Others v City of Tshwane Metropolitan Municipality (2007) ZASCA 70.
Tullow Uganda Operations PTY Ltd v Republic of Uganda, International Centre for Settlement of Investment Disputes No. ARB/12/34 (2012).
Velásquez-Rodríguez v Honduras IACtHR (29 July 1988) Ser C. No 4.
Yordanova & Others v Bulgaria ECHR (24 September 2012).
Zimbabwe Human Rights NGO Forum v Zimbabwe (2006) AHRLR 128 (ACHPR 2006).

Instruments

'1st meeting of the conference of states parties to the Kampala Convention' *African Union (Press Releases)* 3 April 2017.
African Charter on Human and Peoples' Rights, adopted by the Organisation of African Unity, OAU Doc CAB/LEG/67/3 rev 5 (27 June 1981).
African Charter on the Rights and Welfare of the Child, adopted by the Organisation of African Unity, OAU Doc CAB/LEG/153/Rev. 2 (11 July 1990).
African Commission on Human and Peoples' Rights *Model Law on Access to Information in Africa* (2013).
African Commission on Human and Peoples' Rights *State Reporting Guidelines and Principles on Articles 21 and 24 of the African Charter Relating to Extractive Industries, Human Rights and the Environment* (2018).
African Development Bank Group's Policy on the Environment (2004).
African Union Convention for the Protection and Assistance of Internally Displaced Persons in Africa, adopted at the Special Summit of the African Union Heads of States and Government in Kampala, Uganda (19–23 October 2009).
African Union Model Law for the Implementation of the African Union Convention for the Protection and Assistance of Internally Displaced Persons in Africa (2012).
Bandir Regional Administration and Municipality of Mogadishu *Internally Displaced Person and Refugee Returnees Policy* (2019).
Cameroon Constitution: Law No 96–06 of 18 January 1996 to amend the Constitution of 2 June 1972.
Charter of the United Nations 1945 1 UNTS XVI.
Conference of State Parties *Harare Plan of Action for the Implementation of the Kampala Convention (2017–2022)* (2017) IV–V.
Constitution of Kenya (2010).
Convention on the Elimination of All Forms of Discrimination against Women (1979) 1249 UNTS 13.

Convention on the Rights of the Child (1989) 1577 UNTS 3.
Declaration on the Right to Development, adopted by the UN General Assembly, Resolution 41/128, UN Doc A/RES/41/128 (4 December 1986).
Declaration on the Rights of Persons Belonging to National or Ethnic, Religious and Linguistic Minorities, adopted by the UN General Assembly 47/135 (18 December 1992).
Draft Articles on State Responsibility for Internationally Wrongful Acts, adopted by the International Law Commission at its 53rd Session (2001).
First Protocol to the European Convention on Human Rights (1952) 213 UNTS 262.
General Act of the Conference of Berlin (26 February 1885).
General Comment No 3 on art 2(1): the nature of state parties' obligation, adopted by the UN Committee on Economic, Social and Cultural Rights, UN Doc E/1991/23 (14 December 1990).
General Comment No 4 on art 11(1): the right to adequate housing, adopted by the UN Committee on Economic, Social and Cultural Rights, UN Doc E/1992/23 (13 December 1991).
General Comment No 7 on art 11(1): forced evictions, adopted by the UN Committee on Economic, Social and Cultural Rights, UN Doc E/1998/22 (20 May 1997).
General Comment No 14 on art 3(1): the right of the child to have his or her best interests taken as a primary consideration, adopted by the UN Committee on the Rights of the Child, UN Doc CRC/C/GC/14 (29 May 2013).
General Comment No 23 on art 27: the right of minorities, adopted by UN Human Rights Committee, UN Doc CCPR/C/21/Rev.1/Add.5 (26 April 1994).
General Comment No 31: the nature of the general legal obligation imposed on states parties to the Covenant, adopted by the UN Human Rights Committee, UN Doc CCPR/C/21/Rev.1/Add.13 (26 May 2004).
General Comment on art 12(1) of the African Charter on Human and Peoples' Rights (2019).
General Comments on article 14(1)(d) and (e) of the Protocol to the African Charter on Human and Peoples' Rights on the Rights of Women in Africa (2012).
Ghana: Limitation Act 1972.
Human rights and transnational corporations and other business enterprises, adopted by the UN Human Rights Council Resolution 17/4, UN Doc A/HRC/RES/17/4 (6 July 2011).
ILO Convention 107: The Indigenous and Tribal Populations Convention, adopted by the General Conference of the International Labour Organisation (5 June 1957).
ILO Convention 169: Indigenous and Tribal Peoples Convention, adopted by the General Conference of the International Labour Organisation (27 June 1989).
ILO Declaration on Fundamental Principles and Rights at Work, adopted at the 86th International Labour Conference (18 June 1998).
International Covenant on Civil and Political Rights, adopted by the UN General Assembly Resolution 2200A (XXI), UN Doc A/6316 (16 December 1966).
International Covenant on Economic, Social and Cultural Rights, adopted by the UN General Assembly Resolution 2200A (XXI), UN Doc A/6316 (16 December 1966).
Kenya: Limitation of Actions Act Cap 22 2012.
Niger Law No 2018–74 (10 December 2018).
Operational Policy 4.12 – Involuntary Resettlement 2001 (revised in 2013).

Optional Protocol to the International Covenant on Economic Social and Cultural Rights, adopted by the UN General Assembly Resolution 63/117, UN Doc A/RES/63/117 (10 December 2008).

Organisation for Economic Cooperation and Development 'OECD Declaration and Decisions on International Investment and Multinational Enterprises' (1976).

Organisation for Economic Cooperation and Development 'Guidelines for aid agencies on involuntary displacement and resettlement in development projects' (1992).

Organisation for Economic Cooperation and Development 'New OECD guidelines to protect human rights and social development' *OECD Directorate for Financial and Enterprise Affairs* 25 May 2011.

Organisation for Economic Cooperation and Development 'OECD Guidelines for Multinational Enterprises' (2011).

Protocol to the African Charter on Human and Peoples' Rights on the Rights of Women in Africa, adopted by the African Union, OAU Doc CAB/LEG/66.6/Rev 1 (11 July 2003).

Protocol to the African Charter on Human and Peoples Rights on the Rights of Persons with Disabilities, adopted by the AU Assembly at the 30th Ordinary Session in Addis Ababa, Ethiopia (29 January 2018).

Protocol on the Protection and Assistance of Internally Displaced Persons (2006).

Puntland Policy Guidelines on Displacement (2014).

Resolution 1/4: Establishment of an intergovernmental working group on asset recovery, adopted by the Conference of the State Parties to the UN Convention against Corruption, UN Doc CAC/COSP/2006/12 (10–14 December 2006).

Resolution 3/2: Preventive measures, adopted by the Conference of the State Parties to the UN Convention against Corruption, UN Doc CAC/COSP/2009/15 (9–13 November 2009).

Rio Declaration on Environment and Development, adopted at the UN Conference on Environment and Development, Rio de Janeiro, Brazil on 3–14 June 1992 (A/CONF 151/26 I).

Somalia: National Policy on Refugee-Returnees and Internally Displaced Persons (IDPs) (2019).

South Africa: Prescription Act No 68 of (1969).

Tanzania: The Law of Limitation Act Cap 89 1971.

The American Convention on Human Rights (1969) 1144 UNTS 123.

The Covenant of the League of Nations (1919).

The Siracusa Principles on the Limitation and Derogation Provisions in the International Covenant on Civil and Political Rights, endorsed by the UN Commission on Human Rights, UN Doc E/CN.4/1985/4 (28 September 1984).

Tripartite Declaration of Principles concerning Multinational Enterprises and Social Policy, adopted by the Governing Council of the International Labour Office at its 204th Session in Geneva, Switzerland (1977).

Uganda: Limitation Act Cap 80 1959.

UN collaborative initiative on Reducing Emissions from Deforestation and Forest Degradation Programme *Guidelines on Free, Prior and Informed Consent* (2013).

UN Commission on Human Rights, Addendum, 'Guiding Principles on Internal Displacement' *Report of the Representative of the Secretary-General, Mr. Francis M. Deng, submitted pursuant to Commission on Human Rights resolution 1997/39*, UN Doc. E/CN.4/1998/53/Add.2 (11 February 1998).

UN Committee on the Elimination of Racial Discrimination 'General recommendation 23: rights of indigenous peoples' UN Doc A/52/18 annex V (1997).
UN Convention against Corruption, adopted by UN General Assembly Resolution 58/4, UN Doc A/58/422 (31 October 2003).
UN Convention on the Rights of the Child (1989) 1577 UNTS 3.
UN Convention on the Rights of Persons with Disabilities, adopted by the UN General Assembly Resolution 61/106, UN Doc A/RES/61/106 (13 December 2006).
UN Economic Commission for Europe 'Convention on access to information, public participation in decision-making and access to justice in environmental matters' made in Aarhus, Denmark (25 June 1998).
UN Human Rights Council, 'Basic principles and guidelines on development-based evictions and displacement,' *Report of the Special Rapporteur on adequate housing as a component of the right to an adequate standard of living, Mr Miloon Kothari* UN Doc A/HRC/4/18 annex I (5 February 2007).
Universal Declaration of Human Rights, adopted by the UN General Assembly Resolution 217 A(III) of 10 December 1948.
Vienna Convention on the Law of Treaties 1969 1155 UNTS 331.
World Bank 'Revised operational policy 4.01: Environmental assessment' (2013).

Others

Asiimwe, SP 'Peasantry struggles and agriculture modernisation in Uganda: the failed attempt at agriculture transformation for development' Masters of Arts, Institute of Social Studies, Erasmus University, The Netherlands (2011).
Ataguba, JO 'Towards a disturbance-integrated compensation method for land expropriation: a case of Rwanda' Master's Thesis, Faculty of Geo-Information Science and Earth Observation, University of Twente, The Netherlands (2014).
Oxford Dictionaries 'Arbitrary' https://www.lexico.com/synonym/arbitrary (accessed 26 May 2020).
Oxford Dictionaries 'Feasible' https://www.lexico.com/definition/feasible (accessed 24 May 2020).
Sirna, ZT 'Ethiopia: when the gadaa democracy rules in the federal state: bridging indigenous institutions of governance to modern democracy' Master of Philosophy in indigenous studies, faculty of humanities, social sciences and education, University of Tromsø (2012).

Index

For Product Safety Concerns and Information please contact our EU
representative GPSR@taylorandfrancis.com
Taylor & Francis Verlag GmbH, Kaufingerstraße 24, 80331 München, Germany

www.ingramcontent.com/pod-product-compliance
Ingram Content Group UK Ltd.
Pitfield, Milton Keynes, MK11 3LW, UK
UKHW020001200926
475702UK00015B/2404

9780367546250